EDMUND SPENSER

Longman Critical Readers

General Editor:

Stan Smith, Professor of English, University of Dundee

EDMUND SPENSER

Edited and Introduced by

ANDREW HADFIELD

LONGMAN
LONDON AND NEW YORK

Addison Wesley Longman Limited,
Edinburgh Gate,
Harlow, Essex CM20 2JE,
United Kingdom
and Associated Companies throughout the world
Published in the United States of America
by Addison Wesley Longman Inc., New York

First published 1996

ISBN 0 582 247357 CSD
ISBN 0 582 247365 PPR

British Library Cataloguing-in-Publication Data

A catalogue record for this book is
available from the British Library

Library of Congress Cataloging-in-Publication Data

Edmund Spenser/edited and introduced by Andrew Hadfield.
    p. cm. – (Longman critical readers)
    Includes bibliographical references and index.
    ISBN 0–582–24735–7 (csd). – ISBN 0–582–24736–5 (ppr)
    1. Spenser, Edmund, 1552?–1599–Criticism and interpretation.
I. Hadfield, Andrew. II. Series.
PR2364.E36   1996
821'.3–dc20
                                                              96–1992
                                                                  CIP

Phototypeset by 20, in 9/11.25pt Palatino
Produced by Longman Singapore Publishers (Pte) Ltd.
Printed in Singapore

Contents

General Editors' Preface

The outlines of contemporary critical theory are now often taught as a standard feature of a degree in literary studies. The development of particular theories has seen a thorough transformation of literary criticism. For example, Marxist and Foucauldian theories have revolutionised Shakespeare studies, and 'deconstruction' has led to a complete reassessment of Romantic poetry. Feminist criticism has left scarcely any period of literature unaffected by its searching critiques. Teachers of literary studies can no longer fall back on a standardised, received, methodology.

Lecturers and teachers are now urgently looking for guidance in a rapidly changing critical environment. They need help in understanding the latest revisions in literary theory, and especially in grasping the practical effects of the new theories in the form of theoretically sensitised new readings. A number of volumes in the series anthologise important essays on particular theories. However, in order to grasp the full implications and possible uses of particular theories it is essential to see them put to work. This series provides substantial volumes of new readings, presented in an accessible form and with a significant amount of editorial guidance.

Each volume includes a substantial introduction which explores the theoretical issues and conflicts embodied in the essays selected and locates the areas of disagreement between positions. The pluralism of theories has to be put on the agenda of literary studies. We can no longer pretend that we all tacitly accept the same practices in literary studies. Neither is a *laissez-faire* attitude any longer tenable. Literature departments need to go beyond the mere toleration of theoretical differences: it is not enough merely to agree to differ; they need actually to 'stage' the differences openly. The volumes in this series all attempt to dramatise the differences, not necessarily with a view to resolving them but in order to foreground the choices presented by different theories or to argue for a particular route through the impasses the differences present.

The theory 'revolution' has had real effects. It has loosened the grip of traditional empiricist and romantic assumptions about language and literature. It is not always clear what is being proposed as the new agenda for literary studies, and indeed the very notion of 'literature' is questioned by the post-structuralist strain in theory. However, the uncertainties and obscurities of contemporary theories appear much less worrying when we see what the best critics have been able to do with them in practice. This series aims to disseminate the best of recent criticism and to show that it is possible to re-read the canonical texts of literature in new and challenging ways.

RAMAN SELDEN AND STAN SMITH

The Publishers and fellow Series Editor regret to record that Raman Selden died after a short illness in May 1991 at the age of fifty-three. Ray Selden was a fine scholar and a lovely man. All those he has worked with will remember him with much affection and respect.

Acknowledgements

We are grateful to the following for permissions to reproduce copyright material:

Cambridge University Press and the authors for 'The "Sacred Hunger of Ambitious Minds": Spenser's Savage Religion' by Andrew Hadfield from *Religion, Politics and Literature in Reformation and Restoration England* (eds) Hamilton and Strier (1995), 'Mapping Mutability: or, Spenser's Irish Plot' by Julia Reinhard Lupton from *Representing Ireland: Literature and the Origins of Conflict, 1534–1660* (eds) Bradshaw, Hadfield and Maley (1993), and 'Spenser's Complaints: "Into Each Secrete Parte" ' from *Spenser's Secret Career* by Richard Rambuss (1993); The Johns Hopkins University Press for an extract from Chapter 1 in *Endless Worke: Spenser and the Structures of Discourse* by Jonathan Goldberg, (1981) pp. 1–12; the Modern Language Association of America for 'Spenser's Poetics: The Poems of Two Bodies' by David Lee Miller from *Publications of the Modern Language Association of America* 101 (1980); The Pennsylvania State University for 'Praise and Defense of the Queen in *The Faerie Queene*' from *The Invention of the Renaissance Woman: The Challenge of Female Independence in the Literature and Thought of Italy and England* by Pamela Joseph Benson (1993) pp. 291–305. Copyright 1993 by The Pennsylvania State University; The University of Chicago Press and the authors for extracts from Chapter 4, 'To Fashion a Gentleman: Spenser and the Destruction of the Bower of Bliss' from *Renaissance Self-Fashioning: From More to Shakespeare* by Stephen Greenblatt (1980), the essay 'Barbarous Tongues: The Ideology of Poetic Form in Renaissance England' by Richard Helgerson from *The Historical Renaissance: New Essays on Tudor and Stuart Literature and Culture* (eds) Dubrow and Strier (1988), and the essay 'Singing Unsung Heroines: Androgynous Discourse in Book 3 of *The Faerie Queene*' by Lauren Silberman from *Rewriting the Renaissance: The Discourses of Sexual Difference in Early Modern Europe* (eds) Ferguson, Quilligan and Vickers (1987). Copyright The University of Chicago Press; Cork University Press and the author for extracts from the essay (with alterations) 'The Colonization of Language: Narrative Strategies in *A View of the Present State of Ireland* and *The Faerie Queene*, Book VI' by Anne Fogarty from *Spenser and Ireland: An Interdisciplinary Perspective* (ed) Patricia Coughlan (1989); the University of Texas Press for 'The Perfect Paterne of a Poete: The Poetics of Courtship in *The Shepheardes Calender*' by Louis Adrian Montrose from *Texas Studies in Literature and Language* vol. 21 (1979).

Edmund Spenser

Thanks to Diane Watt for suggesting Pamela Joseph Benson's essay to me and for reading and correcting the introduction; to Tim Woods for also reading and correcting the introduction; to Tom Healy for checking the bibliography and making helpful suggestions; to Anne Fogarty for promptly rewriting the beginning and end of her essay when requested; to all the contributors for supplying notes on the composition of their essays which helped me compile the headnotes; to Stan Smith for belief and encouragement; to Longman for seeing the book through the press.

ADH

For Maud Rosa May

1   Introduction

Exiles from the main street: Spenser and Joyce

Edmund Spenser has never fitted easily into critical categories and his contemporaries found it hard to judge his literary merit. A major problem was his style. Even whilst praising his work, critics showed an undercurrent of nervousness and incomprehension. Francis Meres commented that Spenser was one of the poets who had 'the English tongue . . . mightily enriched and georgeouslie invested in rare ornaments and resplendent abilments'; Thomas Churchyard called Spenser 'the spirit of learned speech'; and Richard Barnfield argued in a verse epistle that Spenser's 'deepe conceit is such, / As passing all Conceit, needs no defence'. Ben Jonson was more direct in his criticism: 'Spenser, in affecting the Ancients, *writ no language*' [emphasis added], although he recommended that he be 'read for his matter'.[1]

Early readers were unsure what to make of Spenser: many admired his poetry but they were not at all clear what it meant (as the paradoxical defence by Richard Barnfield suggests) and, like Ben Jonson, were uncertain whether Spenser fitted into any sort of tradition or was a curious one-off. Contemporary reactions to Spenser's poetry, especially his *magnum opus, The Faerie Queene*, bear a curious resemblance to some early responses to two monuments of twentieth-century literary experimentalism, *Ulysses* and *Finnegans Wake*. Jane Heap replied to one puzzled and hostile reader of *Ulysses* that if that person was blind to 'the luminosity of his genius . . . nothing will help you but a work of equal magnitude which no one could write and which you would again not understand', a defence which resembles Richard Barnfield's; Arland Ussher sounds more like Ben Jonson in describing Joyce as 'a Duns Scotus splitting hairs and mangling words' in *Finnegans Wake*.[2]

In many ways, Spenser and Joyce are regarded similarly by academic establishments: both have had a massive influence on a select group of initiates and inspire lifelong critical devotion, but tend to remain outside a central critical tradition because they are largely unread. At the risk

1

of pushing the analogy too far, it is perhaps no accident that both were exiles: Joyce from his native Ireland and Spenser in Ireland, where he lived from 1580 until his death in 1598, the period during which all his majority poetry was published (see below, p. 3).

It is remarkable how F. R. Leavis, probably the single most influential English literary historian, who helped not only to establish a usable canon of English literary texts, but also to gain recognition for the subject itself as a university discipline,[3] treats Spenser and Joyce in almost identical ways. In his study of the English novel, *The Great Tradition* (1948), Leavis acknowledges Joyce as a remarkable stylist, but terms him, ultimately, 'a dead end' whose work has 'no organic principle determining, informing, and controlling into a vital whole, the elaborate analogical structure, the extraordinary variety of technical devices' and leads only to a series of sterile experimental writers. Hence Joyce, for all his linguistic flair, is not considered part of 'the great tradition' of English novel-writing.[4] In his earlier study of the development of English poetry, *Revaluation* (1936), Leavis damns Spenser with faint praise, suggesting that he does not require revaluation as he is 'in his own way a fact of the first importance in the tradition of English poetry ... too simple a fact to need examining afresh'. However, Leavis then associates Spenser with Milton, claimng that 'I think the way in which, as powers in the English tradition, Milton and Spenser are associated is sufficiently conveyed in the chapters on Milton and Keats'.[5] Given that *Revaluation*'s most polemical and influential chapter was Leavis's attempt to *remove* Milton from the canon of English Literature – or, rather, to sum up an already completed process: 'Milton's dislodgement, in the past decade, after two centuries of predominance, was effected with remarkably little fuss'[6] – for his dead experimentalism, his tedious use of language and poisonous influence on the next generation of poets, the association of Milton and Spenser would seem to question Spenser's place within the canon rather than confirm it. Leavis argues that reading Milton is a matter 'of resisting, of standing up against, the verse-movement, of subduing it to something tolerably like sensitiveness' and in the end we are worn down by the monotony of the grand style because Milton 'exhibits a feeling *for* words rather than a capacity for feeling *through* words' [Leavis's emphasis].[7] One has to ask whether Leavis is displaying a sly piece of wit – a quality *Revaluation* endorses, at least in poetry – or simply pulling any trick to avoid discussing Spenser and so contradicting himself. Either way, Spenser is damned by association and silence.

'An Englishman in love with England . . . afraid of Ireland's impenetrability': some contexts for Edmund Spenser[8]

Spenser's paradoxically canonical yet marginalised role – an unread 'classic' – corresponds to his position during his lifetime. His writing displays all the signs of massive ambition: he had the temerity to publish his early correspondence with Gabriel Harvey, announcing plans to reform the whole course of English poetry (see Chapter 2 below): he took the trouble to oversee his works through the press leaving no manuscripts: his progression from pastorals to epic appears to foreshadow Virgil's and set him up as the great English poet of nationhood: he invented his own verse forms, style and vocabulary.[9] His poetry clearly has significant designs upon the reader, as the well-known statement of his intention in the letter to Raleigh published with the first edition of *The Faerie Queene* (1590) indicates – 'The generall end therefore of all the book is to fashion a gentleman or noble person in vertuous and gentle discipline'[10] – to say nothing of the manipulative and dangerous project of presuming to represent the Queen.[11] His works were presented at court, he appears to have been one of the very few writers who was awarded a pension by the Queen and he was buried in Westminster Abbey, near Chaucer, the most celebrated English poet.[12]

But, as has already been noted, Spenser spent most of his adult life in Ireland, something he lamented bitterly on occasions, notably in his poem *Colin Clouts Come Home Againe* (1595), a fictionalised account of his return to London with Sir Walter Raleigh (1589–91).[13] Spenser was appointed to a series of important positions in Ireland, enjoying the colonial government's patronage in Dublin and later Cork, where he lived from about 1588, possessing the substantial estate of Kilcolman despite litigation with the Anglo-Irish Lord Roche. It is a matter of considerable controversy whether Spenser was exiled to Ireland against his will, having committed some sort of misdemeanour – possibly having offended Lord Burghley, Elizabeth's Principal Secretary, in an early manuscript version of the satirical complaint, *Mother Hubberds Tale* – or whether he *chose* to pursue a lucrative career as an official in Ireland.[14] The very facts of Spenser's life seem to mirror the reactions of contemporaries – as well as of later readers – to his poetry. On the one hand Spenser appears to be an important and central figure, both poetically and politically; on the other, an obscure and strange phenomenon, perhaps admired, but certainly kept at arm's length. Perhaps the grand ambition of Spenser's poetry, culminating in the romance epic of *The Faerie Queene*, precluded the widespread audience he expressed a hope for in the letter to Raleigh. Spenser appears to have had in mind three separate poetic traditions: a classical heritage which manifested itself in poetic models to imitate – Virgil, Homer, Ovid, etc. – and legend, via the story of Aeneas's great-grandson, Brutus, who founded and named Britain, thus linking the contemporary English to the legacy of the Trojan Wars and the founding of Rome; a native English tradition of Protestant satire and eclogue, principally Chaucer, Langland and Skelton, the inventor of one of Spenser's most frequently adopted masks, the poet, Colin Clout; and the sophisticated European courtly cultures of France and Italy, principally the poets Ariosto and Tasso, whose work is reformulated in large sections of *The Faerie Queene*'s narrative'.[15] In *The Faerie Queene* he deliberately sets out to employ multitudinous aspects of all three in order to make *English* literature pre-eminent. The trouble may be that in doing so, he lost his English audience and became instead 'the poet's, gentleman's, or scholar's poet'.[16] In the same way, historians dispute whether Spenser's prose tract, *A View of the Present State of Ireland* (c. 1596), was a hugely influential political treatise which affected the course of Irish history and led to the rise of the group identity of the Anglo-Irish, or merely the extremist ravings of an obscure government official, which has been granted more status than it deserves because it happens to have been written by a famous poet.[17]

Growing in mental health or corrupting the imagination? Spenser before the end of the New Criticism

It is important to recognise that a history of Spenser criticism in the twentieth century tells a strange, circular story which does not conform to the narrative of ' "shock of the new" iconoclasm sweeping away the cobwebs of bourgeois liberal humanism', beloved of some radical literary guides. In many ways what has happened has been something of a return to the contextualising criticism which led to the *Variorum Edition* (1932–49). Harry Berger, Jr, has commented, 'When the first waves of the "new criticism" washed across the decks of academe, [Spenser] was quickly swept overboard because of his inability to write like Donne, Eliot, and Allen Tate'.[18] Spenser was assumed to be the author of dead monuments, inorganic and brittle with no relevance to a living literary tradition, as Leavis argued (see above, p. 2). Commenting on *A Hymne in Honour of Beautie*, Derek Traversi opined that 'Within its peculiarly narrow limits it is . . . almost perfect. One can imagine no development from it in terms of human experience'.[19]

Spenser's chief defender and probably the most important Spenser critic of the twentieth century was C. S. Lewis, and it is surely no accident that his posthumously published Spenser lectures were called *Spenser's Images of Life* (1967) as a deliberate challenge to those who saw only arid formal virtues in the poetry: a title which ironically enough, signalled an acceptance of the values of the 'New Critics'.[20] In what was perhaps his most significant book, *The Allegory of Love* (1936), Lewis placed great stress on the need to read Spenser's narrative, commenting on *The Faerie Queene* that 'The things we read about in it are not like life, but the experience of reading it is like living' and, in a deliberate echo of I. A. Richards's recently published comments about critical practice and psychology, 'To read him [Spenser] is to grow in mental health'.[21] Lewis argues for a Spenser who is always one step ahead of his reader: 'Spenser . . . may not always know where he is going as regards the particular stories: as regards the symphony of moods, the careful arrangement of different degrees of allegory and different degrees of seriousness, he is always in command'.[22] This is principally because Lewis shares what he sees as Spenser's values. Poet and reader merge as one composite being, speaking up for married and, by analogy, heavenly, love in a hostile, disbelieving society:

> It is only after centuries that Spenser's position becomes apparent; and
> then he appears as the great mediator between the Middle Ages
> and the modern poets, the man who saved us from the catastrophe of
> too thorough a renaissance . . . In the history of sentiment he is the
> greatest among the founders of that romantic conception of marriage
> which is the basis of all our love literature from Shakespeare to
> Meredith . . . all that Britomart stands for was platitude to our fathers.
> It is platitude no longer. The whole conception is now being attacked.
> Feminism in politics, reviving asceticism in religion, animalism in
> imaginative literature, and, above all, the discoveries of the psycho-
> analysts, have undermined that monogamic idealism about sex which
> served us for three centuries.[23]

Lewis has clearly missed one very obvious irony in his hymn to wedded love, the stubborn fact that the poem was dedicated to a virgin queen, which should perhaps have altered his interpretation of the sexual politics of the poem (see below, pp. 13–17). But if his criticism has no discernible parallels with or influence upon more recent interest in the representations of gender in Spenser's poetry, his stress upon the role of the reader, real and implied, foreshadows and informs – often unacknowledged – contemporary developments in reader-response and deconstructionist criticism (in this volume Miller, Goldberg, Silberman, Hadfield, Fogarty).

There is, however, a further and more seriously limiting irony in Lewis's criticism. Many of the editors of the *Variorum Spenser* – Edwin Greenlaw, Raymond Jenkins, Alexander Judson, Ray Heffner and Rudolf Gottfried – were particularly interested in the historical milieu of Spenser's writings, notably the Irish context, and published considerable research on this issue as well as providing substantial information in the notes to their edition.[24] Lewis, by birth an Ulsterman whose undergraduate career coincided with Irish independence and the Irish Civil War, argued that such detail was not merely irrelevant but harmful: 'Spenser was the instrument of a detestable policy in Ireland, and in the fifth book [of *The Faerie Queene*] the wickedness begins to corrupt his imagination'.[25] Lewis was following the policy of W. B. Yeats, who, in his introduction to a volume of selections from Spenser, had divided the English poet up into a good imaginative writer whose work was resonant with symbolism and a bad colonial official whose desire to control what he could not understand produced flat and dull allegory: 'Like an hysterical patient he drew a complicated web of inhuman logic out of the bowels of an insufficient premise – there was no right, no law, but that of Elizabeth, and all that opposed her opposed themselves to God, to civilisation, and to all inherited wisdom and courtesy, and should be put to death'. Yeats laments that 'When Spenser wrote of Ireland he wrote as an official', with a consequent loss to literature: 'Could he have gone there as a poet merely, he might have found among its poets more wonderful imaginations than even the islands of Phaedria and Acrasia.'[26] Whilst Yeats struggled with what he saw as the warring, Blakean states of Spenser's mind, Lewis was concerned to limit the influence of Ireland to Book V of *The Faerie Queene* and pass over it in virtual silence: having suggested that Artegall is not meant to represent an ideal notion of justice he states, 'The rest of the book needs little comment'.[27] Readers should ignore topical references to current events and concentrate instead on the more universal themes of secular and divine love. In effect, Lewis is drawing a thick line between poetry and politics, insisting that if they do mix, the result can only be bad poetry which students should not bother to study. The process uncomfortably mirrors the ignorant dismissal of Spenser that Lewis was so keen to negate.

Reading the narrative: from New Criticism to Deconstruction

Lewis's stress upon the role of the reader has always been a central concern of Spenser criticism and in the 1960s and 1970s major studies were published by Paul Alpers, Isabel MacCaffrey, Giamatti Bartlett and others, alongside more exegetical and iconographic studies (William Nelson, James Nohrnberg, John Erskine Hankins), most following Lewis in concentrating upon *The Faerie Queene* – particularly the first three books, which were more frequently set on university courses, and ignoring Books IV and V altogether – and expending most energy dealing with Spenser's treatment of love.[28]

In an important review article, 'How to Read *The Faerie Queene*', Paul Alpers anticipated many of the readings of the 'New Historicists' (as well as restating and modifying the judgement of C. S. Lewis). He argues 'that *The Faerie Queene* is *radically undramatic*, and that it therefore defeats all the modern reader's expectations about the primacy of dramatic narration, about the relation of moral generalisation to the specific instances and "evidence" offered, and about the nature of "concrete" details in the verse' [emphasis added] (compare this to Greenblatt's statement, 'Spenser's profoundly *undramatic* art . . . wards off . . . radical questioning of everything that exists' [Greenblatt's emphasis]).[29] Alpers contends that the reader has to trust the verse to lead him or her to the desired aim of the poet and not intervene too hastily to make moral judgements: the desired stance a reader should adopt is 'passivity . . . as the manifestation of a full, humane intelligence'. He illustrates his principles by qualifying C. S. Lewis's reading of a stanza from probably the most frequently debated episode in the poem, Guyon's destruction of Acrasia's Bower of Bliss:

> And over all, of purest gold was spred,
> A trayle of yvie in his natiue hew;
> For rich metall was so coloured,
> That wight, who did not well auis'd it vew,
> Would surely deeme it to be yvie trew:
> Low his lasciuious armes adown did creepe,
> That themselves dipping in the silver dew,
> Their fleecy flowres they tenderly did steepe,
> Which drops of Christall seemed for wantones to weepe.
>
> II. xii. 61

Alpers comments:

> [W]e apprehend the moral clarity of those lines precisely when we respond to the richness and felicity of the verse, and by empathetic participation understand the self-indulgence and self-dissipation of 'wantones'. However, the really difficult aspect of this stanza lies in lines 4 and 5 . . . What is so hard to grasp and *trust* is that Spenser could state these lines so flatly, almost as a warning, and then confirm the persuasiveness of 'yvie trew' by the sudden sensuousness of the next line . . . The sensuous appeal of 'purest gold' and 'rich metall' gets what we may call moral support from the plain and strong meaning of 'natiue hew', and 'trayle' (which is an architectural term for a metal ornament) acquires its usual meaning from the line in which it appears.

These effects keep 'wight' a truly open term, *as it should be in allegory.*
[emphases added][30]

Alpers demonstrates that he is an extremely sensitive close reader of
the poem. His comments are valuable both in terms of his analysis
of the functioning of Spenser's allegory and the creation of an *implied
reader,* and also as a description of the process of a (particularly well-
informed) reader reading. The problem is that he refuses to recognise the
difference between different readers at different times, what Stanley
Fish terms 'interpretative communities'.[31] There is no separation between
the implied readers whom Spenser wished to fashion, and those who were
actually fashioned by their reading of the poem over the four centuries
from its publication to the present day. Concomitantly, there is no
acknowledgement that Spenser might have changed his ideas during the
course of writing *The Faerie Queene,* or have betrayed within the text a
recognition that the poem might mean something different to different
readers.[32] Alpers has simply collapsed all these categories into one
concept of the right reader of the poem, one who coincides with the mind
of the author and refuses to judge the allegory prematurely.

Terry Eagleton has argued that literary critics who dislike theory or
claim to get along better without it are 'simply in the grip of an older
theory', and in some ways it could be argued that Alpers has not
advanced
our theoretical understanding of the role of the reader beyond that of
Lewis.[33] Catherine Belsey's analysis of the way in which 'New Criticism'
constructs an implied reader applies to Alpers's reading of *The Faerie
Queene*:

> Literature for the New Critics is . . . concerned with truth, though it is
> a truth more complex, more paradoxical, more mysterious than the
> truths of every day. It is the truth of *unchanging experience* in all its
> complexity and ambiguity, which the poem as icon 'embodies in
> language' and offers for contemplation. This contemplation, performed
> in isolation, involves only the individual reader and the individual text.
> The poem, self-contained and closed, constitutes a pattern of
> knowledge which leads to a philosophy of detachment. Rising above
> the vicissitudes of the world, 'poems remain and explain' and New
> Critical readers encounter in solitude the paradoxes of human experience
> which leads to a *wise passiveness.* [emphases added][34]

Belsey describes almost exactly the critical assumptions of Alpers, who
uses the same word to articulate his vision of the role of the reader of
The Faerie Queene: 'passiveness' before the great truths of an art which
depicts 'human nature and the human condition'.[35]

The most radical break with these assumptions of authorial control has occurred in the work of Jonathan Goldberg, who published the first post-structuralist reading of *The Faerie Queene, Endlesse Worke* in 1981 – at the same time that New Historicist critics were starting to challenge (New) critical orthodoxies. The title of the book is taken from IV.xii.1 and deserves to be quoted in full:

> O what an endlesse work haue I in hand,
> To count the seas abundant progeny,
> Whose fruitfull seede farre passeth those in land,
> And also those which wonne in th'azure sky?
> For much more eath to tell the starres on by,
> Albe they endlesse seeme in estimation,
> Then to recount the Seas posterity:
> So fertile be the flouds in generation,
> So huge their numbers, and so numberlesse their nation.

The universe might only 'seem' infinite, rather than actually be infinite or endless, but this makes no difference to the writer who has to represent it. At the start of Book VI, Calidore, the Knight of Courtesy, repeats the narrator's fears, describing his quest as 'an endlesse trace, withouten guyde' (VI.i.6), so that the anxiety of the narrator/authorial persona is transferred to the character whom the reader is to follow throughout the quest, and so to the reader him- or herself. The fear is that instead of the text being able to master the series of representations or linguistic signs it uses, these will, in fact, master the text, so that the allegory will not be controlled and reduced to an overall design. Put another way, one might say that the fear of the author is that the reader will take over the sense of the text which will become an impossible project to complete or close, what Goldberg refers to as 'the "endlesse worke" of play'. Or to put it another way still, the copia of rhetoric threatens to engulf the representative power of the text's mimetic function.[36]

Goldberg's book, like David Lee Miller's essay reprinted below, is heavily indebted to Roland Barthes', *S/Z: An Essay* (1970), an extraordinary critical exploration of Balzac's novella, *Sarrasine*. In this work, Barthes produced his enormously influential distinction between the classic, 'readerly text' which aims to represent a fixed and stable reality for the passive reader, who 'is thereby plunged into a kind of idleness' (the text that Lewis and Alpers read which demands a 'passive' reader?), and the 'writerly text', which 'is a perpetual present, upon which no *consequent* language can be imposed; the writerly text is *ourselves writing*, before the infinite play of the world (the world as function) is traversed, intersected, stopped, plasticized by some singular system (Ideology, Genus, Criticism) which reduces the plurality of entrances,

the openings of networks, the infinity of languages' [Barthes' emphasis].[37]
Barthes is not describing real works, but ideal texts which cannot ever
exist: as soon as a writerly text had a reader it would no longer belong
to 'the infinite play of the world' as it would be interpreted and,
therefore, traversed and stopped.[38] *The Faerie Queene* is not so much a
'writerly text' as one subjected by Goldberg to what he terms a 'writerly
reading' which 'aims both at revealing that the text is one that the reader
produces, and at restoring to a text its primacy as language' (see below,
p. 159). Goldberg develops such strategies in his essay on *The Shepheardes
Calender* in *Voice Terminal Echo* (1986), where he suggests, following
Jacques Derrida, that 'The scene of writing is the fantasy of reading, the
horror of incorporation that the alluring, charming text proffers'.[39]

Spenser and the dawn of New Historicism

Just as it is difficult to narrate the origin, rise, spread and theoretical
hegemony of New Criticism, pigeon-holing and circumscribing a
complex group of interrelated writings and institutional methodologies
in doing so, it is also a problematic enterprise to try and tell the story
of 'New Historicism'. Stephen Greenblatt, widely taken to be the
movement's founding father, has written that he coined the term to
describe a group of diverse essays he was commissioned to edit 'out of
desperation' and that the subsequent proliferation of articles, references
in dissertations, attacks, etc., has made him 'quite giddy with amazement'.
Greenblatt further suggests that New Historicism should be described as
'a practice rather than a doctrine, since as far as I can tell (and I should
be the one to know) it's no doctrine at all'.[40]

In the same volume, the editor, H. Aram Veeser, provides an outline of
the 'key assumptions [which] continually reappear and bind together
the avowed practitioners':

1 That every expressive act is embedded in a network of material
  practices;
2 That every act of unmasking, critique, and opposition uses the tools
  it condemns and risks falling prey to the practice it exposes;
3 That literary and non-literary 'texts' circulate inseparably;
4 That no discourse, imaginative or archival, gives access to
  unchanging truths nor expresses inalterable human nature;
5 Finally . . . that a critical method and a language adequate to describe
  culture under capitalism participate in the economy they describe.[41]

The point that needs to be made is not that these principles of criticism can usefully be applied to Spenser – although, of course, they can be and have been – but that they were formulated as a result of attempts to read Renaissance authors, specifically Spenser. The theoretical apparatus used and the critical interest in the subject itself emerge at the same time, rather than independently. In this collection I have included two highly important essays in the story of both interrelated enterprises: Louis Adrian Montrose's ' "The perfect paterne of a poete": the poetics of courtship in *The Shepheardes Calender*' (1979) and a substantial section from Stephen Greenblatt's chapter, 'To fashion a gentleman: Spenser and the destruction of the Bower of Bliss' from *Renaissance Self-Fashioning: From More to Shakespeare* (1980).

These essays can be seen to exhibit most of the characteristics of New Historicism outlined by Veeser (although Greenblatt is far more indebted to the cultural anthropology of Clifford Geertz, another crucial point of reference for New Historicists[42]): both acknowledge that every expressive act cannot be separated from a network of material practices, Montrose reading *The Shepheardes Calender* in terms of 'a dialectic of poetic aspirations and constraints, to articulate his awareness of a discrepancy between the myth of the poet's high calling and the functions to which his skills are relegated in his own society', Greenblatt analysing the temptation of Guyon in Acrasia's Bower in terms of a perceived threat to civilisation's power from art, colonisation and Ireland, and arguing that Spenser had 'a field theory of culture'; both show that the texts studied are closer to what they wish to define themselves against than they would desire, Montrose arguing that the would-be Virgilian poet eventually seeks a 'release from his compromised song', Greenblatt, that Spenser's ideological position forces him to dramatise the destruction of art as an ironic means of affirming its value; both locate the value of their subject in contingent historical ways, Greenblatt in particular reminding the reader of his or her own historical position ('To say that Spenser worships power . . . is not, in the heady manner of the late '60s, to condemn his work as shallow, craven, or timeserving.'); neither reads literature as a separate or separable phenomenon, but examines the texts under study as part of an emerging culture which links them to the present day.

New Historicism has not, of course, been without its critics. British cultural materialists have been vociferous in their attacks on the ways in which they have felt that many New Historicists 'hermeticised culture . . . into a self-sustaining sign system' rather than reading Renaissance texts in terms of 'the material struggles inscribed in literature' and intervening in turn in that struggle: 'We inherit a narrative of oppression . . . but our duty as re-readers is to show that "It did not, and still does not, need to be so".' In other words, both groups of critics agree that 'Representations do shape history', but cultural materialists recognise that the converse is also true.[43]

Spenser has not been a central concern of cultural materialist analysis, although an essay by Alan Sinfield and Jonathan Dollimore in an influential radical collection of essays on Shakespeare explicitly linked the politics of *Henry V* to Spenser's often-cited comments on the starving Irish in *A View of the Present State of Ireland* (Act V of *Henry V* opens with the chorus comparing Henry's French wars to the Earl of Essex's expedition to Ireland whence he will bring 'rebellion broached on his sword').[44]

'they were brought to such wretchedness, as that any stony heart would have rued the same. Out of every corner of the woods and glens they came creeping forth upon their hands, for their legs would not bear them . . . They did eat of the dead carrions'. The human cost of imperial ambition protruded through even its ideological justifications, and the government felt obliged to proclaim that its intention was not 'an utter extirpation and rooting out of that nation'. The claim of the state to be the necessary agent of peace and justice was manifestly contradicted. Ireland was, and remains, its bad conscience.[45]

One might well object to the rather idealist distinction between textual narrative and real feeling,[46] but the theoretical model employed recognises a potential conflict between authorites endorsed within the text itself, as well as sides which the reader of either historical/literary or critical text might be persuaded to take. Sinfield's reading of the destruction of Acrasia's Bower in *Faultlines* (1992) is notably more straightforwardly oppositional than Greenblatt's as he locates 'an excess, an instability, in the puritan humanist project': 'The violence with which Guyon breaks up the bower may not only be religious fervor, therefore, but an anxiety that the place of pagan letters, together with the palaces, arbours, banqueting halls, and fine workmanship of courtly culture, is not altogether settled'.[47] Sinfield's reading is an attempt to locate a contradiction in Spenser's ideological employment of two opposed systems of discourse – a critical practice which owes a great deal to the work of Althusser, Foucault and Raymond Williams[48] – in the name of a radical disaffection with prevailing hegemonies: 'Cultural materialism seeks to discern the scope for dissident politics of class, race, gender, and sexual orientation, both within texts and in their roles in cultures'.[49] Sinfield's textual politics are a long way from Greenblatt's seeming acceptance of the inevitability of the status quo, both in his reading of Spenser's art as an affirmation of 'the existence and inescapable moral power of ideology' and his pronouncements elsewhere in his essays on the early modern period. Greenblatt's celebrated analysis of *Henry V* concludes, 'we are free to locate and play homage to the play's doubts only because they no longer threaten us. There is subversion, no end of subversion, only not for us'.[50] Sinfield and Dollimore conclude their essay on *Henry V* by alleging that it 'can be read to reveal not only the strategies of power but also the anxieties informing both them and their ideological representation . . . we might conclude that the ideology which saturates his [Shakespeare's] texts, and their locations in history are the most interesting things about them'.[51] Both provide readings which are clearly historical, but Greenblatt treats the text as a distant historical object which affirms the twentieth-century reader's difference from the concerns and struggles of the 1590s: Sinfield and Dollimore read the same text contiguously, as part of an ongoing struggle which has not yet exhausted itself.[52]

A considerable lacuna in Spenser criticism is the absence of a cogent and informed Marxist reading. Simon Shepherd has blazed a trail, but his *Spenser* (Harvester New Readings series, 1989) relies upon a simplistic model of historical determinism which owes little to the actual writings of Marx or his commentators and reinterpreters.[53] This is all the more remarkable given Marx's own comments on Spenser, whom he describes as 'Elizabeth's arse-kissing poet' because of his involvement in Ireland.[54]

How much of Spenser's poetry Marx had actually read is open to question, and he may well have been relying on Spenser's nineteenth-century reputation as 'the most poetical' of poets and assuming that he concerned himself with literary beauty whilst administering colonial cruelty.[55] Certainly Marx's comment responds to one tradition which assumes that Spenser must be an official apologist *because he is a canonical poet*, a position Marx clearly detests.[56] Neither Spenser's potentially anomalous position as a colonial official who relied upon central power yet detested its intrusion into his sphere of influence, nor the group of radical protestant writers in England who derived inspiration from his example were historical phenomena that Marx could have been expected to appreciate.[57]

It is much more likely that Marx had read *A View of the Present State of Ireland*; certainly, Friedrich Engels was familiar with that text and refers to it on numerous occasions in his notes for his highly ambitious but never completed 'History of Ireland' (1869–70), noting that Spenser criticised the greedy Irish clergy and that 'Artegal in Spencer's [*sic*] Faery Queen is Lord Deputy Gray [*sic*]'.[58] A reinvestigation of such writings, which are virtually never cited by Spenser scholars, and a subsequent rereading of Spenser after Marx appears long overdue.

Sex, glamour and armour: Spenser's gender trouble

Spenser's sexual politics are yet another matter for considerable debate. To take only the most obvious example: *The Faerie Queene* is a poem dedicated to a virgin which appears to promote chastity as a virtue within marriage in the figure of Britomart, the heroine of Book III. Far from being a poem of arse-licking as Marx would have had it, Spenser was actually sticking his neck out in aggressively criticising Elizabeth's cult of virginity in the poem.[59] Spenser was certainly critical of Elizabeth in the 'Two Cantos of Mutabilitie', which were discovered after his death and published in the First folio edition of the poem (1609). One notorious verse appears to be an explicit attack on the Queen for failing to secure a successor:

> Even you, faire *Cynthia*, whom so much ye make
> *Joves* dearest darling . . .
> Then is she mortall borne, how-so ye crake;
> Besides, her face and countenance every day
> We changed see, and sundry forms partake,
> Now hornd, now round, now bright, now brown and gray:
> So that *as changefull as the Moon* men use to say.
>
> VII.viii.50

In the letter to Raleigh appended to the first edition of *The Faerie Queene*, Spenser had stated that 'in some places' he represented the Faerie Queene as 'the most excellent and glorious person of our sovereigne the Queene . . . fashioning her name according to your own excellent conceit of Cynthia' (p. 737). The question is not so much whether Spenser criticises Elizabeth, but when he starts to do so in his work.[60]

At times, it could be argued, this criticism lapses into a more general misogyny and disgust at the sight of women's bodies, as in the description of the stripping of Duessa (I. viii. 46–9), and more disturbingly and pruriently, in the overtly pornographic description of Serena's body offered up to the gaze of the cannibals and, therefore, the reader:

> Her yvorie necke, her alablaster brest,
> Her paps, which like white silken pillowes were,
> For love in soft delight thereon to rest;
> Her tender sides, her bellie white and clere,
> Which like an Altar did it selfe uprere,
> To offer sacrifice divine thereon;
> Her goodly thighes, whose glorie did appeare
> Like a triumphal Arch, and thereupon
> The spoiles of Princes hang'd, which were in battel won.
>
> VI.viii.42

Serena is displayed with her legs wide apart in this lascivious adaptation of the common poetic device of the blazon (a poem describing a woman's body) and the reader is tempted to imagine what lies between them. What, then, are these spoils of princes? By making the reader complicit with the savage cannibals, is Spenser exposing the usual focus of the male gaze and answering the unspoken question of what men really want? Or, is he himself unconscious of such complexities and is simply putting his own desires on display, depicting Serena as a ball-busting butterfly collector?

In themselves, such questions raise further problems as both of them assume that the reader is a heterosexual male.[61] Elsewhere, the poem seems to invite very different gendered readings. At the start of Book III, Britomart is pursued by the lustful lady of the Castle Joyeous, Malecasta, who is unaware that Britomart is actually female because she has not yet removed her armour. The narrator describes Britomart as 'full of amiable grace, / And *manly* terrour mixed therewithall, / So that as the one stird up affections bace, / So th'other did *mens* rash desires apall, / And hold them backe, that would in errour fall' [emphasis added] (III.i.46). The most obvious irony of this nuanced description is that Britomart is not provoking a man's but a woman's desire. Her female appearance is seen to trigger male desire, yet her own masculine virtue thwarts that incontinence, the word that is used to describe Malecasta's passion for Britomart (48). The scene ends with Britomart declaring her sex, Malecasta bursting into tears, the would-be seducer being comforted by her intended victim and bonds of mutual sympathy being established between the two women:

> Full easie was for her [Britomart] to have beliefe,
> Who by self-feeling of her feeble sexe,
> And by long triall of the inward griefe,
> Wherewith imperious love her hart did vexe,
> Could judge what paines do loving harts perplexe.
> Who meanes no guile, be guiled soonest shall,
> And to faire semblance doth light faith annexe;
> The bird, that knowes not the false fowlers call,
> Into his hidden net full easily doth fall.

> III.i.54

These lines – which probably refer back to traditional imagery of seduced women as trapped birds[62] – equate the two women's experience of love, placing them as victims in a hostile erotic world, thus qualifying the interim statement of the narrator that Malecasta was an exceptionally lustful creature who should be ignored by all virtuous ladies as an irrelevance (49).

The encounter is indeed complex – and really needs to be read in terms of the discussion of sexuality which takes place throughout Book III[63] – involving the representation of both homoerotic desire and hermaphroditic existence in the form of Britomart, the Amazon warrior woman.[64] Certainly, the stated aim of the poem articulated in the letter to Raleigh, that 'The generall end therefore of the booke is to fashion a *gentleman* or noble person in vertuous and gentle discipline' [emphasis added] appears either inadequate or deliberately misleading, or else involves a reading of 'noble person' as specifically female.[65]

Camille Paglia has argued, in her controversial and hugely popular book on Western artistic representations of sexuality, that Spenser's poem characteristically possesses 'a sermonizing voice earnestly comment[ing] on disturbing pornographic images', and that in this struggle between Protestant control and pagan freedom (shades of Nietzsche here?), 'the eye in Spenser always wins'. Paglia concludes:

> Britomart's shiny armour and Belphoebe's Byzantine glitter are attempts to polish and perfect the eye and keep it free. Spenser longs for the Apollonian woman . . . Spenser turns medieval allegory into pagan ostentation . . . Spenser's pictorialism is a compulsive Apollonian thing-making. And the most glamorous of these made things is the female warrior, who combats fallen nature, where the vampire drains maleness and the rapist annihilates femaleness.[66]

Rhetorically overblown and unproblematically endorsing Spenser's sexual politics this might seem (especially in the light of Paglia's well-publicised disagreements with eminent feminist critics[67]), but it does represent one significant type of response to Spenser's intervention in Renaissance debates on issues of sexual identity.

Feminist and gender-conscious readings of the poem have often concentrated on these images of androgynous women: Britomart, Radigund, Amoret and Belphoebe in the Garden of Adonis. In more scholarly ways, Lauren Silberman's reading of Book III in this collection comes to similar conclusions to Paglia, as does Pamela Benson's analysis of Radigund and Britomart (although neither shares Paglia's post-feminist agenda). Silberman suggests that Spenser is keen to break down traditional male conceptions of virtue and construct a reader who will accede to this demand; Benson, that *The Faerie Queene* mounts a spirited defence of female government – rather than a defence of women *per se* – and so participates in a whole line of male pre-feminist representations of women in Renaissance Italy and England. Works by writers such as Thomas More, Ariosto, Boccaccio and Thomas Eliot, according to Benson, debated whether women possessed virtues which were identical to those of men or had their own specific integrity, without actually acknowledging that women might have the same rights as men. Benson claims that Spenser's work displays a similar mixture of sympathy and resistance.

In direct contrast one might cite Patricia Parker's reading of *The Faerie Queene*, which claims that the poem narrates a male desire to 'escape from female power and the anxiety of castration' and, in Guyon's destruction of the Bower of Bliss, finally to master and surpass a threatening female ruler who resembles Spenser's own Queen, a woman Spenser felt had reduced him to the status of the paralysed captives of Acrasia. Simon Shepherd argues that Spenser's misogynist works often represent woman as 'one who displaces a male partner to form a triangle of never-ending desire'. The problem is that 'the sexual effect of woman makes masculine identity unstable'.[68]

Selecting the volume

As I hope the above account makes clear, Spenser criticism is inextricably bound up with some important modern movements in literary and cultural analysis. I have therefore chosen to represent these – New Historicist, deconstructionist, feminist and reader-response informed studies – more heavily than other approaches – Marxist, psychoanalytical – which are less important in terms of recent developments in Spenser studies and rereadings of his poetry and prose.

In this respect David Lee Miller's suggestive essay marks something of a watershed, eschewing more traditional psychoanalytical decodings of Spenser's allegory like Benjamin G. Lockerd, Jr.'s rather limited Jungian account of the narrative of *The Faerie Queene, The Sacred Marriage*, which appeared to be quite impervious to the irony that the poem was dedicated to a virgin.[69] Miller follows in the wake of Jonathan Goldberg's post-structuralist reading of the poem, employing Lacan's rereading of Freud in order to explore the politics of the body – sacred, sexual, political – in Spenser's major work. Spenser's strange romance, like Freud's son playing the *fort-da* game with a cotton reel, is haunted by the loss of an unrecoverable whole body, represented most clearly by Arthur's sexual dream of the Faerie Queene in Book I, canto 9.

I have also sought to achieve other impossible balancing acts: my aim was to concentrate on *The Faerie Queene*, but to have three essays dealing with Spenser's other works: *The Shepheardes Calender, The Complaints* and the Spenser-Harvey letters. The essays on *The Faerie Queene* deal with all seven books of the poem, which are arranged in ascending order, with my own essay providing something of an overview. I was also concerned to include a number of essays dealing with *A View of the Present State of Ireland* and Spenser's role in Ireland – Greenblatt, Hadfield, Fogarty, Lupton – as a subject of major critical importance in recent years and one which is inextricably linked with theoretical developments. Finally, I wanted to highlight some other themes and historical concerns which have assumed importance in the last fifteen years: national identity (dealt with in Richard Helgerson's important essay), the relationship between Spenser's career and his poetry (Richard Rambuss), mapping (Julia Lupton), colonisation (Stephen Greenblatt and Anne Fogarty) and religion (Hadfield). I hope that the resulting compromise and mixture of these demands – which has involved significant omissions, most notably of essays dealing with a wider range of Spenser's poetry – leaves the reader at least partially satisfied and eager to find out more.

Notes

1. All cited in R. M. CUMMINGS, ed., *Edmund Spenser: The Critical Heritage* (London: Routledge, 1971), pp. 96, 77, 94, 294.
2. Both cited in MARVIN MAGALANER and RICHARD M. KAIN, *Joyce: The Man, the Work, the Reputation* (London: John Calder, 1956), pp. 164, 295.
3. TERRY EAGLETON comments – with some polemical exaggeration – on the influence of Leavis's circle: 'In the early 1920s it was desperately unclear why English was worth studying at all; by the early 1930s it had become a question of why it was worth wasting your time on anything else', *Literary Theory: An Introduction* (Oxford: Basil Blackwell, 1983), p. 31.
4. F. R. LEAVIS, *The Great Tradition: George Eliot, Henry James, Joseph Conrad* (Harmondsworth: Penguin, 1972, rpt. of 1948), p. 37.
5. F. R. LEAVIS, *Revaluation: Tradition and Development in English Poetry* (Harmondsworth: Penguin, 1972, rpt. of 1936), p. 12. Incidentally, Spenser is mentioned only once in the chapter on Keats (p. 249).
6. Ibid., p. 46.
7. Ibid., pp. 47, 53. For a discussion of 'the Milton Controversy', see CHRISTOPHER RICKS, *Milton's Grand Style* (Oxford: Clarendon Press, 1963), ch. 1.
8. ROBERT WELCH, *The Kilcolman Notebook* (Dingle, Co. Kerry: Brandon, 1994), p. 10.
9. For analysis of Spenser's self-presentation and self-promotion see RICHARD HELGERSON, *Self-Crowned Laureates: Spenser, Jonson, Milton and the Literary System* (Berkeley: University of California Press, 1983), ch. 2; MICHAEL MCCANLES, 'The Shepheardes Calender as Document and Monument', *Studies in English Literature* 22 (1982), 5–19; MICHAEL O'CONNELL, *The Mirror and the Veil: The Historical Dimension of Spenser's Faerie Queene* (Chapel Hill: The University of North Carolina Press, 1977), pp. 1–5.
10. *The Poetical Works of Edmund Spenser*, ed. J. C. SMITH and E. DE SELINCOURT (London: Oxford University Press, 1912), p. 407. All subsequent references to this edition in parentheses.
11. See LOUIS MONTROSE, 'The Elizabethan Subject and the Spenserian Text', in PATRICIA PARKER and DAVID QUINT, eds, *Literary Theory/Renaissance Texts* (Baltimore: The Johns Hopkins University Press, 1986), pp. 303–40; PHILIPPA

BERRY, *Of Chastity and Power: Elizabethan Literature and the Unmarried Queen* (London: Routledge, 1989), pp. 153–65.

12. For details of Spenser's life see WILLY MALEY, *A Spenser Chronology* (London: Macmillan, 1994). See also A. C. JUDSON, *The Life of Edmund Spenser* in EDWIN GREENLAW *et al.*, eds, *The Works of Edmund Spenser: A Variorum Edition*, 11 vols (Baltimore: The Johns Hopkins University Press, 1932–49), vol. 11 (1945), although some of the more speculative passages should be read with caution.

13. For analysis of the poem in terms of its Irish location see ANDREW HADFIELD, *Literature, Politics and National Identity: Reformation to Renaissance* (Cambridge: Cambridge University Press, 1994), pp. 188–90. See also SAM MEYER, *An Interpretation of Edmund Spenser's 'Colin Clout'* (Cork: Cork University Press, 1969); NANCY JO HOFFMAN, *Spenser's Pastorals: The Shepheardes Calender and 'Colin Clout'* (Baltimore: The Johns Hopkins University Press, 1977), ch. 5.

14. The former case is argued in MURIEL BRADBROOK, 'No Room at the Top: Spenser's Pursuit of Fame', in *The Artist and Society in Shakespeare's England: The Collected Papers of Muriel Bradbrook, Volume I* (Hassocks: Harvester, 1982), pp. 19–36; the latter in ANDREW HADFIELD and WILLY MALEY, 'Introduction: Irish Representations and English Alternatives', in BRENDAN BRADSHAW, ANDREW HADFIELD and WILLY MALEY, eds, *Representing Ireland: Literature and the Origins of Conflict, 1534–1660* (Cambridge: Cambridge University Press, 1993), pp. 1–23, at pp. 10–11.

15. O'CONNELL, *Mirror and Veil*; ANTHEA HUME, *Edmund Spenser: Protestant Poet* (Cambridge: Cambridge University Press, 1984), ch. 7; JOHN N. KING, *Spenser's Poetry and the Reformation Tradition* (Princeton: Princeton University Press, 1990); GRAHAM HOUGH, *A Preface to the Faerie Queene* (London: Duckworth, 1962), pt. 1.

16. HARRY BERGER, Jr, 'Introduction' in BERGER, ed., *Spenser: A Collection of Critical Essays* (Englewood Cliffs, NJ: Prentice-Hall, 1968), pp. 1–12, at p. 2.

17. NICHOLAS CANNY, 'Edmund Spenser and the Development of an Anglo-Irish Identity', *Yearbook of English Studies* 13 (1983), 1–19; CIARAN BRADY, 'Spenser's Irish Crisis: Humanism and Experience in the 1590s', *Past and Present* 111 (May, 1986), 17–49; BRADY and CANNY, 'Debate: Spenser's Irish Crisis: Humanism and Experience in the 1590s', *Past and Present* 120 (1988), 201–15.

18. BERGER, ed., *Spenser*, p. 2.

19. See, for example, *Derek Traversi*, 'Spenser's *Faerie Queene*' in BORIS FORD, ed., *The Pelican Guide to English Literature: Vol. 1, The Age of Chaucer* (Harmondsworth: Penguin, 1978, rpt. of 1954), pp. 211–26, at p. 226.

20. C. S. LEWIS, *Spenser's Images of Life*, ed. ALASTAIR FOWLER (Cambridge: Cambridge University Press, 1967). Lewis died in 1963.

21. C. S. LEWIS, *The Allegory of Love: A Study in Medieval Tradition* (Oxford: Oxford University Press, 1979, rpt. of 1936), pp. 358, 359. RICHARDS has commented '[T]he critic is as closely occupied with the health of the mind as the doctor with the health of the body', *Principles of Literary Criticism* (London: Routledge, 1983, rpt. of 1924), p. 25. For Richards's massive influence on the growth of 'New Criticism' see EAGLETON, *Literary Theory*, pp. 44–6.

22. C. S. LEWIS, *English Literature in the Sixteenth Century, excluding drama* (Oxford: Oxford University Press, 1973, rpt. of 1954), p. 381.

23. LEWIS, *Allegory of Love*, p. 360.

24. For details see WILLY MALEY, 'Spenser and Ireland: A Select Bibliography', in *Spenser Studies 9* (1991), 227–42.

25. LEWIS, *Allegory of Love*, p. 349.

26. W. B. YEATS, 'Edmund Spenser' (1902), in *Essays and Introductions* (London: Macmillan, 1961), pp. 356–83, at pp. 361, 372.

27. LEWIS, *Allegory of Love*, p. 349.

28. PAUL J. ALPERS, *The Poetry of 'The Faerie Queene'* (Princeton: Princeton University Press, 1967); A. BARTLETT GIAMATTI, *Play of Double Senses: Spenser's 'Faerie Queene'* (Englewood Clifs, NJ: Prentice-Hall, 1976); ISABEL G. MACCAFFREY, *Spenser's Allegory: The Anatomy of Imagination* (Princeton: Princeton University Press, 1976); WILLIAM NELSON, *The Poetry of Edmund Spenser: A Study* (New York: Columbia University Press, 1963); JAMES NORHNBERG, *The Analogy of 'The Faerie Queene'* (Princeton: Princeton University Press, 1976); JOHN ERSKINE HANKINS, *Source and Meaning in Spenser's Allegory: A Study of 'The Faerie Queene'* (Oxford: Clarendon Press, 1971).

29. PAUL ALPERS, 'Review Article: How to Read *The Faerie Queene*', *Essays in Criticism* 18 (1968), 429–43, at p. 437: STEPHEN GREENBLATT, *Renaissance Self-Fashioning: From More to Shakespeare* (Chicago: The University of Chicago Press, 1980), p. 192 (below, pp. 129–30).

30. ALPERS, 'How to Read *The Faerie Queene*', p. 440. Lewis's well-known reading of the Bower of Bliss is to be found in *Allegory of Love*, pp. 324–31.

31. See ROBERT HOLUB, *Reception Theory: A Critical Introduction* (London: Methuen, 1984), pp. 150–2 for a brief, critical analysis.

32. For one interpretation of Spenser changing his mind during the course of the poem, see THOMAS H. CAIN, *Praise in 'The Faerie Queene'* (Lincoln, Nebr.: University of Nebraska Press, 1978); on the different audiences of *The Faerie Queene*, see HADFIELD, *Literature, Politics and National Identity*, pp. 173–4.

33. EAGLETON, *Literary Theory*, p. viii.

34. CATHERINE BELSEY, *Critical Practice* (London: Methuen, 1980), p. 20.

35. ALPERS, 'How to Read *The Faerie Queene*', p. 434.

36. See TERENCE CAVE, *The Cornucopian Text: Problems of Writing in the French Renaissance* (Oxford: Clarendon Press, 1979).

37. ROLAND BARTHES, *S/Z: An Essay*, trans. Richard Miller (New York: HIll & Wang, 1974), pp. 4–5.

38. For a further development of this distinction see Barthes' essay, 'From Work to Text', in JOSUÉ HARARI, ed., *Textual Strategies: Perspectives in Post-Structuralist Criticism* (London: Methuen, 1979), pp. 73–81.

39. JONATHAN GOLDBERG, 'Consuming Texts: Spenser and the Poet's Economy', in *Voice Terminal Echo: Postmodernism and English Renaissance Texts* (London: Methuen, 1986), pp. 38–67, at p. 66. Goldberg is referring to DERRIDA's highly influential essay, 'Freud and the Scene of Writing', in *Writing and Difference*, trans. Alan Bass (London: Routledge, 1978), pp. 196–231.

40. STEPHEN GREENBLATT, 'Towards a Poetics of Culture', in H. ARAM VEESER, ed., *The New Historicism* (London: Routledge, 1989), pp. 1–14, at p. 1. A useful interpretation of the intellectual antecedents and development of 'New Historicism' is provided in RICHARD WILSON and RICHARD DUTTON, eds, *New Historicism and Renaissance Drama* (Harlow, Essex: Longman, 1992), 'Introduction: Historicising New Historicism', pp. 1–18.

41. H. ARAM VEESER, 'Introduction', in VEESER, ed., *New Historicism*, pp. ix-xvi, at p. xi.
42. GREENBLATT, *Renaissance Self-Fashioning*, pp. 3–4; VEESER, ed., *New Historicism*, p. xi.
43. WILSON, 'Introduction', in WILSON and DUTTON, eds, *New Historicism and Renaissance Drama*, p. 15.
44. ALAN SINFIELD and JONATHAN DOLLIMORE, 'History and Ideology: the instance of *Henry V*', In JOHN DRAKAKIS, ed., *Alternative Shakespeares* (London: Methuen, 1986), pp. 206–27. On the disastrous failure of Essex's expedition, see STEVEN G. ELLIS, *Tudor Ireland: Crown, Community and the Conflict of Cultures, 1470–1603* (London: Longman, 1985), pp. 306–7.
45. SINFIELD and DOLLIMORE, 'History and Ideology', p. 226. The quotations are taken from *A View of the Present State of Ireland*, ed. W. L. RENWICK (Oxford: Clarendon Press, 1970), p. 104: PAUL L. HUGHES and JAMES F. LARKIN, eds, *Tudor Royal Proclamations*, 3 vols (New Haven: Yale University Press, 1969), III, p. 201.
46. For a different reading of this passage see ANDREW HADFIELD, 'Spenser, Ireland and Sixteenth-Century Political Theory', *The Modern Language Review* 89 (1994), 1–18, at pp. 8–9.
47. ALAN SINFIELD, *Faultlines: Cultural Materialism and the Politics of Dissident Reading* (Oxford: Clarendon Press, 1992), pp. 197, 196.
48. Ibid., p. 9.
49. Ibid., pp. 9–10.
50. STEPHEN GREENBLATT, 'Invisible Bullets', in *Shakespearean Negotiations: The Circulation of Social Energy in Renaissance England* (Oxford: Clarendon Press, 1988), pp. 21–65, at p. 65.
51. DOLLIMORE and SINFIELD, 'History and Ideology', pp. 226–7.
52. For a related discussion of modes of reading see A. J. POLAN, *Lenin and the End of Politics* (London: Methuen, 1984), ch. 1.
53. SIMON SHEPHERD, *Spenser* (Hemel Hempstead: Harvester, 1989). For further (hostile) analysis see my review, *Textual Practice* 8 (1994), pp. 156–9.
54. KARL MARX, *Ethnographical Notebooks*, ed. L. KRADER (Assen: Van Gorcum, 1974), p. 305. The full quotation reads: 'D. Lausige Sir John Davies was King James Attorney-General for Ireland u. fur diessen posten war naturlich entsprechender Lump gewahlt ein ebenso "vorurtheilsfreeier" u. uninteressirter Patron wie der Elizabeth's ArschKissende Poet Spenser' ('The lousy Sir John Davies was King James' Attorney-General for Ireland and for this post was of course a corresponding rogue chosen like a similarly unprincipled and disinterested Patron (fellow?), Elizabeth's Arse-Kissing Poet Spenser). Shepherd rather creatively interprets the phrase (*Spenser*, p. 3).
55. WILLIAM HAZLITT, *Lectures on the English Poets*, cited in PETER BAYLEY, ed., *Spenser: The Faerie Queene: A Casebook* (Basingstoke: Macmillan, 1977), pp. 34–40, at p. 34.
56. Compare the judgement of EDWIN GREENLAW that Spenser's advocation of harsh methods in Ireland was justified because 'this enemy was making war not honourably but by the methods of a sneak and a coward', 'Spenser and British Imperialism', *Modern Philology* 26 (1911–12), 347–70, at p. 361. Such a judgement is repeated by ALASTAIR FOWLER, 'Spenser and War', in J. R. MULRYNE and MARGARET SHEWRING, eds, *War, Literature and the Arts in*

Sixteenth-Century Europe (Basingstoke: Macmillan, 1989), pp. 147–64, at pp. 158–9.

57. See ANDREW HADFIELD, ' "Who Knowes not Colin Clout?" The Permanent Exile of Edmund Spenser', in *Literature, Politics and National Identity: Reformation to Renaissance* (Cambridge: Cambridge University Press, 1994), pp. 170–201; DAVID NORBROOK, *Poetry and Politics in the English Renaissance* (London: Routledge, 1984), ch. 8; WILLIAM B. HUNTER, ed., *The English Spenserians: The Poetry of Giles Fletcher, George Wither, Michael Drayton, Phineas Fletcher and Henry More* (Salt Lake City: The University of Utah Press, 1977).

58. FREDERICK ENGELS, 'From *The Preparatory Material for the "History of Ireland"* ', in KARL MARX and FREDERICK ENGELS, *Ireland and the Irish Question* (London: Lawrence & Wishart, 1971), pp. 303–82, at pp. 378, 362.

59. See BERRY, *Of Chastity and Power*, ch. 6; FRANCES A. YATES, *Astraea: The Imperial Theme in the Sixteenth Century* (London: Routledge, 1975); ROY STRONG, *The Cult of Elizabeth: Elizabethan Portrait and Pageantry* (London: Thames & Hudson, 1977).

60. See CAIN, *Praise in The Faerie Queene*; MONTROSE, 'Elizabethan Subject and Renaissance Text', HADFIELD, 'The Permanent Exile of Edmund Spenser'.

61. For a sophisticated interpretation of Spenser's implied reader who 'may, in fact, be female', see MAUREEN QUILLIGAN, *Milton's Spenser: The Politics of Reading* (Ithaca, NY: Cornell University Press, 1983), pp. 38–40.

62. See, for example, GEOFFREY CHAUCER, *Troilus and Criseyde*, III, stanzas 171, 177. For analysis of this image see JILL MANN, *Geoffrey Chaucer* (Hemel Hempstead: Harvester, 1991), p. 22.

63. See the entry by THOMAS ROCHE, Jr, in A. C. HAMILTON, ed., *The Spenser Encyclopedia* (London and Toronto: Routledge and Toronto University Press, 1990), pp. 270–3.

64. See SIMON SHEPHERD, *Amazons and Warrior Women: Varieties of Feminism in Seventeenth Century Drama* (Brighton: Harvester, 1981), ch. 1.

65. For a recent argument that the letter should be treated with caution as it is unlikely to express Spenser's views, see DARRYL J. GLESS, *Interpretation and Theology in Spenser* (Cambridge: Cambridge University Press, 1994), pp. 48–9.

66. CAMILLE PAGLIA, 'Spenser and Apollo: *The Faerie Queene*', in *Sexual Personae: Art and Decadence from Nefertiti to Emily Dickinson* (New Haven: Yale University Press, 1990), pp. 170–93, at pp. 192–3.

67. See ELAINE SHOWALTER, 'The Divine Miss P.' (review of *Sex, Art and American Culture*), *The London Review of Books* 15, 3 (11 Feb. 1993), 7–8.

68. PATRICIA PARKER, 'Suspended Instruments: Lyric and Power in the Bower of Bliss', in *Literary Fat Ladies: Rhetoric, Gender, Property* (London: Methuen, 1987), pp. 54–66, at pp. 65, 63; SHEPHERD, *Spenser*, pp. 88, 85. See also SHEILA T. CAVANAGH, *Wanton Eyes and Chaste Desires: Female Sexuality in The Faerie Queene* (Bloomington: Indiana University Press, 1994).

69. BENJAMIN G. LOCKARD, Jr, *The Sacred Marraige: Psychic Integration in The Faerie Queene* (Lewisburg: Bucknell University Press, 1987).

2 'Barbarous Tongues': The ideology of poetic form in Renaissance England*

RICHARD HELGERSON

'Barbarous Tongues' was originally published in a collection of essays designed to illustrate the historical turn scholarship had taken in the early modern field in the last decade or so, but was written as part of a larger project, namely, the study of English national self-writing (*Forms of Nationhood* (1992)). The interest throughout that book is in showing how certain 'forms' of writing came to be associated, sometimes quite arbitrarily, with certain distributions of power and privilege within the newly reconstructed national state. The book discusses rivalry between chivalric romance and epic, between common-law reports and Roman-law institutes, between carto-graphic description and chronicle history, between collections of voy-ages and epic narrative, between Shakespeare's kind of history play and the very different history plays of his contemporaries, and finally between the apocalyptic narrative of John Foxe and Richard Hooker's apologetic discourse. The insistence on form suggests the 'New His-toricist' bent of the work and the discussion of meaning in terms of difference suggests the debt to Saussurian semiotics. The term 'his-torical semantics' best describes this combination of approaches.

I

Midway through one of his letters to Harvey, Spenser exclaims, 'Why a God's name may not we, as else the Greeks, have the kingdom of our own language?'[1] For years bits of this sentence have been running through my head. Here, it has seemed to me, Spenser gave voice to the generative impulse that lay behind not only his own career but also the whole

*First published in HEATHER DUBROW and CLARK HUSE, eds, *The Historical Renaissance: New Essays on Tudor and Stuart Literature and Culture* (Chicago: Chicago University Press, 1988), pp. 273–8.

23

extraordinary development of English poetry in his time – and, indeed, the very emergence of England itself as an autonomous and powerfully self-conscious realm. This is, I realise, a large claim to make for so little, but the more closely I have looked at the sentence itself and the further I have gone in tracing its reverberations the more fully justified my initial feeling has seemed. Spenser had, of course, only a limited responsibility for all those momentous events. Not even the shape of his own poetic career depended entirely on him. But he was very much a part of what was happening to him and around him, and he here expressed with marvelous economy both the ambition and the situation of those of his own generation who shared his involvement.

Consider for a start those last six words, 'the kingdom of our own language.' They carry us from an essentially dynastic conception of communal identity ('the kingdom') to an assertion of what we recognise as one of the bases of postdynastic nationalism ('our own language'). A kingdom whose boundaries are determined by the language of its inhabitants is no longer a kingdom in the purely dynastic sense, but neither, so long as it goes on identifying itself with the person of a hereditary monarch, is it quite a nation. Nor are the representational resources of this phrase exhausted by the extremes of 'kingdom' and 'language,' for between them comes that first-person plural 'our' with its suggestion of shared participation and possession. King, people, and language – which is in charge? From this formulation it is impossible to tell. But even a small acquaintance with the history of England in the next century or so will remind us that conflict was to develop along precisely the lines suggested by these few words, between royal prerogative, subjects' rights, and the cultural system.[2]

So attached have I become to this phrase that I feel a pang each time I must reinsert it into its original context, for immediately it loses its even-handed representational character and is captured by a purpose that upsets the delicate dynamic equilibrium that had been so finely achieved. In Spenser's impatient question, 'the kingdom' does not, after all, initiate the semi-autonomous noun phrase we have been regarding, a stable syntactic and conceptual entity to which further qualification (as, for example, 'the *glorious* kingdom of our own language') might be added. No, rather it belongs with the verb *have*. Spenser wants to 'have the kingdom' of his own language, he wants to exercise sovereignty over English, wants to make it do what he wants it to do. Of the triangularly balanced forces that weigh against one another in 'the kingdom of our own language,' Spenser selects one and asserts its priority. 'Our' makes a claim to omnipotence which reduces 'kingdom' to the role of action and 'language' to that of object. But if there is semantic loss here, there is also gain. Instead of an ideal representation, the larger sentence presents a dramatic expression of ambition, cultural envy, and frustration. The Greeks had the kingdom of their own language. Why, Spenser asks, can't we? Why must we be consigned to perpetual subjection and inferiority? This pressure, this tension, this conflict of aspiration and insecurity, brings us close to the crisis from which Elizabethan poetry emerged, close to the desperately hopeful sense that, were England to rival the greatness of Greece or of Rome, something decisive needed to be done.

And what was that something? To have the kingdom of our own language. To govern the very linguistic system, and perhaps more generally the whole cultural system, by which our own identity and our own consciousness is constituted. To remake it, and presumably ourselves as well, according to some ideal pattern. An extraordinary ambition! But, for most readers, its edge will be blunted, its momentous significance reduced to antiquarian peculiarity, as we step back further to take in more of the surrounding context. 'I like your late English hexameters so exceedingly well,' Spenser writes to Harvey,

> that I also inure my pen sometime in that kind, which I find indeed, as I have heard you often defend in word, neither so hard, nor so harsh, that it will easily and fairly yield itself to our mother tongue. For the only or chiefest hardness, which seemeth, is in the accent, which sometime gapeth and, as it were, yawneth ill-favoredly, coming short of that it should, and sometime exceeding the measure of the number, as in *carpenter*, the middle syllable being used short in speech, when it shall be read long in verse, seemeth like a lame gosling that draweth one leg after her . . . But it is to be won with custom and rough words must be subdued with use. For why a God's name may not we, as else the Greeks, have the kingdom of our own language and measure our accents by the sound, reserving the quantity to the verse?
>
> (10:16)

So *that* is what Spenser was talking about: the comically misguided effort to base English prosody on the rules of ancient quantitative meters. How can anything said in such a context be taken seriously?

Yet Spenser himself seems to have been quite serious about it. The greater part of both his published letters to Harvey is given over to detailed and enthusiastic discussion of this project. He assures Harvey that he is 'of late more in love with my English versifying than with rhyming' (10:6), gives several brief examples of his work in this reformed mode, promises to send a more substantial 'token' of 'what and how well therein I am able to do' (10:17), and names as fellow partisans not only Harvey himself but also Sidney and Dyer. That Harvey and Dyer should have been mistaken in this way causes us no concern. Nor are we much bothered at finding elsewhere in these letters and in other documents the names of Drant, Preston, and Still, of Stanyhurst, Puttenham and Webbe associated with the quantitative movement. Even Greville and Campion are figures small enough to have erred thus greatly without provoking much alarm. But Sidney and Spenser! If, as I have been assuming and as most commentators since the end of the sixteenth century itself have agreed, modern English literature got its first solid foundation in the second half of Elizabeth's reign, these two men have the best claim to being its founders. A project that concerned them deeply just at the moment when their careers were beginning and their most significant works were being written is perhaps less negligible than we are sometimes inclined to think.

To a student of English literary history, the correspondence between Spenser and Harvey comes heavy with the promise of things shortly to be known. When the first of Spenser's letters was written toward the end of 1579, *The Shepheardes Calendar* was as yet unpublished. Indeed, the question of whether to publish at all is among the issues he most worriedly discusses. In those letters, too, we find the earliest reference to *The Faerie Queene*, mentioned along with Spenser's *Slomber*, his *Dying Pellicane*, his nine comedies, and a whole collection of other works that, like these, have disappeared leaving no other trace behind. What if their fate had been shared by *The Shepheardes Calendar* and *The Faerie Queene*? How different the course of our literature would have been! The future that to us is known as a secure past, so familiar that it seems inevitable, was in those years no less laden with uncertainty than with promise. Harvey, who, like Spenser, then stood on the threshold of what appeared a likely, even brilliant, career and whose ambition was, if anything, still greater than Spenser's, went on to a series of failures and public humiliations that have made him a near joke to posterity, saved from total ridicule by little more than his association with Spenser.

A similar fate has, of course, overtaken the quantitative movement. It now seems no less foolish than Harvey, no less futile than the *Dying Pellicane*. Success has a way of making failure look silly. But what if success needs failure as the guarantor of its own identity, the comic (yet still fearful) double that tells what success is not but might have been, tells of the historical abyss into which all ambition threatens to fall? The works that were finally not written, the vocational ambition that was not rewarded, the verse form that was not adopted stand to their successful counterparts as the sounds and meanings that we don't make or intend stand to those that we do. They enable by their absence and difference the production and reception of an intelligible message. For Spenser and Harvey it was, of course, not yet clear which of their many projects would succeed and which would fail – indeed, not clear that any would surely succeed or fail. But already they were ascribing meaning to various attitudes and undertakings by opposing them to others. Harvey does this

when he prefers Spenser's 'nine English comedies' to *The Faerie Queene*.
The meaning of each is defined by its difference from the other. In a
similar but more elaborate way, the two correspondents define
themselves in terms of their differences, Spenser playing giddy Petrarchan
love poet to Harvey's wise counselor and learned scholar, 'our age's
great Cato.' So, to quote Harvey, 'our new famous enterprise for the
exchanging of barbarous and balductum rhymes with artificial verses'
(10:463) derives its intelligibility as much from what it opposes as from
what it supports. Rhyme can be seen as crude and trashy only in
contrast to the fine artifice of quantitative verse.

In the more than four centuries since the letters between Harvey and
Spenser were published, *The Faerie Queene*, Spenser's poetic identity,
and English rhyming verse have entered into many new systems of
difference, altering their meanings as they prospered, while the nine
comedies, Harvey's reputation for wisdom, and the dream of English
verse in quantitative meters have dropped almost completely from
memory, to be recalled only with amusement and wonder. But if we are
to understand why in 1580 Spenser would have so ardently wished to
have the kingdom of his own language and what that ambition meant
for the development of his career and for the more general development
of English poetry and English national self-consciousness, we need at
least to entertain the possibility of valuing the terms that have failed, as
both Spenser and Harvey apparently did, over those that have succeeded.

Not that the two letter writers always agreed with one another in their
own valuation. On the crucial matter of having the kingdom of their own
language, Harvey, though the earlier and keener partisan of the
quantitative movement, thought Spenser went too far.

> In good sooth and by the faith I bear to the Muses, you shall never
> have my subscription or consent (though you should charge me with
> the authority of five hundred Master Drants) to make your *carpĕnter*,
> our *carpĕnter*, an inch longer or bigger than God and his English
> people have made him. Is there no other policy to pull down rhyming
> and set up versifying but you must needs correct *magnificat* and
> against all order of law and in despite of custom forcibly usurp
> and tyrannise upon a quiet company of words that so far beyond the
> memory of man have so peaceably enjoyed their several privileges and
> liberties without any disturbance or the least controlment?
>
> (10:473–74)

Where Spenser had used the language of sovereign power eager to
subdue rough words and have the kingdom of them, Harvey responds in
terms made familiar by centuries of resistance to royal encroachment,
terms that would become still more familiar in the first half of the next

century. He accuses Spenser of usurpation and tyranny, locates authority not in the king but in 'God and his English people,' proclaims the value of custom and the order of law, supports the peaceful enjoyment of immemorial privileges and liberties. Against Spenser's version of the absolutist cultural politics of antiquity, he sets, without quite calling it that, a Gothic, common law tradition. If quantitative verse means correcting *magnificat*, Harvey opposes it. His is, of course, a local response to a very particular provocation. He never develops its implications. Indeed, his arguments elsewhere contradict them. But the intervention is nevertheless significant. For here Harvey discovers, almost inadvertently it would seem, an oppositional politics of national literary self-representation, a politics that would later become far more open and explicit. And in doing so, he suggests one way of reversing the Renaissance hierarchy of values that had prompted him to try quantitative verse in the first place.

In the debate over quantitative meter, as perhaps nowhere else in Elizabethan literary history, the great issues of national self-making came into focus – issues that would prove central to such diverse cultural phenomena as the establishment of the Anglican church, the defense of the common law tradition, the spread of English antiquarian study, the neo-chivalric cult of Elizabeth and the Jacobean reaction to it, the cartographic and chorographic description of Britain, the celebration of British navigation, and the dreams of an English overseas empire. In each of these areas the contribution of men born within just a few years of Spenser and Harvey was especially large. Richard Hooker, Sir Edward Coke, William Camden, John Norden, John Speed, Richard Hakluyt, and Sir Walter Ralegh, all belong to the generation that came of age in the second half of Elizabeth's reign, and all were involved, to a degree that could be equaled by only a very few men of any preceding generation and with a success that could be equaled by none, in a complex and multifaceted articulation of England, a generational project of national self-fashioning in which the effort to found an art of English poetry had a significant, but by no means isolated, place. When Spenser, upset at his inability to make *carpenter* scan the way the rules of classical versification told him it should, impatiently asks why the English can't have the kingdom of their own language as the Greeks had the kingdom of theirs, he evokes a model of self-making that was widely shared by his contemporaries and that for a while governed many of their attempts to lift England to the status of its ancient and modern competitors. And when Harvey answers in the name of immemorial custom, he draws on what would shortly emerge as the principal countermodel. Between these two models, these two ways of asserting and maintaining identity, the struggle for supremacy that we saw latent in the last six words of

Spenser's question, the struggle between king, people, and cultural system, would be waged.

Notes

1. *The Works of Edmund Spenser: A Variorum Edition*, 11 vols., ed. EDWIN GREENLAW et al. (Baltimore: Johns Hopkins Press, 1932–57), 10:16. Subsequent quotations from this edition will be identified in the text. Spelling and punctuation have been modernised throughout, with the single exception of titles of Spenser's individual works which I have allowed to retain their familiar archaic appearance. Titles in the notes follow the spelling of the edition cited.
2. Compare King James's formula, 'king, people, law' (*law* here representing the cultural system, as language does in Spenser), in the preface to his *Basilikon Doron* (*The Political Works of James I*, ed. C. H. McIlwain [Cambridge, Mass. Harvard University Press, 1918]), p. 7.

3 'The perfecte paterne of a poete': the poetics of courtship in *The Shepheardes Calender*[*][1]

LOUIS MONTROSE

The purpose of this essay is to contextualise the matters of literary convention, genre, mode, etc., in which *The Shepheardes Calendar* was being read by literary historians, in terms of such socio-political issues as ambition, patronage, upward mobility, and sovereign-subject relations. The aim is to give a materialist grounding to Petrarchan and other forms of erotic rhetoric, and to link Spenser's programme of literary aspiration with his programme of social advancement.

Louis Montrose is one of the foremost New Historicist critics working in the Renaissance. In his more recent work he has continued his explorations into the nature of power and sexuality in the Renaissance and also produced an often-cited defence of New Historicism, arguing that 'the newer historical criticism is *new* in its refusal of unproblematised distinctions between "literature" and "history", between "text" and "context"; new in resisting a prevalent tendency to posit and privilege a unified and autonomous individual – whether an Author or a Work – to be set against a social or literary background' ('Professing the Renaissance: The Poetics and Politics of Culture', in H. Aram Veeser, ed., *The New Historicism* (London: Routledge, 1989), pp. 15–36, at p. 18).

First among the verses which commend Spenser's heroic poem to its royal audience is Ralegh's graceful vision of 'The grave, where Laura lay':

> All suddenly I saw the Faery Queene:
> At whose approach the soule of *Petrarke* wept,
> And from thenceforth those graces were not seene.
> For they this Queene attended; in whose steed
> Oblivion laid him downe on *Lauras* herse.[2]

---

*First published in *Texas Studies in Literature and Language*, 21:1 (Spring 1979), 34–67.

Ralegh envisions Spenser as overgoing not Vergil or Chaucer but Petrarch
– not the epic poet of the *Africa* but the visionary love poet of the
Canzoniere and *Trionfi*. The Faerie Queene supplants Laura as the supreme
image of the poet-lover's power to sublimate desire. Ralegh does not
envision *The Faerie Queen* as an exemplary heroic poem but as the verbal
courtship of an exalted female whose patronage can satisfy the poet's
material ambitions and those whose Idea is a spur to his moral and poetic
aspirations. In other words, Ralegh is suggesting that *The Faerie Queene*
and his own *Cynthia* poems are parallel in strategy and purpose. Spenser
had declared a public, Vergilian vocation in his *Letter* to Ralegh; by
transforming Spenser's declaration into intimate Petrarchan terms, Ralegh
illuminates a characteristic stance of the Spenserian persona: a humble
poet celebrates a sublime female figure – a Petrarchan mistress, great
lady, goddess, or saint. This *topos* is a conspicuous one in Spenser's
poetry. He uses it to express a dialectic of poetic aspirations and
constraints, to articulate his awareness of a discrepancy between the
myth of the Poet's high calling and the functions to which his skills are
relegated in his own society. These Spenserian preoccupations appear
in incipient form in *The Shepheardes Calendar*, shadowed in the pastoral
simplifications of Colin Clout's 'great misadventure in Love' (*Aprill*,
Argument). My object is to explore the implications of Ralegh's conceit
for an understanding of Colin's role in the *Calendar*. Colin's courtships
unfold a sequence exemplifying 'the perfecte paterne of a Poete' set forth
in the dialogue of *October*. He enacts an amorous courtship of Rosalind,
a social courtship of Eliza, a spiritual courtship of Dido. Each of Colin's
wooings is also Spenser's exploration of a particular mode of poetic power
and form; each is a manifestation of the arduous courtship of the Muse.

I

In *The Shepheardes Calender*, Spenser inventories and analyses the heritage
of the English poet; he assesses the aims and resources, the limitations
and dangers, of the poetic vocation. The poem is a vehicle for the highest
personal aspirations and public significance a poet can claim: a vatic
role, sanctioned by the artistic and ethical idealism of Renaissance
Humanism but frustrated by the constraints of a social order controlled
by powers for whom poetry is, at worst, morally corrupting and
politically subversive; at best, a useful instrument of policy or an
innocuous diversion. Colin's courtships of Rosalind, Eliza, and Dido are
permutations of the *Calender's* recurrent attempt to transform language
into power, to animate the word as a force in the world, to create the

personal and social harmony which, for Renaissance poets and
rhetoricians, is figured in the responsiveness of nature to the music of
Orpheus.

The Shepheardes Calender is something more than a skillful poetic
restatement of ethical, political, and religious orthodoxies. Its
publication in 1579 demonstrated the capacity of the vernacular to
produce a poetry 'well grounded, finely framed, and strongly trussed
up together' (Epistle). Spenser's conspicuous concern with the creation
and projection of a poetic persona and his thematic emphasis on erotic
desire and social ambition proffered to readers a range of verbal strategies
that could give formal expression to the complexity and ambivalence
of an emergent generational consciousness. The *Calender*'s catalytic power
is attested by the vigorous growth of an Elizabethan pastoral tradition
in its wake; by its immediate and continued popularity during the 1580s
and 1590s; and by other poets' elevation of Spenser's Colin to the status
of *genius loci* in their pastoral worlds. Colin is a poet, lover, and courtier;
a would-be mover of trees and waters, mistresses and rulers, in a world
in which the degree of success to which he aspires is beyond reach.[3] Colin
can be identified neither as a simple allegorical projection of Spenser
nor as a pathetic and unenlightened antithesis to his sage and serious
creator. 'Immerito,' the persona of the poet who has written the *Calender*,
presents himself within the eclogues in the persona of 'Colin Clout.'
'Touching the generall dryft and purpose' of Immerito's self-presentation,
E. K. writes that 'his unstayed yougth had long wandred in the common
Labyrinth of Love, in which time to mitigate and allay the heate of his
passion, or els to warne (as he sayth) the young shepheards .s. his equals
and companions of his unfortunate folly, he compiled these xii
Aeglogues' (Epistle). Colin's pattern of prodigality and misfortune has
its origin precisely in his successful embrace of the Renaissance poet's
pastoral role; the literary shepherd's otiose environment of eroticism and
poetry is being viewed through the stern spectacles of Tudor patriarchal
morality. In a Reformation society whose ideology reinforces strict control
by personal, political, academic, and ecclesiastical fathers, sexual passion
and love poetry signify waste and idleness, a dangerous lack of bodily
and spiritual self-discipline, a potential threat of insubordination and
rebellion.[4]

The Vergilian progression puts pastoral at the beginning of the poet's
career; the principle of decorum puts it at the bottom of the hierarchy
of poetic kinds. Pastoral is persistently associated with new poets and
with poets who are young. In the Epistle to the *Calender*, E. K. speculates
on Immerito's motives for writing eclogues:

doubting perhaps his habilitie, which he little needed, or mynding to
furnish our tongue with this kinde, wherein it faulteth, or following

the example of the best and most auncient Poetes, which devised this kind of wryting, being both so base for the matter, and homely for the manner, at the first to trye theyr habilities: and as young birdes, that be newly crept out of the nest, by little first to prove theyr tender wyngs, before they make a greater flyght. . . . So finally flyeth this our new Poete, as a bird, whose principals be scarce growen out, but yet as that in time shall be hable to keepe wing with the best.

This conjunction of humility and pride exemplifies the pastoral poet's capacity to strike ambivalent poses. Spenser articulates a tense relationship to literary and social patriarchy shared by many in his literary generation: poetic progenitors have shaped a literary tradition within which the new poet must find a place by creative imitation; the elder Tudor generation has shaped and still controls the social institutions and cultural values within which the young, educated gentleman or would-be gentleman must live and write and try to advance himself.

Tensions between generations and between cultural values that are observable in later Elizabethan society are mirrored in the uneasy mixture of two currents within the *Calender*. Spenser's moral eclogues persistently oppose youth and age, ambition and contentment, recklessness and caution, insolence and deference, eroticism and asceticism. The youthful figures in the moral eclogues manifest crude analogues of Colin's refined obsessions, though they can in no way emulate his verbal skill. E. K.'s Epistle suggests that the way to unify one's moral experience of this heterogeneous poem is to read the relationship between Immerito and Colin in terms of the moral eclogues' dichotomies: the sage, serious, and mature moral poet confronts and condemns the image of his own unstayed youth, turning the unfortunate folly of his past to the public good and redeeming poetry from wantonness. But the debates in the moral eclogues are between limited perspectives.[5] Spenser does not provide an easy validation of his reader's stock homiletic responses; he encourages them to interpret and evaluate dialectically. The relationship between Immerito and Colin involves a similar strategy. Spenser's work fuses the sober Tudor Humanism of his rigorous formal education at the Merchant Taylors' School and Cambridge with the elegant romanticism, restless expansiveness, and troubled introspection that characterise the later Elizabethan cultural milieu. In both *The Shepheardes Calender* and *The Faerie Queene*, Spenser attempts to transcend the cultural opposition that he is articulating; the poems repeatedly evidence the strains and contradictions involved in this attempt. In *The Faerie Queene*, erotic and poetic fertility come to be celebrated as complementary heroic virtues that have emanated from the pastoral environments of The Garden of Adonis and Mount Acidale. But Spenser must continue to defend his celebratory vision against 'these Stoicke censours' (*FQ*, IV. Proem. 3) and against The Blatant Beast. Colin's life within the *Calender* projects a poetic vocation of the kind upon which Spenser himself is ambitiously embarking – but one which runs its course toward that failure which the aspiring minds of Elizabethan society are forever being warned to expect. Spenser readies for his greater flight by apprising himself of its hazards, not by eliminating them.

II

E. K. divides the eclogues 'into three formes or ranckes. For eyther they be Plaintive . . . or recreative, such as al those be, which conceive matter of love, or commendation of special personages, or Moral: which for the most part be mixed with some Satyrical bitternesse' (Generall Argument). The eclogues that E. K. classifies as 'Moral' depict potential conflicts between narrow self-interest and common profit, and explore the difficulty of creating an effective, morally motivated rhetoric to do battle against the perversions of language that can mislead the susceptible human will. 'Recreative' poetry is celebratory. It commends the virtue of its subject and signifies a harmonious relationship between subject and poet; it creates a joyful circumstance in which poetry itself can be celebrated. 'Complaint' is the poetry of frustrated desire, unfulfilled longing, alienation; it is a protest against an irremediable reality that obtrudes into a vision of happiness, harmony, perfection. Colin's complaints bemoan the absence, loss, or irretrievability of the recreative state in its idealised personal form, as the fulfillment of sexual love. The refinements of mood and expression in Colin's plaintive poetry transform its subject – the loss of recreative experience – into a new form of recreative experience; the frustration of erotic desire offers an occasion for the perfection of imaginative form. Colin is not the image of a man in history but rather the image of a poet in literary history. He experiences the joys and sorrows of aspiration and suffers conflict and desire in the intimate terms of love and poetry. It is largely through Colin's experience that Spenser relates poetics to the other forms of verbal expression and coercion that the *Calender* mirrors. The moral mode complements the plaintive, for it originates in the denial or loss of erotic recreation's authentic social form: a community organised on the principle and practise of charity.

Immerito begins his cycle of eclogues with Colin's plaintive invocation: 'Ye Gods of love, that pittie lovers payne,/ (If any gods the paine of lovers pittie:),' and with the initial allusion to the poem's underlying plaintive/ recreative myth: 'And Pan thou shepheards God, that once didst love,/

Pitie the paines, that thou thy selfe didst prove' (*Januarye*, 13–14, 17–18). Pan is an archetype of the creative power of the human spirit, for he accomplishes his own transformation of what the Olympian gods have already transformed: Syrinx is metamorphosed into reeds; Pan makes a musical instrument from the reeds, turns nature into art, creates culture.[6] Pan brings forth music from the artifact he has made; he is able to transform erotic frustration into the consolation of an art that can recreate the senses and the spirit, that can turn the plaintive into the recreative and turn sorrow into celebration.

In *Januarye*, the irony of Colin's situation is that he is unable to transform the pain of love into the plaintive solace of poetic creation. Colin's poetry has been the expression of his love and the medium of his courtship. The disappointment of his erotic aspirations manifests the rhetorical failure of his erotic poetry: 'She deignes not my good will, but doth reprove,/And of my rurall musick holdeth scorne' (63–4). The pain of longing and denial impels Petrarchan creativity, but it renders Colin poetically sterile:

> Wherefore my pype, albee rude *Pan* thou please,
> Yet for thou pleasest not, where most I would:
> And thou unlucky Muse, that wontst to ease
> My musing mynd, yet canst not, when thou should:
> Both pype and Muse, shall sore the while abye.
>
> (67–71)

It is conventional for oncoming night to end an eclogue. Here nightfall implies an ironic relationship between Colin and Apollo: 'So broke his oaten pype, and downe dyd lye./By that, the welked *Phoebus* gan avail' (72–3). The transition from 'rude *Pan*' to 'the welked *Phoebus*' is the *Calender*'s initial, oblique allusion to the singing contest between Pan and Apollo. It suggests Colin's failure to accomplish a critical vocational transition from the pastoral already mastered and outgrown to the higher poetic calling which remains above his reach. Colin's Apollonian aspirations are frustrated, and this frustration is beyond the powers of Pan to sublimate into recreative pastoral art.[7]

III

The *Aprill* eclogue, which E. K. classifies as 'Recreative,' interrelates 'matter of love' and 'commendation of special personages,' transforms sexual into social courtship, and connects the celebratory mode to the

plaintive and moral modes which frame Colin's lay by providing
the circumstances of its performance and reception. It is a historical
circumstance of immense political and cultural significance that, for the
second half of the sixteenth century, England's sovereign is a virgin queen
who is governor of both state and church, and whose personal
mythology is contrived to be a national and Protestant substitute for a
cult of the Blessed Virgin. One literary consequence is the production of
royal encomia which assimilate to the public celebration of an earthly
ruler both the sacred psalm or hymn of praise and the private love
sonnet, which itself was often classed as a species of encomiastic poetry.[8]
The relationship between courtier-poet and Queen is idealised as a love
that has been purified of physical desire; its erotic energy has been
transformed into art and service. The public ritualisations of intimate
relationship in encomia of Elizabeth serve effectively as instruments of
policy, as romantic mystifications of the motives of the Queen and her
councillors. But they can also function as idealisations of the motives of
courtier-poets. The rhetoric of royal encomium provides an allowable
occasion for the cultivation of love poetry, and a purified medium for the
pursuit of socio-economic advancement. The Elizabeth cult can serve
the personal aesthetic and material ends of her worshippers.

The crux of the *Aprill* eclogue's strategy is in the second stanza of
Colin's song. Here the poet metamorphoses an Ovidian aetiology into
a Tudor genealogy: 'For shee is *Syrinx* daughter without spotte,/Which
Pan the shepheards God of her begot' (50–1). E. K. glosses Pan variously
as God, Christ, and Henry VIII. Spenser's myth alludes to the immaculate
conception of a blessed virgin, cleverly countering Catholic insinuations
of Elizabeth's bastardy with an insinuation of her divinity. If we follow
out the Ovidian logic of the myth, which E. K. retells concisely in his
gloss, it becomes obvious that Elisa is also a personification of pastoral
poetry: the 'offspring' of the love chase and the nymph's transformation
were the reeds from which Pan created his pipe.[9] The myth of *Aprill* is a
variation on the myth of *Januarye*.

Sannazaro, one of the 'excellent . . . Poetes, whose foting this Author
every where followeth' (Epistle), has re-created the myth of the origins
and history of pastoral poetry in the Tenth Prose of his *Arcadia*. There the
shepherds are led to a sacred grove by a priest who is the genius of
the pastoral world. They see a great pipe of seven reeds hung up before
a cave: it is the pipe of Pan. The priest narrates the myth of Syrinx's
metamorphosis and Pan's creation of the pipes from the reeds into which
she has been changed, the descent of the pipes into the hands of
Theocritus ('a shepherd of Syracuse') and thence into the hands of Vergil
('Mantuan Tityrus'). The priest alludes to Vergil's fourth eclogue: the
celebration of an unborn child and a new age of peace and plenty,
subsequently interpreted as a prophecy of the Advent of Christ. The priest

concludes by recounting Vergil's restlessness within the pastoral's narrow and lowly confines, and his progression from eclogues through georgics to epic. The implication of the episode is that the pipes of Pan have passed into the hands of Sincero, Sannazaro's Petrarchan persona, who is only sojourning in the pastoral world.

Spenser's fourth eclogue incorporates and complicates Sannazaro's strategy; it re-creates the myth of Pan and Syrinx in the context of a royal encomium which is being advanced as an English and Protestant fulfillment of Vergil's fourth eclogue. The myth of Elisa's generation from the union of Pan and Syrinx is a re-creation of the original Ovidian myth, in which the desire for sexual union was first frustrated, then sublimated into a union of Pan's breath with the reeds into which Syrinx had been changed. The subject of Colin's recreative encomium is an act of poetic re-creation. The first stanza is an invocation to the Muses; the second stanza expresses the conception of an image through a genealogical procreation myth; in the third stanza, the unfolding of the image commences with the imperative, 'See, where she sits upon the grassie greene' (55); the final stanza bids the perfected image to go forth into the world, to be received by the Queen: 'Now ryse up *Elisa*, decked as thou art,/in royall array' (145–6). The poet has transformed *Eliza* into *Elisa*. Elisa, the special personage which has been the subject of his celebration, he commends to Elizabeth, the special personage from whom he hopes a commendation in return: 'Let dame *Eliza* thanke you for her song' (150). Spenser emphasizes Elisa's status as an ideal image created by the poet, rather than her status as a poetic reflection of Elizabeth:

> So sprong her grace
> Of heavenly race,
> No mortall blemishe may her blotte.
>
> (52.4)

The effect is to discriminate the ideal image from the actual personage who is the nominal subject of celebration.

The genealogical myth is repeated from a different perspective in the seventh stanza, the numerical center of the encomium:

> *Pan* may be proud, that ever he begot
>   such a Bellibone,
> And *Syrinx* rejoyse, that ever was her lot
>   to bear such an one.
> Soone as my younglings cryen for the dam,
> To her will I offer a milkwhite Lamb:
>   Shee is my goddesse plaine,

> And I her shepherds swayne,
> Albee forswonck and forswatt I am.
>
> (91–9)

The lowly pastoral deities, shepherd-poet and muse, have engendered a great goddess. The poet shifts into a suppliant style of courtship. At the center of the idealising form within which the poet has boldly re-created the human personage of Elizabeth in his own inspired image, the courtier humbly worships his Queen. In *Aprill*, the triumphant first occurrence of the myth of Pan and Syrinx blazes the praise of the Orphic poet who articulates a vision of perfection toward which humanity may strive. In its poignant recurrence, the myth ushers in a pastoral image of the poet's status in the actual social order; it suggests the subservience of poetic to political power, and the poet's economic dependency on the patronage system manipulated by the Queen and her regime. The poet's gift is a rhetorically powerful symbolic form, an illusion that sanctifies political power; the poet's expectation is a reciprocal, material benefit. Spenser qualifies a visionary conception of poetry by placing it within the context of his own historical and social existence and by expressing it as the erotic idealisation of a power relationship.

Colin's 'laye of Fayre *Elisa*' is a poem-within-a-poem, a framed performance; the responses of the fictional auditors within the eclogue condition the reader's responses to Colin's song. According to its prefatory 'Argument,' the eclogue's intention is encomiastic; it is recreative, in E. K.'s sense of the term, and its subject is the Queen. Within the eclogue's fiction, however, Hobbinoll's purpose in singing Colin's song is to celebrate not the subject but the poet, not Elisa but Colin. The occasion of composition was recreative but the occasion which gives rise to Hobbinoll's performance is plaintive. The poem lives in the memory of those who have heard and admired it; it is now a public trust, a document of cultural history. The poet himself is now lost in love melancholy, alienated from his creative sources and from the society which he has endowed: 'Hys pleasant Pipe, whych made us meriment,/ He wylfully hath broke' (14–15). In the ambiguous commentary of the shepherds which follows Colin's song, Spenser insinuates that Colin's relationships to Rosalind and Eliza are permutations of an underlying problematic of desire:

> THENOT.
> And was thilk same song of *Colins* owne making?
> Ah foolish boy, that is with love yblent:
> Great pittie is, he be in such taking,
> For naught caren, that been so lewdly bent.

HOBBINOLL.
Sicker I hold him, for the greater fon,
That loves the thing, he cannot purchase.

(154–9)

The poetic power manifested in the song is now lost because love for
Rosalind is debilitating. But there is also the implication that the song
itself was the manifestation of a reckless aspiration for which Colin now
suffers. Within the fiction of the *Aprill* eclogue, Colin's recreative song
is being revived in a plaintive pastoral world where love breeds pain as
well as joy. *Januarye's* plaintiveness provides the context for our
experience of *Aprill's* recreation.

IV

The charming *August* eclogue is a qualified celebration of the therapeutic
powers of poetry. Perigot's love pangs lightly parody the plaintiveness
of Colin Clout; Willye has the recreative shepherd's perfect response: 'But
and if in rymes with me thou dare strive,/Such fond fantsies shall soone
be put to flight' (21–2). What the 'Argument' calls the 'delectable
controversie' of their singing match is the sublimation of the political,
intellectual, and emotional strife of the moral and plaintive eclogues into
harmonious counterpoint. Enchased on the mazer that Willye pledges is a
shepherd saving a lamb from the jaws of a wolf: the scenario of the moral
eclogues is re-created in the happy stillness of art. The singing contest
between rude Pan and great Apollo – Colin's myth of vocational anxiety
– is replaced by a game between youthful, rustic equals. Cuddie is a
delighted auditor whose appreciation is gracefully manifested in his
refusal to disrupt the present harmony by a partial judgment. The
interplay of songs is concluded in the exchange of gifts; this is a model
of perfect reciprocity, in which there are no losers.

Cuddie repays the shepherd's entertainment by rehearsing 'a doolefull
verse/of Rosalend . . . That Colin made' (140–2). The powerful, plaintive
sestina is framed by the recreative expectations and responses of its fictive
audience. The sestina distills an experience of alienation antithetical to
the experience of community pervading the framing eclogue. The
shepherd's response is not empathy with Colin's anguished spirit but
awed delight in his skill: 'O Colin, Colin, the shepheards joy,/How I
admire ech turning of thy verse' (190–1). The sestina is proof of Colin's
skill in making, and of his power to recreate the spirit of his audience;
but its performance reveals a profound disjunction between poet and

poem. Colin's *Aprill* encomium is an ideal image toward which Elizabeth may aspire; its creator remains a suppliant shepherd. Colin's *August* sestina delights its hearers and elicits their admiration, yet it cannot heal his anguish. The sestina's power to elicit its listeners' admiration for Colin's art is undercut by its failure to elicit their empathy with his sufferings. The rhetoric of ornamentation displaces the rhetoric of persuasion; action is sacrificed to admiration. The poet's capacity for verbal idealisation is no longer a medium of tangible power; it degenerates into a strategy for the obfuscation and compensation of frustrated desires and ambitions. (In *June*, Colin's craving for vituperative poetic power to revenge himself upon the actual Rosalind is the destructive result of his inability to console himself with her ideal image.) The failures of rhetorical efficacy within *The Shepheardes Calender* are projections of the frustrations that a poet with Orphic pretensions must experience in a world not moved by his song.

V

The thematic nucleus of the *October* eclogue is formed out of the poet's inability effectively to refashion his audience 'in vertuous and gentle discipline,' and his failure to elicit the gracious and bountiful thanks which the ideals of courtesy proclaim to be his due. Colin's plaintiveness is parodied in the disappointment impeding Cuddie's production of the verbal confections that pleasure his fellow shepherds. Like Colin's love songs, Cuddie's rhymes and riddles have not elicited from their audience the return which his own poetic gift was devised to procure:

> The dapper ditties, that I wont devise,
> To feede youthes fancie, and the flocking fry,
> Delighten much: what I the bett for thy?
> They han the pleasure, I a sclender prise.
>
> (13–16)

Cuddie is a purely recreative versifier; his appeal to the baser instincts of youth befits the baseness of his own conception of the poet's proper reward.[10]

Piers responds to Cuddie's complaint with the moralised Elizabethan defense of poetry and poets: the right poet is a persuader to virtue who seeks only the reward of honor. This initial opposition of poetic stereotypes – purely recreative and debased by materialistic ambitions; purely moral and elevated by virtuous aspirations – generates a dialectic

of reformulated positions at successively higher generic levels. The
absolute values of the initial positions become more ambivalent as the
dialogue unfolds. Cuddie's first response is to deflate Piers' idealism by
a commonsensical insistence on life's material necessities:

> But who rewards him ere the more for thy?
> Or feedes him once the fuller by a graine?
> Sike prayse is smoke, that sheddeth in the skye,
> Sike words bene wynd, and wasten soone in vayne.
>
> (33–6)

Piers' counter-response is to counsel poetic aspirations synonymous with
vicarious social elevation: the more elevated the poetic kind, the more
elite its subjects and audience. Cuddie is advised to abandon 'the base
and viler clowne,' whom Piers has previously declared to be the object of
the moral poet's reforming power. Now Cuddie is to sing of love and
war in an encomiastic epic which celebrates the heroic virtue of Eliza
and 'the worthy whome shee loveth best' (47) – Elizabeth and Leicester
as E. K.'s gloss informs us.

As the poet's subject becomes more exalted, his audience more
powerful, and his own chance for fame and material reward more
tangible, his Orphic powers become correspondingly confined. The higher
the poet aspires, the more he becomes encomiast rather than teacher
and reformer. The idealistic Piers attributes this phenomenon to the
identity of moral and social hierarchies. The crucial change conditioning
the poetic subject is in the nature of the poet's audience: the base and
vile clown must be instructed; virtuous and gentle lords and princes
elicit only praise. The modern poet's situation is seen from a less idealising
perspective in *The Teares of the Muses*. There Polyhymnia laments the
Elizabethan poet's decline in power from his prototypes:

> Whilom in ages past none might professe
> But Princes and high Priests that secret skill,
> The sacred lawes therein they wont expresse,
> And with deepe Oracles their verses fill:
> Then was shee held in soveraigne dignitie,
> And made the noursling of Nobilitie.
> But now nor Prince nor Priest doth her maintayne.
>
> (*TM*, 559–65)

In the beginning was the word. In an ideal mythic past, poetry was the
profession of society's leaders; and, by implication, poets enjoyed
the perquisites of a social elite. Intellectual and imaginative power were
then synonymous with political and metaphysical power. The historical

conditions of Spenser's society have reduced the Poet-Priest to an inferior and dependent position in relation to the aristocratic patron and poetaster.

Queen Elizabeth, of course, is lauded as 'Most peereles Prince, most peereles Poetresse' (577). And

> Some few beside, this sacred skill esteme,
> Admirers of her glorious excellence,
> Which being lightened with her beawties beme,
> Are thereby fild with happie influence:
> And lifted up above the worldes gaze,
> To sing with Angels her immortall praize.
>
> (*TM*, 583–8)

The Queen's perfection inspires the poet's praise – but does not the poet's praise create her perfection? A rhetorical strategy of the encomiastic poet is to establish his own greatness through his praise of the prince's greatness. Becoming one with the angels, he restores to himself the title of high priest. Yet the wailing burden of *The Teares of the Muses* is that the poet's claim to his inheritance goes unrecognised, and that its material fruits are not forthcoming. The Muse of epic, Calliope, laments,

> For noble Peeres whom I wont to raise,
> Now onely seke for pleasure, nought for praise.
>
> Their great revenues all in sumptuous pride
> They spend, that nought to learning they may spare;
> And the rich fee which Poets wont divide,
> Now Parasites and Sycophants doo share.
>
> (*TM*, 467–72)

In the clear view from Parnassus, the Muse can distinguish Sycophant and Poet as antitheses; for the poet who invokes his queen as his muse, the distinction becomes profoundly problematic.

Cuddie's response to Piers in *October* echoes the complaint of Calliope in *The Teares of the Muses*. The patronage of Maecenas drew Vergil from pastoral and georgic to the epic song of which Augustus was worthy. But the moral virtue which was once synonymous with temporal power has fallen off:

> But after vertue gan for age to stoupe,
> And mighty manhode brought a bedde of ease:
> The vaunting Poets found nought worth a pease,
> To put in preace among the learned troupe.

Tho gan the streames of flowing wittes to cease,
And sonnebright honour pend in shamefull coupe.
And if that any buddes of Poesie,
Yet of the old stocke gan to shoote agayne:
Or it mens follies mote be forst to fayne,
And rolle with rest in rymes of rybaudrye:
Or as it sprong, it wither must agayne:
Tom Piper makes us better melodie.

(67–78)

Cuddie implies that, at least in part, the debasement of poetry into idle
fripperies is the result of the political and socioeconomic constraints
placed upon the poet. The predicament of the heroic poet in the present
age is that he has no subject worthy of celebration and is not free to
reprehend his audience so as to refashion them into subjects worthy of
praise. Heroic poetry's lack of a worthy subject becomes the subject
of moral pastoral mixed with some satirical bitterness. Such pastorals
must use allegory, 'to insinuate and glaunce at greater matters, and such
as perchance had not bene safe to have beene disclosed in any other
sort.'[11] In *A Discourse of English Poetrie* (1586), William Webbe lauds the
Calender as the equal of Vergil's *Eclogues*, and calls Spenser 'the rightest
English Poet that ever I read.' In addition to its

> many good Morall lessons . . . there is also much matter uttered
> somewhat covertly, especially the abuses of some whom he would
> not be too playne withall: in which, though it be not apparent to every
> one what hys speciall meaning was, yet so skillfully is it handled, as any
> man may take much delight at hys learned conveyance, and pick out
> much good sense in the most obscurest of it.[12]

Allegory is not only a veil to prevent the profanation of spiritual mysteries
but also an obfuscation of meaning and intention necessary to
circumvent governmental hostility to all expressions of dissent or
controversy.

The degeneration of the great into luxury and corruption is the thematic
link between *October* and the eclogues which attack clerical abuses. A
primary function of the *Calender*'s pastoral metaphor is to link poet and
priest together through a common signifier, the persona of shepherd.
June and *Julye*, the central eclogues of the *Calender*, are complementary
dialogues on the temptations and dangers of aspiration faced by shepherd-
poets and shepherd-priests. In *June*, Hobbinoll recounts that Calliope, the
Muse of epic and mother of Orpheus, was moved and shamed by the skill
of Colin's 'oaten Pype.' Colin responds by rejecting the Vergilian
progression:

> For sith I heard, that *Pan* with *Phoebus* strove,
> Which him to much rebuke and Daunger drove:
> I never lyst presume to *Parnasse* hyll,
> But pyping lowe in shade of lowly grove,
> I play to please my selfe, all be it ill.
>
> (68–72)

Julye employs the pastoral debate between humility and ambition in an ecclesiastical allegory. The eclogue distinguishes between the self-aggrandising ambitions of worldly prelates and the selfless aspirations of good pastors who teach their flocks and reprehend corruption in high places. Colin's ambivalence toward poetic aspiration and commitment is put into a social context by *Julye*. It may be presumptuous of a humble shepherd-poet to answer the call of Calliope. But refusal of the poet's calling, or the priest's, may be the dereliction of a higher duty.

Spenser's allusions to Archbishop Grindal ('Algrind') in *Maye* and *Julye* suggest his sympathy with Grindal's reformist convictions, his resistance to the corrupting effects of high ecclesiastical office and defiant support of 'prophesyings.' These bible discussion groups were strongly opposed by the queen on the grounds that they bred 'variety of dangerous opinions' among 'the vulgar sort.' She saw clearly that prophesyings fostered Puritanism and that Puritanism undermined royal supremacy and the hierarchical social principles of privilege and deference.[13] *Julye* concludes with a boldly explicit allusion to Elizabeth's reprisal for Grindal's outspokenness that is thoroughly sympathetic to the archbishop. By combining within his *Calender* moral and recreative eclogues, politics and poetics, Algrind and Colin, Spenser implies analogies between religious and poetic visions, and between the burdens of religious and poetic vocations. In his study of liberty and authority in Elizabethan England, Joel Hurstfield has concluded 'that the measure of private freedom . . . was small; that the government tried where it could to condition men's minds and where it could not, to repress diversity of opinion . . . It thought that to preserve social stability and national freedom it must suppress private freedom.'[14] The Elizabethan social order is one in which the expression of personal opinions – and in matters of policy, the very possession of personal opinions – is no right at all but rather a privilege granted conditionally and tenuously to a very few. Spenser's poetry is the instrument of an extraordinarily comprehensive and subtle speculation on the nature and limits of Elizabethan ideals and actualities. The expression of such a poetic vision is subject to constraints like those imposed upon the exercise of personal conscience and conviction in matters of politics and religion. Spenser himself is confronted by the specter of which he writes, the Poet's tongue, 'nayld to a post':

> Thus there he stood, whylest high over his head,
> There written was the purport of his sin,
> In cyphers strange, that few could rightly read,
> BON FONT: but *bon* that once had written bin,
> Was raced out, and *Mal* was now put in.
>
> (*FQ*, V. ix. 26)

In *October*, Piers first champions the poet's Orphic power to teach his fellows, then shifts his emphasis to the poet's skill in praising his betters. Finally, he responds to Cuddie's indictment of the present age by urging transcendence:

> O pierlesse Poesye, where is then thy place?
> If nor in Princes pallace thou doe sitt;
> (And yet is Princes pallace the most fitt)
> Ne brest of baser birth doth thee embrace.
> Then make thee winges of thine aspyring wit,
> And, whence thou camst, flye backe to heaven apace.
>
> (79–84)

Piers accepts Cuddie's critique and is led to reformulate substantially his own conception of poetic vocation. An implicit concurrence seems now to exist between the interlocutors: 'fayre *Elisa* [and] the worthy whome shee loveth best' – Spenser's queen and his patron – are unfit subjects for an uncompromising and uncompromised poetry of praise.

Cuddie's final outburst wanes quickly; he recognises his own limits and rejects aspiration for the comforts and safety of mediocrity:

> For thy, content us in thys humble shade:
> Where no such troublous tydes han us assayde,
> Here we our slender pipes may safely charme.
>
> (116–18)

Cuddie's final response to the poet's social responsibilities echoes Hobbinoll's response to Diggon's sustained and impassioned attack on ecclesiastical abuses:

> Now Diggon, I see thou speakest to plaine:
> Better it were, a little to feyne,
> And cleanly cover, that cannot be cured.
> Such il, as is forced, mought nedes be endured.
>
> (*September*, 136–9)

Shepherd poets can maintain their *otium* only by closing their eyes and

45

ears to the unpleasant actualities impinging upon the pastoral world. The shepherds begin by opposing materialistic and idealistic perspectives on the social place of poetry and poets; they end by jointly abandoning heroic poetry, the poetry of virtuous action-in-the-world. Cuddie's resignation to the poetry of pastoral triviality complements Piers' gesture toward the poetry of spiritual transcendence; both tacitly acknowledge the modern poet's inability to transform society, to turn a brazen world to gold.

VI

The pastoral elegy sung by Colin in *November* is filled with echoes of the previous eclogues in which he has had a role. Thenot urges Colin to awake his sorrowful Muse, 'Whether thee list thy loved lasse advaunce,/ or honour *Pan* with hymnes of higher vaine' (7–8). But Colin remains steadfast in his rejection of the recreative, Panic persona: 'Thenot, now nis the time of merimake./Nor *Pan* to herye, nor with love to playe' (9–10). In challenging Colin to overgo his performance of the *August* sestina (43–6), Thenot is also challenging him to transcend the situation that the sestina distills. The *Aprill* lay and the *August* sestina were rehearsed by other shepherds because Colin no longer sang; the *November* elegy is a spontaneous creation sung by Colin in the eclogue's narrative present. Colin now refrains from the sublimated eroticism of *Aprill* and the frustrated eroticism of *August*. In this public performance, the poet includes himself within the poem among those who have been formed into a community of mourners by Dido's death: 'So well she couth the shepherds entertayne,/ . . . Als *Colin cloute* she would not once disdayne' (95–101). Dido is remembered as a public fulfillment of the private audience Rosalind refused to be: 'She deignes not my good will, but doth reprove,/And of my rurall music, holdeth scorne' (*Januarye*, 63–4); and as a courteous and bounteous fulfillment of the public audience that Colin hoped Eliza would be: 'Let dame *Eliza* thanke you for her song' (*Aprill*, 150).

Why is the subject of this crucial elegy within Spenser's neo-Vergilian poem named Dido? The *November* eclogue has been thought to be an obscure topical allegory. It has been proposed that, because Vergil's Dido is also named Elissa, Spenser's Elisa and Dido are projections of Elizabeth.[15] Little attention has otherwise been paid to the significance of the name change in Spenser's imitation of Marot's *elegie* for Loyse de Savoye. The effect, however, is to make Spenser's pastoral elegy a conspicuous allusion to and revision of the critical episode of recreative truancy in Vergil's epic. Vergil's Dido embodies all those passionate, private needs and desires that must be repudiated by the hero who is destined to refound civilisation on principles of law and reason; Aeneas' private person must be subsumed by the public role and its collective burdens. After her suicide, Dido wanders among the shades of other unfortunate lovers in the fields of mourning. Aeneas passes the fields of mourning on his journey to the Elysian fields, the exclusive preserve of heroes, where he is to receive prophetic knowledge from the spirit of his father. Aeneas greets Dido and is spurned by her; she is now reunited with her first husband. In the *November* elegy, Colin's Dido has found her own rightful place in the field of heroes, where the poet hopes to join her. Dido's apotheosis inspires in Colin the desire for a transcendent object which will make him one of the community of saints:

> I see thee blessed soule, I see,
> Walke in *Elisian* fieldes so free.
>   O happy herse,
> Might I once come to thee (O that I might)
>   O joyful verse.

(179–82)

Spenser's is a Christian elegy, whose Elysian fields figure the heavenly bliss of blessed souls. *November*'s Christian poetry is a revision of both Vergil's *Aeneid* and Spenser's Vergilian *Aprill*, of both pagan imperial epic and Anglican dynastic eclogue. Elisa upon her 'grassie greene,' an idealising pastoral emblem of Elizabethan England, is succeeded by Dido in the '*Elisian* fieldes so free,' a vision of the spiritual reality Elisa is claimed to prefigure. 'Fayre *Eliza*, Queene of shepheardes all,' reigns at the center of *Aprill*; 'Christ, the very God of all shepheards', reigns at the center of *Maye*. In *November*, Dido 'raignes a goddesse now among the saintes,/ That whilome was the saynt of shepheards light' (175–6).[16] The 'forswonck and forswatt' *Aprill* celebrant no longer looks for patronage from one who is far above him in the social hierarchy but for a communion of transfigured souls. The great reversal upward that is the central strategy of Christian elegy – 'Dido nis dead, but into heaven hent./O happye herse' (169–70) – follows immediately upon the revelation that worldly ambition is the pursuit of an illusion. Colin's version of Dido's apotheosis does not provide him with an image to be adored but rather with a model to be emulated. The strategy of the elegy is to transform the 'earthlie mould' of a literal Dido into a symbolic vehicle of the poet's own aspiration. In his creation of the *November* elegy, Colin enacts 'the perfecte paterne of a Poete' that Piers had advanced in *October*: 'Then make thee winges of thine aspyring wit,/And, whence thou camst, flye back to heaven apace.' Colin now sings in a visionary, prophetic mode that leaves the courtships of Rosalind and Eliza behind.

The sequence of Colin's presences in the *Calender* explores the problematics of poetic vocation. These explorations constitute a progression that culminates in *November*'s revaluation of the whole enterprise in the light of eternity. *Januarye* sets out the framing biographical fiction of Colin's erotic frustration and the Pan/Syrinx and Pan/Apollo myths that inform his imaginative life. Colin attempts to deal with his Rosalind-problem by emulating Pan's metamorphosis of life into art; his failure suggests that Pan's resources and pastoral's range are inadequate effectively to manage complex human needs. Colin rejects his vocation as recreative pastoral poet by breaking his pipe. The song re-created in *Aprill* returns us to an earlier recreative state; Pan's powers had then been sufficient for Colin to enact symbolically a genealogical myth of metamorphosis *within* a pastoral world. At the outset of the *November* eclogue, Colin keeps to his *Januarye* vow: he will sing neither of Rosalind nor Pan. Through his power to enact symbolically a myth of sacrifice and apotheosis that *transcends* the pastoral world, he demonstrates his progression towards a higher kind of poetry and his emulation of a higher poetic genius.

In *November*, Colin spurns Pan's paradigm of metamorphosis:

> The sonne of all the world is dimme and darke:
> The earth now lacks her wonted light,
> And all we dwell in deadly night
>   O heavie herse.
> Breake we our pypes, that shrild as lowde as Larke,
>   O carefull verse.
>
> (68–72)

The poem's repetition of the breaking of the pipe re-emphasizes the inadequacy of Pan's myth of change and fixity. But the conditions of separation from the beloved object are more radical than before: the context is neither the lady's refusal nor her metamorphosis but her physical extinction. The poem is in the process of articulating a sacred mystery of death and rebirth that can guarantee not merely displacement and consolation but rejoicing and the expectation of a sanctified future union. In *Januarye*, Colin is symbolically associated with a declining Phoebus. In *November*, Colin builds his elegy by transfiguring solar myth into Christological symbol:

> She hath the bonds broke of eternall night,
> Her soule unbodied of the burdenous corpse.
>   . . .

Dido nis dead, but into heaven hent.
O happye herse,
Cease now my Muse, now cease they sorrowes sourse,
O joyfull verse.

(165–6, 169–72)

In turning from Rosalind-Eliza to Dido, Colin turns from Pan to Apollo-Christ, a greater Pan. 'O heavie herse . . . O carefull verse' is transformed into 'O happy herse . . . O joyfull verse' at the point at which the poet's spirit is liberated from the lure of the mutable earthly things that have held it in its ceaseless cycle of desire and frustration. *November* is the antitype of *Januarye*; it records the authentic spiritual experience that the aesthetic paganism of *Januarye* merely adumbrates. Complaint becomes Recreation through an act of transfiguration, through the spiritual re-creation of subject, singer, and audience.

VII

E. K.'s hybrid 'Recreative' category – 'matter of love or commendation of special personages' – is an explicit acknowledgement of the analogy of sexual and social modes of literary courtship. Eliza and Rosalind are realisations of the dual aspect of the Petrarchan mistress: Eliza of her virtue and purity, which are the source of the lover's aspiration and the poet's inspiration but which, at the same time, put her beyond his reach; Rosalind, of her cruelty and pride, which frustrate the lover and inhibit the poet. Underlying the encomiastic song of *Aprill* is a tension between the poet's power to create and control an ideal image within his poem and his dependency upon the actual personage whom it perfects. This paradox of power and powerlessness characterises Colin's plaintive state. Spenser is exploring the metaphorical transactions between the private poetry of love and the public poetry of praise, and he uses them in such a way as to reveal the rhetorical principles upon which personal and political relations are organised in courtly society.

In the fictional experience of Colin Clout, the political and the personal are superficially characterised as the pure and polluted forms of erotic relationship; each is more ambivalent than its conventionalised presentation implies. As lover, Colin is in thrall to the cruel Rosalind, but he struggles to purge his plaintiveness by re-creating it as plaintive poetry. As courtier, Colin re-creates Elizabeth's ideal image within the forms of celebratory poetry but he remains wholly impotent to effect a re-creation of poetic vision as a social fact. The breakthrough that occurs in the *November* elegy is the verbal enactment of a rite of transition. The problematic carnal and political complexities of Rosalind and Eliza are separated out from the pure spirit of Dido through the sacramental symbolism of death and rebirth. The poet uses the lady as a sacrificial victim, to mediate between his present 'trustless state of earthly things, and slipper hope' (153) and his desired future 'in *Elisian* fields so free' (179).

In Petrarch's *Canzoniere*, as in Dante's *Vita Nuova*, the lady's death is the turning point in the poet-lover's life and in its poetic record. That death makes possible, or symbolises, the resolution of a war between the antithetical inclinations of body and spirit that has wracked the lover during the lady's lifetime. The lady's sublimation into spirit brings about the lover's purification by obliterating the object of his earthly desires. Few Elizabethan sonnet cycles elaborate the spiritual aspect of the lady and in none does she die. But these elements of the Petrarchan experience are present in *The Shepheardes Calender* – which precedes the main wave of Elizabethan sonnets by over a decade – as aspects of the spiritual biography of Colin Clout. Colin yearns for the recovery of a mode of relationship which is truly recreative, which is based on love rather than on power, and is grounded in a spiritual model of creaturely communion rather than in a sociopolitical model of strict hierarchical statuses. Colin's elegy for Dido is a displacement of the Rosalind-Eliza problem in which Spenser attempts a radical solution by symbolic means: kill the lady, thus sending her spirit to heaven, where the lover's spirit might hope eventually to join her in a communion free from the accidents and constraints that characterise earthly life – life within the body and the body politic. The tensions and contradictions underlying the plaintive and moral impulses of the shepherds in Spenser's *Calender* are versions of an essential thematic antithesis that the Renaissance imagination habitually embodies in pastoral form. Dissatisfactions with the way things are can be assuaged by the artistic generation of pastoral counter-worlds. But the act of imaginative transformation is always suspect – potentially dangerous, escapist, or regressive. The 'transcendence' achieved by Colin's *November* elegy is an ambiguous, melancholic, and symbolic remedy for actual problems. To make poetry a vehicle of transcendence is tacitly to acknowledge its ethical and political impotence.

Spenser's *Amoretti* are more closely related to the poetry of the *dolce stil nuovo* than are any of the other Elizabethan sonnet cycles. Spenser departs from, revises, and re-creates the tradition by resolving the antithesis of body and spirit not by exclusion but rather by a reconciliation of apparent opposites in sacramental sexual love.[17] Spenser melds Reformation Humanism with Renaissance eroticism. He can celebrate the mysteries of incarnation in an Easter love sonnet because

God's courtship of humanity sanctifies the courtship of lovers: 'So let us love, deare love, lyke as we ought,/love is the lesson which the Lord us taught.' (*Amoretti*, LXVIII). The identification of poet with lover is complete in the *Epithalamion*; Spenser's own marriage song celebrates the transformation of lady and courtier into wife and husband, and the incarnation of spirit in wedded love. The success of the erotic poet in reconciling tensions within the private world of *Amoretti* is contrasted to the epic poet's inability to work such a reconciliation within the larger public world. Indeed, the tensions of the public world sometimes exert a direct and intrusive pressure upon the private world itself. In *Amoretti*, XXXIII, the poet confesses that the perturbations of love make him neglect his 'taedious toyle,' his duty to 'that most sacred Empresse my dear dred,/not finishing her Queene of faery.' In *Amoretti*, LXXX, the earthly paradise of personal love is hemmed in by a public world of toil and obligation:

> After so long a race as I have run
> Through Faery land, which those six books compile,
> give leave to rest me being halfe fordonne,
> and gather to my selfe new breath awhile.
> Then as a steed refreshed after toyle,
> out of my prison I will breake anew:
> and stoutly will that second worke assoyle,
> with strong endeavour and attention dew.
> Till then give leave to me in pleasant mew,
> to sport my muse and sing my loves sweet praise:
> the contemplation of whose heavenly hew,
> my spirit to an higher pitch will rayse.
> But let her prayses yet be low and meane,
> fit for the handmayd of the Faery Queene.

Amoretti-Epithalamion perfects the erotic courtship which in the *Calender* could only be resolved by death and sublimation. At the same time, the incarnation of love sustains the poet's attempt to perfect the public courtship which in the *Calender* had been conflated with the erotic and resolved by the same means. *Amoretti*, LXXX, records the splitting of the synthetic recreative mode; it opposes the 'matter of love' that creates joy and refreshment to the 'commendation of special personages' that generates anxiety and exhaustion.

In the *Calender*, *Colin Clouts Come Home Againe*, Book VI of *The Faerie Queene*, Colin seems always to embody a Spenserian motive that can be identified variously as desire, ambition, or aspiration. Beginning in lowliness, isolation, or privation, it is a movement outward and upward, an attempt at persuasion, possession, or communion. Pastoral's lowly status in the hierarchy of literary kinds admirably suit it to the celebration of humility but also to expressing the aspirations of a confined spirit. The endemic plaintiveness of Elizabethan and Spenserian pastoral points not to its function as a freely chosen rejection of the aspiring mind but to its function as an expression of, protest against, or (perhaps) catharsis of the frustration of the aspiring mind. The shepherd-poet complains against forces or circumstances indifferent or hostile to the strivings to better his social or sexual, economic or spiritual, lot.[18] In the *Calender*, Colin's only expectation of communion is with the spirit of Dido 'in *Elisian* fieldes so free,' after death. The private and public courtships of Rosalind and Eliza do not admit of any relationship other than a strictly hierarchical one, in which unfulfilled desire is purged in complaint or sublimated in encomium. In *Colin Clouts Come Home Againe*, these variant forms of worship of the remote and unobtainable object of desire are counterbalanced by Colin's ecstatic celebration – at the poem's center – of an unnamed lady who inspires her poet-lover. The shepherd of the Ocean (Spenser's pastoral mask for Ralegh) sings plaintively 'of great unkindnesse, and of usage hard,/of *Cynthia*' (*CCCHA*, 165–6), his cruel royal mistress; Colin himself emerges not as an emblem of self-destructive passion – as E. K. represents him in the *Calender* – but as a mystagogue, an Orphic priest of love as well as a satirist exposing the abuses of desire and the abuses of poetry at Cynthia's court.

Colin and his love reappear in Spenser's Legend of Courtesy, apotheosized upon Mount Acidale. The figure at the center of the concentric circles of nymphs and graces to whom Colin pipes is a lass unparalleled. The Graces themselves have advanced her 'to be another Grace':

> Another Grace she well deserves to be,
>   In whom so many Graces gathered are,
>   Excelling much the meane of her degree;
>   Divine resemblance, beauty soveraine rare,
>   Firme Chastity, that spight ne blemish dare;
>   All which she with such courtesie doth grace,
>   That all her peres cannot with her compare,
>   But quite are dimmed, when she is in place.
> She made me often pipe and now to pipe apace.
>
> Sunne of the world, great glory of the sky,
>   That all the earth doest lighten with thy rayes,
>   Great *Gloriana*, greatest Majesty,
>   Pardon thy shepheard, mongst so many layes,
>   As he hath sung of thee in all his dayes,
>   To make one minime of thy poore handmayd,

> And underneath thy feete to place her prayse,
> That when thy glory shall be farre displayd
> To future age of her this mention may be made.
>
> (*FQ*, VI. x. 27–8)

Spenser's Colin alludes conspicuously to his earlier vision in *The Shepheardes Calender*, so as to draw attention to his process of re-vision:

> Lo how finely the graces can it foote
>   to the Instrument:
> Thy dauncen deffly, and singen soote,
>   in their meriment,
> Wants not a fourth grace, to make the daunce even?
> Let that rowme to my Lady be yeven.
>
> (*Aprill*, 109–14)

Whereas the female figures celebrated by Colin in the *Calender* are transformations of each other, the fourth grace on Mount Acidale is clearly distinguished from and opposed to the idealised imperial type of the queen. In the heroic persona of Gloriana, as in the pastoral and erotic personae of Eliza and Cynthia, Queen Elizabeth and the public world of constraints, obligations and frustrations that she personifies are linked in an anxious tension with the poet's interior life, a life that is fulfilled in poetry and love.

The 'countrey lasse' (*FQ*, VI. x. 25) celebrated by Colin upon Acidale recalls not only the Elisa of *Aprill* but also the poet's beloved and loving mistress and spouse, who is celebrated in *Amoretti-Epithalamion* even though she must merely be 'fit for the hand-mayd of the Faery Queene' (*Amoretti*, LXXX). Colin's strategy complicates that of the sonneteer:

> that little that I am, shall be all spent,
> in setting your immortall prayses forth.
> Whose lofty argument uplifting me,
> shall lift you up unto an high degree.
>
> (*Amoretti*, LXXXII)

In virtue and beauty, and in the grace and courtesy with which she reciprocates his devotion, Colin's love transcends her status in the social hierarchy. Gloriana must be begged to excuse the humble pastoral poet's violation of both poetic and social decorum. The praise of Colin's country lass is to endure as a manifestation of Gloriana's enduring glory. But Gloriana's name will endure – so the poet implies – because she has been raised in his poem. And, as the whole episode has so splendidly proclaimed, the source of Colin's inspiration is not the imperial vision of Gloriana but the personal vision at the recreative center of his experience. Ultimately, then, Gloriana owes her enduring glory to the poor handmaid whose praise is placed beneath her feet. Spenser momentarily touches pastoral's radical sociospiritual strain. 'He hath put down the mighty from their seat, and hath exalted the humble.' But at this point in the narrative, Calidore has already intruded upon and dispelled the vision of the Graces: and Colin has – for the last time – broken his pipe. The Sixth Book and the whole poem are shortly to terminate with the intrusion of the Blatant Beast into the poet's consciousness and into his text:

> Ne spareth he most learned wits to rate
> Ne spareth he the gentle Poets rime,
> But rends without regard of person or of time.

> Ne may this homely verse, of many meanest,
> Hope to escape his venomous despite.
>
> (*FQ*, VI. xii. 40–1)

Cosmic mutability and the personal and social perversion of grace and courtesy, of love and poetry, are the persistent forces of negation in Spenser's vision. It is in the face of these forces that the union of the poet and his bride in *Epithalamion* and the reciprocity of Colin and his country lass upon Mount Acidale achieve their profound but circumscribed, transient, and fragile triumphs.

VIII

The formal and stylistic achievement of *The Shepheardes Calender* is original, brilliant, and wide-ranging. The thematic effect of this achievement is to create a disjunction between poetry's excellence as ornament and its inadequacy as persuasion, between the poet as maker and mover. At the beginning of the *Calender*, at the threshold which conducts readers into the eclogues, stands E. K.'s bold, ambitious, and optimistic Epistle. Despite the Epistle's expectant tone and despite the occasional moments of triumph recorded within the eclogues themselves, their predominant tone is wary, plaintive, anxious, bitter. Epistle and eclogues seem to be intentionally juxtaposed in mood, as are the figures they contain: Immerito, the brilliant debutant, and Colin, the frustrated and rapidly aging shepherd.

In *December*, Colin directs his last plaintive hymn to 'soveraign *Pan*

thou God of shepheards all'; he is addressing the God of *November*, not
the pastoral genius of *Januarye*. Colin's complaint is a purified version of
Cuddie's frustrated materialism, tracing the intertwined fortunes of his
life and his vocation beyond their innocent beginnings in the spontaneous
world of creative play. The critical point in Colin's life has been the
initiation of poetic aspiration:

> To *Pan* his own selfe pype I needed not yield.
>   For if the flocking Nymphes did follow *Pan*,
>   The wiser Muses after *Colin* ranne.
>
> (46–8)

In *June* (65–72), Colin had invoked Pan's defeat by Apollo as a fable
exemplifying the dangers of poetic aspiration. In *December*, the genius
of pastoral poetry is contrasted with an Apollonian Colin, a leader of the
Muses who is only passing through the pastoral world. Yet the dangers
of aspiration prove real enough:

> But ah such pryde at length was ill repayde,
> The shepheards God (perdie God was he none)
> My hurtlesse pleasaunce did me ill upbraide,
> My freedome lorne, my life he lefte to mone.
>
> (49–52)

Ambition is now moralised as pride; Pan is revenged upon Apollo when
Colin is enkindled with love, with desire to possess the 'blasing starre,
meant of beautie' (*December*, Gloss) that ties him to its train. The curse of
love that ends his freedom is the insatiable desire for the unattainable
object, a desire variously expressed in each of his preceding songs.
   In Spring, Colin is a worshipper of the natural world that embraces
him: 'the chaunting birds luld me a sleepe' (71). In the Summer of his
age, Colin applies himself 'to things of ryper reason' (76). From a world
of recreative pastoral, he passes into a rural world of labor, art, and
understanding that is reminiscent of Vergil's *Georgics*: he plants, hunts,
fishes, and studies the cycles and secrets of nature. These achievements
constitute a continued metaphor for his development as a poet. No longer
immersed within nature, Colin works to overcome his alienation – to
repair the ruin of his fall – through the arts of civilisation. Autumn is the
time of Colin's bitter harvest. He has rightfully expected a return for
the creative energy he has expended in summer but it is not forthcoming:

> The eare that budded faire, is burnt and blasted,
> And all my hoped gaine is turned to scathe.
>
> (99–100)

> The flattring fruite is fallen to grownd before,
> And rotted, ere they were halfe mellow ripe:
> My harvest wast, my hope away dyd wipe.
>
> (106–8)

> The fragrant flowres, that in my garden grewe,
> Bene withered, as they had bene gathered long.
> Theyr rootes bene dryed up for lacke of dewe.
>
> (109–11)

Through punning images ('eare,' 'flattring fruite,' 'fragrant flowres,' 'lacke of dewe'), the fates of husbandman and poet, crops and poems, merge. The lost harvest includes the disappointed hopes of material and spiritual sustenance, of patronage and verbal efficacy.

Although Colin's final emblem appears to be missing from the printed texts of the *Calender*, E. K. provides its gloss: 'The meaning whereof is that all thinges perish and come to theyr last end, but workes of learned wits and monuments of Poetry abide for ever.' Colin's emblem has perished with its speaker but Immerito's *Calender* remains. Immerito is separated from Colin in the crucial transition from final eclogue to envoi. We are confronted by an odd shifting of generations as the *Calender* moves from beginning to end: the Epistle presents Colin as an image of the sage Immerito's wayward youth; the mensal succession of eclogues suggests a larger movement in time that is brought sharply into focus by *December*'s retrospective; in the wake of old Colin's withdrawal, Immerito returns on the threshold of maturity. The old poet of *December* who resignedly hangs up his pipe is not the young pastoralist of *Januarye* who petulantly breaks his pipe: 'tryed time [has] taught [him] greater thinges' (85). *October* seems finally to deny that the Vergilian progression can be the modern poet's 'perfecte paterne'; *November* suggests a radical revision of the progression's goal. In *December*, pastoral eclogue modulates into georgic while suggesting a final failure to progress to epic. Colin is the pastoral poet whose Vergilian aspirations have been stifled; his life is enclosed within a poetic form that the pastoral poet who has created him now declares to be perfected. The process of Immerito's testing is coterminous with the process of Colin's creativity, suffering, and decline. Immerito, the persona of the fledgling poet who mediates between Colin Clout and Edmund Spenser, has tested his wings and finds them sound.

It is easy to underestimate how extraordinary and bold are the lightly veiled claims to the mantles of Vergil and Chaucer made by 'Immerito' in 1579. Both the *Calender* and the contemporaneous Harvey-Spenser correspondence leave no doubt that Spenser believes the shape of his whole future to lie in the fortunes of the present moment. 'Whiles the yron is hote, it is good striking, and minds of Nobles varie, as their

Estates.'[19] Spenser's soaring ambition for a major place in literary history
and in Elizabethan society, and his equally audacious commitment to
express his mind (however cryptically) on the critical political and
religious issues of the day, cannot have failed to generate a concomitant
anxiety about personal failure and official displeasure. The current pattern
of a courtier-poet was George Gascoigne, who died in 1577 having tried
half a dozen vocations in the vain pursuit of glory and reward. His last
writings are filled with compulsive repentances for his wayward
youth.[20] The current pattern of a self-appointed royal advisor was the
strident Puritan and Elizabethan loyalist, John Stubbs; his right hand
was chopped off in the marketplace at Westminster by order of Eliza,
only a month before the printer of his anonymous *Gaping Gulf* brought
out Immerito's *Calender*.[21] However dark their precise intendments,
Spenser's moral and satiric eclogues of *Februarie, Julye*, and *September*
make clear enough that 'harme may come of melling' (*Julye*, 208) in
matters of church and state.

The ambiguity of *December* is generated by the contrary significations
of Colin's final act, for Colin's end is merely the end of Spenser's
beginning. We are told that, under the name of Colin Clout, 'this Poete
secretly shadoweth himself, as sometime did Virgil under the name of
Tityrus' (*Januarye*, Gloss). Thus, when Colin hangs up his pipe, his
apparent resignation is also an imitation of the triumphant act of
Sannazaro's 'Mantuan Tityrus,' who left the woods and his pipes for the
fields, the city, and a sonorous trumpet:

> Which reed (when having abandoned his goats he set himself to instruct
> the rustic tillers of the soil, perhaps with a hope of later singing with
> more sonorous trumpet the arms of Trojan Aeneas) he hung up there,
> where now you see it, in honor of this God who had shown him favor
> in his singing. After him came never a soul to these woods that has
> been able to play it with accomplishment, though many, spurred by
> ambitious daring, have attempted it oftentimes and attempt it still.[22]

Drayton interprets Colin's hanging up of his pipe precisely as Spenser's
challenge to future pastoral poets. In *The Shepheards Garland* (1593),
Rowland (Drayton's pastoral persona) is urged to awake his drowsy
muse, 'And sing a while of blessed *Betas* prayse':

> In thy sweete song so blessed may'st thou bee,
> For learned Collin laies his pipes to gage,
> And is to fayrie gone a Pilgrimage.[23]

A few months after the publication of *The Shepheardes Calender*, Spenser
is urging Harvey to return drafts of *The Faerie Queene* with a detailed

reader's report.[24] By the time the *Calender* is published, the conspicuously Vergilian opening lines of the epic have probably been written:

> Lo I the man, whose Muse whilome did maske,
> As time her taught, in lowly shepheards weeds,
> Am now enforst a far unfitter taske,
> For trumpets stern to chaunge mine Oaten reeds.
>
> (*FQ*, I. Proem. i)

The same symbolic act of hanging up the pipe conveys both Colin's resigned withdrawal from the Vergilian progression and Immerito's declaration of intention to succeed in the attempt. Poetic and social anxieties about the possible insufficiency or rejection of Spenser's own aspiring mind are given refined expression and symbolic containment in the pattern of Colin's experience that is developed within the *Calender*'s encompassing form. *The Shepheardes Calender* is the vehicle of a young man's poetic and social ambitions that incorporates within itself a projection of the possibility of its own failure.

Colin is reincarnated in the context of the epic undertaking, in *Colin Clouts Come Home Againe* and in Book VI of *The Faerie Queene*. In the allegorical fiction of *The Faerie Queene*, the heroic poet attempts to combine a celebration of the Elizabethan social order and courtly culture with an imaginative exploration of their morally ambiguous nature and a critique of their claims to metaphysical sanction. Spenser's poetry of courtship evinces a tension between its educative and encomiastic functions, between the ethical imperative that the Orphic poet enlighten his audience and the politic necessity that the court poet flatter them.

Spenser can unite the mythic role of seer with the immediate role of servant only tenuously and ineffectually; the characteristics of Spenserian style and tone are created by the interaction of tradition and the individual talent with the circumstances of the historical moment. The self-assurance to emulate and overgo 'our sage and serious Poet *Spenser*' is as evident in the work of Milton's pastoral apprenticeship as in his epic. The Elizabethan political mythology of *Aprill*, Spenser's re-creation of Vergil's 'messianic' eclogue, is transcended in Milton's sacred December song:

> This is the Month, and this the happy morn
> Wherein the Son of Heav'n's eternal King,
> Of wedded Maid, and Virgin Mother born,
> Our great redemption from above did bring.
>
> ('On the Morning of Christ's Nativity,' 1–4)

Spenser inserts his pastoral elegy into a November eclogue; *Lycidas* is an elegiac spring song, mourning a fellow shepherd rather than a great lady, and ending in a consecration of poetic skill to a spiritual commitment *in the world*. Later, when Milton turns within to hail the Holy Light in *Paradise Lost*, he transforms the failure of political activism into the triumph of poetic power and personal conscience. No poet but the prophetic poet who serves only God can sing the authentic heroic poem – a poem that ends by gesturing us back into our own world, armed with vision.

In the envoi to Spenser's lowly pastoral, Immerito proudly claims to have encompassed all of time within his poem:

> Loe I have made a Calender for every yeare,
> That steele in strength, and time in durance shall outweare:
> And if I marked well the starres revolution,
> It shall continewe till the worlds dissolution.

The framing devices of *The Shepheardes Calender* emphasise the poet's act of perfecting, not God's. Immerito's concern is not transcendence of time so much as endurance within time. His hope is to achieve existence 'eterne in mutabilitie' (*FQ*, III. vi. 47) through the enduring significance and compelling craft of the symbolic form that he himself has made. Within Immerito's *Calender*, it is Colin who comes to yearn for transcendence. And echoes of Colin's plaintive counter-voice from within the *Calender* continue to ring in the voice of Spenser's epic narrator as he travails through Faery-land to the *October*-like, bitter and ironic final lines of Book VI of *The Faerie Queene* – 'Therfore do you my rimes keep better measure,/And seeke to please, that now is counted wisemans threasure' (*FQ*, VI. xii. 41) – and beyond to the *November*-like prayer in the last lines of the *Mutabilitie* cantos. In the envoi to Spenser's lofty epic, the humble poet-narrator looks forward to the infolding of self and work into the 'stedfast rest of all thinges firmely stayd/Upon the pillours of Eternity' (*FQ*, VII. viii. 2). Spenser is not a medieval poet constructing an artifice of eternity; he is a poet of Renaissance and Reformation creating endless monuments for short time. Such poets cannot truly emulate 'the perfecte paterne.' As he turns away from time, change, and history in the last extant lines of his 'unperfite' *Mutabilitie* cantos, the poet is necessarily turning away from poetry. This is not a triumph of the Elizabethan Orpheus but rather a release from his compromised song.

Notes

1. The reading text of a paper based on an earlier version of this study has been published on microfiche in *Spenser at Kalamazoo: Proceedings from a Special Session at the Thirteenth Conference on Medieval Studies in Kalamazoo, Michigan, May 5–6, 1978*, ed., DAVID A. RICHARDSON (Cleveland, 1978), 254–66. I am grateful to those who have heard or read versions of this study and have improved it by their comments; above all, I thank Thomas K. Dunseath.

2. References are to the often reprinted one-volume *Oxford Standard Authors* edition of Spenser's *Poetic Works*, eds J. C. SMITH and E. DE SELINCOURT. In quotations from this and other Elizabethan texts, I have modified obsolete typographical conventions.

3. The ambiguous mixture of progress and failure that characterises Colin's life within the *Calender* has led to various critical perspectives. Readings which emphasise rigorous moral choices between fleshly and spiritual values rely upon a distinction between Colin's mutable, spiritually unfulfilled existence within the eclogues and the order, harmony, and plenitude of being figured in the encompassing calendrical form: See ROBERT ALLEN DURR, 'Spenser's Calendar of Christian Time,' *ELH*, 24 (1957), 269–95; S. K. HENINGER, Jr., 'The Implications of Form for *The Shepheardes Calender*,' *Studies in the Renaissance*, 9 (1962), 309–21; ISABEL G. MACCAFFREY, 'Allegory and Pastoral in *The Shepheardes Calender*,' *ELH*, 36 (1969), 88–109; MICHAEL MURRIN, *The Veil of Allegory* (Chicago, 1969), 156–63. A. C. HAMILTON's classic essay, 'The Argument of Spenser's *Shepheardes Calender*,' *ELH*, 23 (1956), 171–83, emphasises the ethics of Christian Humanism rather than theology and eschatology: Colin's appearances enact a rejection of the otiose pastoral life and the recreative values of pastoral poetry for the active, morally committed life of heroic poetry. In 'Mode and Diction in *The Shepheardes Calender*,' *Modern Philology*, 67 (1969), 140–9, HARRY BERGER, Jr. revises Hamilton's argument by discriminating Colin's level of poetic and ethical achievement from Spenser's: Colin is 'the fledgling imagination . . . disporting itself in the Muses' garden of conventions and reluctant to pass . . . into the world' (147); Spenser himself is in the process of forging a mature union of life and art. PATRICK CULLEN, *Spenser, Marvell, and Renaissance Pastoral* (Cambridge, Mass: Harvard University Press, 1970), 76–98, proposes that Colin fails within the pastoral world because he does not realise his vocation as its great poet; he fails through frailty rather than through sin. PAUL ALPERS, 'The Eclogue Tradition and the Nature of Pastoral,' *College English*, 34 (December, 1972), 365–6, rejects judgmental criticism: Colin's end is neither a failure nor a transcendence but a submission 'to the nature of things'; he is an Everyman coming to terms with experiential reality. My own understanding of Colin and of his creator is most indebted to the work of HARRY BERGER, Jr., notably the seminal essay, 'The Prospect of Imagination: Spenser and the Limits of Poetry,' *Studies in English Literature, 1500–1900*, I (1961), 93–120.

4. See LAWRENCE STONE, *The Family, Sex and Marriage in England 1500–1800* (New York: Harper & Row, 1977), Pt III, ch. 5; KEITH THOMAS, 'Age and Authority in Early Modern England,' *Proceedings of the British Academy* LXII (1976), 205–48. The fullest generational study of the period is ANTHONY ESLER, *The aspiring*

mind of the Elizabethan younger generation (Durham, North Carolina: Duke University Press, 1966).

5. See CULLEN, *Spenser, Marvell, and Renaissance Pastoral*, 29–76; and compare MICHAEL F. DIXON, 'Rhetorical Patterns and Methods of Advocacy in Spenser's *Shepheardes Calender,*' *English Literary Renaissance*, 7 (1977), 131–54.

6. Spenser's literary source for the myth is Ovid, *Metamorphoses*, I. 698–712. Lucretius (*De rerum natura*, V) interprets the myth as an aetiology of song, which began among primitive pastoralists whose poetry manifested their *otium*. George Sandys, *Ovid's Metamorphosis Englished, Mythologised, and Represented in Figures* (1632; ed. KARL K. HULLEY and STANLEY T. VANDERSALL, Lincoln, Nebraska: University of Nebraska Press, [1970]), quotes Lucretius and euhemerises Pan as the first pastoral poet – a human shepherd who, for his invention of the pipes, 'was esteemed a God, as others were for other inventions' (77).

7. For other interpretations, see JOHN W. MOORE, Jr., 'Colin Breaks His Pipe: A Reading of the "January" Eclogue,' *English Literary Renaissance*, 5 (1975), 3–24: Colin's rejection of Pan is 'a renunciation of his quest to serve society as a divine pastoral poet' (22); and DAVID R. SHORE, 'Colin and Rosalind: Love and Poetry in the *Shepheardes Calender,*' *Studies in Philology*, 73 (1976), 176–88: Colin's 'rejection of the pipe is a sign of sorrow and of loss, not . . . a sign that his love is in some way morally culpable' (180).

8. This paragraph borrows from my 'Celebration and Insinuation: Sir Philip Sidney and the Motives of Elizabethan Courtship,' *Renaissance Drama*, N. S. 8 (1977), 3–4. On the theory and practise of encomium, see O. B. Hardison, Jr., *The Enduring Monument* (Chapel Hill: University of North Carolina, 1962), esp. 95–102; and BARBARA KIEFER KEWALSKI, *Donne's Anniversaries and the Poetry of Praise* (Princeton, N.J.:Princeton University Press, 1973), 11–41. On the ideology of the Elizabeth cult and its iconography, see FRANCES A. YATES, *Astraea* (London: Routledge & Kegan Paul, 1975), 29–120; and ROY STRONG, *The Cult of Elizabeth* (London: Thames & Hudson, 1977). ELKIN CALHOUN WILSON, *England's Eliza* (Cambridge, Mass.: Harvard University Press, 1939), usefully surveys the literary idealisations of Elizabeth.

9. Compare CULLEN, *Spenser, Marvell, and Renaissance Pastoral*, 114; and THOMAS H. CAIN, 'The Strategy of Praise in Spenser's *Aprill,*' *Studies in English Literature 1500–1900*, 9 (1968), 45–58.

10. Harvey quotes Cuddie's complaint (*October*, 7–18) from the 'famous new Calender,' in a letter 'to my very friend *M. Immerito.*' Harvey's context is the pursuit of personal ambitions through poetry: 'Master *Colin Clout* is not every body, and albeit his olde Companions, Master *Cuddy*, and Master *Hobbinoll* be as little beholding to their *Mistresse Poetrie*, as ever you wilt: yet he peradventure, by the meanes of hir special favour, and some personall priviledge, may . . . purchase great landes, and Lordshippes, with the money, which his *Calender* and *Dreames* have, and will affourde him' (*A Gallant familiar Letter*, etc. [1580], reprinted in Spenser, *Poetical Works*, 627–8). Harvey's tone is ironic, but Spenser's life and works suggest that his aspirations were permeated by the thoroughly materialistic concerns that he projected and censured in the figure of Cuddie. For a reading of the eclogue that embraces the perspective of Piers' moral idealism, see RICHARD F. HARDIN, 'The Resolved Debate of Spenser's "October",' *Modern Philology*, 73 (1976), 257–63.

11. GEORGE PUTTENHAM, *The Arte of English Poesie* (1589), eds GLADYS DOIDGE WILLCOCK and ALICE WALKER (Cambridge: Cambridge University Press, 1936), 38. Puttenham is characterising the eclogue, which he classes with satire, comedy, and tragedy as reprehensive *'drammatick* poems.'

12. Reprinted in *Elizabethan Critical Essays*. ed. G. GREGORY SMITH, 2 vols. (Oxford: Oxford University Press, 1904), I, 245, 264.

13. 'A letter from the queen's majesty sent to the bishops through England' (8 May, 1577) reprinted in CLAIRE CROSS, *The Royal Supremacy in the Elizabethan Church* (London: George Allen & Unwin, 1969), 191; Grindal's letter to the queen (20 December 1576) is reprinted on pages 171–4. For a narrative and analysis of the controversy, see PATRICK COLLINSON, *The Elizabethan Puritan Movement* (London: Jonathan Cape, 1967), 159–207. For Grindal as 'Algrind,' see PAUL E. MCLANE, *Spenser's Shepheardes Calender: A Study in Elizabethan Allegory* (Notre Dame, Ind.: University of Notre Dame Press, 1961), 140–57.

14. JOEL HURSTFIELD, *Freedom, Corruption and Government in Elizabethan England* (London: Jonathan Cape, 1973), 64.

15. See *The Works of Edmund Spenser: A Variorum Edition*, ed. EDWIN GREENLAW, et al. (Baltimore: Johns Hopkins University Press, 1932–49). *The Minor Poems, Volume One*, 402-4 and MCLANE, *Spenser's Shepheardes Calender*, 47–60.

16. Dido has a central place in Petrarch's 'Triumph of Chastity,' where she is celebrated as an example of honor, led to a virtuous suicide by faithful love for her husband rather than by despair and shame following Aeneas' desertion. YATES, *Astraea*, 112–19, explores the political use of the Triumph of Chastity in the iconography of Elizabeth. Dido is a negative antithesis to Troynovant's heroic virgin queen; Elizabeth is a female Aeneas. Yates identifies the vastly influential *Trionfi* as the source of the Elizabethan icon while ignoring the apparent contradiction between the censoriously moralised Elizabethan image of Dido and Petrarch's very sympathetic treatment. Spenser's Dido *triumphans*, presumably conceived in opposition to Vergil's Dido, is in fact close in spirit to Petrarch's.

17. See O. B. HARDISON, Jr., 'Amoretti and the *Dolce Stil Novo*,' *English Literary Renaissance*, 2 (1972), 208–16.

18. Here I am taking issue with HALLETT SMITH's thesis that 'the central meaning' of Elizabethan pastoral is 'the rejection of the aspiring mind,' and that 'the shepherd demonstrates that true content is to be found in this renunciation.' See his seminal study of Spenserian and Elizabethan pastoral in *Elizabethan Poetry* (1952; reprinted, Ann Arbor: University of Michigan Press, 1968), 1–63; I quote from page 10.

19. From a letter addressed to 'Maister G. H.' from 'Immerito,' dated from 'Leycester House. This. 5. of October, 1579,' and printed in *Two other very commendable Letters*, etc., in 1580; reprinted in Spenser, *Poetical Works*, 635. For the few facts and much speculation about the critical period 1579–80 in Spenser's career, see EDWIN GREENLAW, *Studies in Spenser's Historical Allegory* (Baltimore: Johns Hopkins University Press, 1932), 104–32; and ALEXANDER C. JUDSON, *The Life of Edmund Spenser* (Baltimore: Johns Hopkins University Press, 1945), 54–72.

20. See C. T. PROUTY, *George Gascoigne: Elizabethan Courtier, Soldier, and Poet* (New York: Columbia University Press, 1942). E. K. calls Gascoigne 'the very chefe of our late rymers, who and if some partes of learning wanted not (albee it is

well knowen he altogyther wanted not learning) no doubt would have
attayned to the excellencye of those famous Poets' (*November*, Gloss).

21. See *John Stubbs' Gaping Gulf with Letters and Other Relevant Documents*, ed.
    LLOYD E. BERRY (Charlottesville: University of Virginia Press, 1968). The
    occasion of Stubbs' pamphlet, the bitterly controversial projected marriage of
    Elizabeth to Alençon, a French Catholic prince, is also outlined in McLANE,
    Spenser's Shepheardes Calender, 13–26. McLane argues, often convincingly, that
    the *Calender* is permeated by allegorical references to this religious and
    political crisis.
22. *Arcadia and Piscatorial Eclogues*, trans. RALPH NASH (Detroit: Wayne State
    University Press, 1966), 104–5. Sannazaro's Sincero finally abandons Arcadia
    and returns to his own city, having originally exiled himself because his erotic
    desires were disappointed. The shift that scholars have noted in the sources
    of Sannazaro's imitations in the last sections of *Arcadia*, a shift from the bucolic
    poets to the *Georgics* and the epic poets, insinuates an assumption of the
    Vergilian mantle that is paralleled in Spenser's *December* eclogue.
23. 'The Third Eglog,' 11–15, in *The Works of Michael Drayton*, ed. WILLIAM HEBEL,
    et al., 5 vols. (Oxford: Basil Blackwell, 1961), I, 55. Rowland proceeds to praise
    'Beta,' imitating Colin's praise of 'Elisa' in Spenser's *Aprill*.
24. See the letter, signed 'IMMERITO,' and dated from '*Westminster. Quarto Nonas
    Aprilis* 1580,' printed in *Three Proper, and wittie, familiar Letters*, etc. (1580);
    reprinted in Spenser, *Poetical Works*, 612.

4 Spenser's *Complaints*: 'Into each secrete part'*

RICHARD RAMBUSS

In this essay, part of a longer, innovative interpretation of Spenser's career, Richard Rambuss takes issue with prevailing conceptions of Spenser as a poet who modelled his writing on a classical, Virgilian notion of laureateship, progressing from pastoral to epic, and single-mindedly following this literary trajectory. In the section included here, Rambuss concentrates on the *Complaints*, a volume of distinctly non-laureate-style verse, usually omitted from accounts describing Spenser as a laureate court poet or representing a new kind of author. Including the *Complaints* within a narrative of Spenser's personal literary development does not discount the Virgilian contours of Spenser's self-fashioning as a poet, but, rather, serves to complicate and problematise what has been assumed to be a simple relationship, suggesting a multiplicity of poetic models (Ovid and Chaucer), as well as considering the poetry in the light of Spenser's other career as an Irish civil servant and bureaucrat. Rambuss provides two salutary reminders to the modern reader. Firstly, that Elizabethan writers often had other interests and that it is a partial enterprise to assess them as if they lived only for their literature; secondly, that one needs to pay attention to the conditions of textual production in the early modern period as well as the form and content of the individual text itself: here, specifically, the *volumes* which Spenser published and their contexts.

Theoretically, Rambuss attempts to refract a historicist concern with topical references and historical context through a practice of deconstructionist reading, teasing out the instabilities, the doubleness, and the ambivalences of contextual, as well as textual, significations.

The proems to the 1590 *Faerie Queene* tell one story about the origins of

---

*Reprinted from RICHARD RAMBUSS, *Spenser's Secret Career* (Cambridge: Cambridge University Press, 1993), pp. 78–95, 143–6.

the poem and the career of its poet, who seems to have proceeded directly, if uneasily, from his pastoral pipes to the higher strains of epic. Another story is suggested, however, by the seventeen dedicatory sonnets to various nobles (though, significantly, *not* to the queen) Spenser appends to his epic.[1] The recurring allusions in these sonnets to labor and husbandry repoint the economies of poetic production and consumption in *The Faerie Queene* by supplanting the court, the ostensible locus of the proems and their insistent regiocentricity, with a rural scene of agrarian industry that is more pertinent to the domain of georgic than epic. To the Earl of Oxford, Spenser offers his poem as 'the vnripe fruit of an vnready wit' (2); to the Earl of Essex as 'these first labours' (14); to the Earl of Ormond as 'the fruit of barren field' (14); and so on. These tokens of premature harvesting – terms which Milton's *Lycidas* will apply so violently to pastoral, the usual genre of beginnings – imply both Spenser's familiar seeming reluctance about publication, as well as an alternative view of his epic as a continuation of poetic apprenticeship rather than its culmination – a move, once again, which presages Milton's repositioning of *Paradise Lost* as a prefatory work in the opening lines of *Paradise Regained*, the poem which comes after his epic.

As Jane Tylus has shown, in this period the language of husbandry speaks patronage, and Spenser's object in these georgically-inflected dedications of maintaining his circle of patrons (and perhaps even expanding it) is apparent enough.[2] But the terms of Spenser's patronising agrarianism are further loaded in this context by the way he repeatedly calls attention to the laborious cultivation of his epic in a 'sauadge soyle' ('To Grey,' 12; 'To Ormond,' 2), too far removed from the established centers of cultural production, where there is 'Not one *Parnassus*, nor one *Helicone*/Left for sweete Muses to be harboured' ('To Ormond,' 6–7). Moreover, the qualities attributed to the produce of this savage (Irish) soil hint at something potentially more disruptive than a callow harvest or an untimely prolongation of poetic apprenticeship. For the fruit that is merely 'vnripe' in the sonnet addressed to Oxford turns 'wilde' in the sonnet to Ormond, only to become positively noxious in the sonnet to Ralegh, the sequence's final dedication to a male patron. There Spenser recharacterises his poetic offering as menacingly 'vnsauory and sowre' (8).

If such declarations, which manage to strike at once registers of humility, compliance, and complaint, can be said to anticipate the volume of poems Spenser would publish next, they also turn back to the first book of *The Faerie Queene* and the career of its hero, the Redcrosse Knight. In his letter to Ralegh, Spenser relates the awkward episode of this same 'tall clownishe younge man' putting himself forward at Gloriana's court to demand his first chivalric adventure, and 'that being graunted, *he rested him on the floore*, vnfitte through his

rusticity for a better place' (p. 408; emphasis added). The clownishness
and 'rusticity' of this emblematically named Redcrosse Knight might
bring to mind any of the various country naifs of *The Shepheardes Calender*.
But the same qualities also link him to that poem's author, who likewise
makes a nameless debut as Immerito, as well as to the narrator of *The
Faerie Queene*, another 'rustick' ('To Grey,' 11), who represents himself
as similarly green in the chivalric arena.[3] Of course everything changes
for the Redcrosse Knight when his career is reconstructed at a climactic
moment near the end of Book 1. There the lowborn knight, seemingly
hatched out of the earth itself 'in an heaped furrow' (10.66.2) is renamed,
not once, but twice – progressing from Georgos (*geos*, earth, but also
georgic) to 'Saint *George* of mery England' (st. 61.9), from one
'brought . . . vp in ploughmans state to byde' (st. 66.5) to a national hero
of apocalyptic stature.

The careerist fantasy that is conceived here is, I suggest, a particularly
charged one for Spenser. It is the fantasy of being able to change places
in the social order, of the outsider moving inside, of the lowborn gaining
entrance to the Faery Queen's court and subsequently being reinvested
there as a figure of cultural authority. Thus it hardly seems coincidental
that in *The Faerie Queene*'s dedicatory sonnet to the Countess of
Pembroke Spenser describes the inaugural gesture of his poetic career as
being '*lift[ed] out of the flore*' (6), just as Redcrosse sits on the floor waiting
for the boon that will initiate his advancement from plowman to patron
of England. That the romance narrative adumbrated in the career of
Redcrosse may be understood as one about the position of the poet in
the culture is further suggested by its epiphany on canto 10 atop Mount
Contemplation:

> That done, he leads him to the highest Mount;
>   Such one, as that same mighty man of God,
>   That bloud-red billowes like a walled front
>   On either side disparted with his rod,
>   Till that his army dry-foot through them yod,
>   Dwelt fortie dayes vpon; where writ in stone
>   With bloudy letters by the hand of God,
>   The bitter doome of death and balefull mone
> He did receiue, while flashing fire about him shone.
>
> Or like that sacred hill, whose head full hie,
>   Adorned with fruitfull Oliues all arownd,
>   Is, as it were for endlesse memory
>   Of that deare Lord, who oft thereon was fownd.
>   For euer with a flowring girlond crownd:
>   Or like that pleasaunt Mount, that is for ay

Through famous Poets verse each where renownd.
On which the thrise three learned Ladies play
Their heauenly notes, and make full many a louely lay.

(10.53–4)

Through the sort of topographical and tropological condensation figured
here, the site of poetic inspiration can be analogised to other loci of
legal and religious authority: Mount Contemplation is like the poet's
Parnassus, *and* it is like Sinai (itself a scene of writing, where divine law
was 'writ in stone / With bloudy letters'), *and* it is like Olivet (where
Christ himself wears a flowering crown that resembles the poet's laurel).
The elision of this trio of peaks in Mount Contemplation is of a piece
with Spenser's larger project – one which he shared with the likes of
Sidney, Gascoigne, Puttenham, Jonson, and others, whatever varying
investments and conceptions of poetry differentiate their individual
agendas – of attempting to resituate poetry from a marginal position
where it exists only as 'ydle rimes' ('To Burleigh,' 7) to a place of high
cultural importance.

Spenser may have hoped to see just such an ambition realised when
he returned to England in 1590, the first three books of *The Faerie Queene*
in hand, after nearly a decade of civil service toil in Ireland.
Accompanying Walter Ralegh, his new-found patron and Irish neighbor,
he traveled to London in order to oversee the publication of the opening
installment of his epic, but also, as the poem's mass of dedicatory
sonnets testify, to renew in person and in print his court connections.
And under the sponsorship of Ralegh, Spenser, one of the lowest born
of all the major Elizabethan poets, was indeed received at court. There,
like a few privileged poets before him, he was able to present the queen
with his *Faerie Queene*. According to *Colin Clouts Come Home Againe* (1595),
Spenser's regressively pastoralised account of his reception at court as
'a simple silly Elfe' (371), Elizabeth was pleased with the gift, 'And it
desir'd at timely houres to heare' (362). Even so, no preferment, no courtly
office, was directly forthcoming, and after about a year's waiting Spenser
returned to Ireland and his interests there. Once back in Ireland, he was
granted a royal pension of fifty pounds, a reward which he seems to
have felt was too hardfought and too long deferred.[4] Moreover, while
fifty pounds made at the time an enviable stipend *for a poet*, it was a trifle
compared to the wealth accrued by many courtly entrepreneurs.[5] And
Spenser, I have argued, never seems to have set his sights on being 'only'
a poet.

Probably before he left England for what must have looked more and
more like a permanent station in Ireland, Spenser's *Complaints* was
entered on the Stationers' Register. *Mother Hubberds Tale*, one of the poems
in this collection, is also in large part a story about a pilgrimage to court

67

– though in this account the court no longer functions as the cynosure of potential reward and approbation, but rather as the site of institutionalised self-abasement and humiliation:

> Most miserable man, whom wicked fate
> Hath brought to Court, to sue for had ywist,
> That few haue found, and manie one hath mist;
> Full little knowest thou that hast not tride,
> What hell it is, in suing long to bide;
> To loose good dayes, that might be better spent;
> To wast long nights in pensiue discontent;
> To speed to day, to be put back to morrow;
> To feed on hope, to pine with feare and sorrow;
> To haue thy Princes grace, yet want her Peeres;
> To haue thy asking, yet waite manie yeeres;
> To fret thy soule with crosses and with cares;
> To eate thy heart through comfortlesse dispaires;
> To fawne, to crowche, to waite, to ride, to ronne,
> To spend, to giue, to want, to be vndonne,
> Vnhappie wight, borne to desastrous end,
> That doth his life in so long tendance spend.

(892–908)

In this self-perpetuating, ever more wildly excessive economy of disappointment, each hopeful sign of reward is instantaneously transvalued as its own negation – so that, for instance, 'To feed on hope' actually means 'to pine with feare and sorrow.' And even when this seemingly interminable system of frustration at last does give way, it is only to be replaced by a potentially endless paratactic cataloging of unabated, and ultimately ruinous, postures of abjection: 'To fawne, to crowche, to waite . . . / To spend, to giue, to want, to be vndonne.'

Notwithstanding the bile of this complaint, which is nowhere answered or mitigated in the poem or elsewhere in the volume, *Mother Hubberds Tale* resembles in some other important respects the journey-to-court narratives we have been examining. Its central characters, the Fox and the Ape, fit the pattern of lowborn laborers, who (not unlike the aspiring Redcrosse Knight) are cavaliers in search of adventures that will improve their station:

> Wide is the world I wote and euerie streete
> Is full of fortunes, and aduentures straunge.
> Continuallie subject vnto chaunge.
> . . .
> Abroad where change is, good may gotten bee.

(90–2, 101)

Despite, or perhaps because of, contemporary anxieties about the stability of class structures when families were moving up and down in the social and economic scale more rapidly than at any time before the nineteenth and twentieth centuries, the mutable world of *Mother Hubberd* allows for nearly boundless social mobility and self-improvisation.[6] Moreover, changing one's place in this world appears to be no more difficult than changing one's clothing.[7] By donning the appropriate garb, the Fox and the Ape trade occupations upwards from near the bottom of the social hierarchy all the way to the top, progressing from vagrants to shepherds to clerks to courtiers to minister and monarch. The implication here is that if one knows how to strike the right poses, every position in the social order, even the highest, can be impersonated. The alternate title of the poem, *Prosopopoia*, in fact means impersonation.

Correspondingly in *The Faerie Queene*, Redcrosse's 'taking on him knighthood' ('A Letter of the Authors,' p. 408) is originally effected at the level of taking on a change of attire. Putting on the spiritual armor St. Paul details in Ephesians 6 transforms him from a clownish upstart into a Protestant warrior. Redcrosse becomes what he wears. Of course, one would want to distinguish the knight from the similarly upwardly mobile Fox and Ape inasmuch as the latter are a pair of rogues, given to deceit, thievery, and even murder. But what is not usually registered in discussions of *Mother Hubberds Tale* is that the poem gives little indication that the enterprising pair had always been unredeemably corrupt.[8] Rather, it opens with an account of their dutiful, though ultimately unrewarded, service in what we are given no reason to question are legitimate occupations. Thus the Ape complains of years of being passed over for a deserved promotion:

> For I likewise haue wasted much good time,
> Still wayting to preferment vp to clime,
> Whilest others always haue before me stept,
> And from my beard the fat away haue swept.
> That now vnto despaire I gin to growe,
> And meane for better winde aboute to throwe.
>
> (75–80)

The story is much the same for the Fox. Unlike his aristocratic predecessor Renard, who is an important nobleman in the various medieval story cycles which provide a central source for *Mother Hubberds Tale*, Spenser's Fox has been toiling in an unfulfilling track as what appears to be a career civil servant:

> Thus manie yeares I now haue spent and worne,
> In meane regard, and basest fortunes scorne,
> Dooing my Countrey seruice as I might,
> No lesse I dare saie than the prowdest wight;
> And still I hoped to be vp aduaunced,
> For my good parts, but still it hath mischaunced.
> Now therefore that no lenger hope I see,
> But froward fortune still to follow mee,
> And losels lifted high, where I did looke,
> I meane to turne the next leafe of the booke.
>
> (59–68)

I want to make two points about these passages. The first is that, at least at the beginning of the poem, the complaints of the Fox and the Ape are presented not unsympathetically. The second point, following from this recognition, is that their subsequent commitment to a life of rapaciousness is figured as an extension into action of justifiable complaints about their lack of career advancement. The word *complaint*, derived from the Latin *planctus*, is related to *plaintiff*, an etymology which suggests one version of complaint as a form of recrimination, legal or otherwise. In this case, the treachery of the Fox and Ape is a retributive act, their spoils a way 'to finde due remedie' (57) against a system grown disfunctional in its distribution of favor and reward.

The possibility of an 'ironic coding' in *Mother Hubberds Tale* of Spenser and Ralegh's 1590 trip to the English court has been suggested by Jonathan Crewe in his extraordinary reading of *Complaints*.[9] Whether or not the poet intended such a parallel to be drawn, I follow Crewe's lead in situating the poet within the context of this 'middle' period in Spenser's career. Such positioning stands in contrast, of course, to the longstanding practice (dating back to Edwin Greenlaw's influential essays of the 1900s and 1910s) of reading *Mother Hubberds Tale* as an index only to Spenser's *early* court dealings and particularly to his standing in relation to the Leicester and Burghley factions.[10] For, although some version of the poem possibly circulated in manuscript around 1579–1580 (in Greenlaw's view as a protest and warning concerning the proffered match of Queen Elizabeth and the French Catholic Duc d'Alençon), and although Spenser himself claims in his preface to the poem that it was 'long sithens composed in the raw conceipt of my youth' (p. 495), *Mother Hubberds Tale* did not appear in print until the 1591 *Complaints*. Let us consider then what it means for the poem – whether recycled, rewritten, or even newly penned – to be published at this date. For if we take the poem as occasional and instrumental, as both 'new' and 'old' historicisms would have us regard all texts, we must also recognize that the poem is not bound to a static or even necessarily stable context. Contexts shift as texts are recycled, revised, reprinted. As Crewe puts it in short: *'Mother Hubberd* could not mean or have meant in 1591 what it could have meant *ca.* 1580.'[11]

The question I want to address in view of potential new investments and encodings in the 1591 *Mother Hubberds Tale* is what it means for this poem to be published *after* the appearance of the first installment of *The Faerie Queene*. Indeed, that question needs to be opened up to a consideration of the entire *Complaints* volume, a text which resists assimilation to overly streamlined accounts of Spenser's Virgilian laureateship and is consequently often ignored or minimized in those accounts. What kind of career gesture, then, is being staged – midway (as it happened) through Spenser's epic in honor of the Elizabethan regime – in the publication of this manifestly non-laureate tome, which bluntly critiques court values, exposes the shortcomings of the system of court patronage and advancement as it exists under the sway of Lord Treasurer Burghley, and confidently predicts the eventual ruin of the powerful?

The preface to *Complaints* seems written to dodge just such questions. There William Ponsonby, who had been responsible for 'setting foorth' the first three books of *The Faerie Queene* just the year before, now assumes full responsibility for compiling (purportedly without Spenser's approval or knowledge) the nine 'smale Poemes' that make up the book:

> Since my late setting foorth of the *Faerie Queene*, finding that it hath found a fauorable passage amongst you; I haue sithence endeuoured by all good meanes (for the better encrease and accomplishments of your delights,) to get into my handes such smale Poemes of the same Authors: as I heard were disperst abroad in sundrie hands, and not easie to bee come by, by himselfe; some of them hauing bene diuerslie imbeziled and purloyned from him, since his departure ouer Sea. Of the which I haue by good meanes gathered togeather these few parcels present, which I haue caused to bee imprinted altogeather, for that they al seeme to containe like matter of argument in them: being all complaints and meditations of the worlds vanitie, verie graue and profitable.
>
> ('The Printer to the *Gentle Reader*,' p. 470)

Such disavowals of authorial involvement and investment in publication are, it is well known, quite conventional in Elizabethan literary texts. Here the disclaimer, along with Ponsonby's insistence on a generalizable moral ('the *worlds* vanitie') that discourages particularized applications, seems primarily to be a screen erected (unsuccessfully as it turns out) against the possibility of censorship. Indeed, the portrait of the enterprising publisher scurrying around in pursuit of Spenser's purloined texts and dealing with assorted embezzlers and literary pirates sounds fanciful, and few have doubted at least Spenser's complicity in (if not direction of) the volume's publication.[12] More than an impromptu attempt to cash in on the recent success of *The Faerie Queene*, as Ponsonby alleges, *Complaints* appears to be a fully authorized Spenserian retrospective – the only one published during the poet's lifetime.[13]

Spenser's auto-anthologization contains some recent compositions (*The Ruines of Time*, for instance, must have been written after Walsingham's death in April, 1590), but the impulse of the volume is thoroughly retrogressive. We have already noted Spenser's own assignment, whether ingenuous or not, of *Mother Hubberds Tale* to 'the raw conceipt of my youth.' These terms are echoed in *Virgils Gnat*, 'Long since dedicated' to the Earl of Leicester (p. 486), though likewise here published for the first time. Spenser's impulse to recycle extends even further back to the inclusion of such juvenilia as the *Visions of Bellay* and the *Visions of Petrarch*. They were 'formerly translated' (p. 525) and are now reprised from the 1569 *Theatre for Worldlings*, which predates by a full decade *The Shepheardes Calender* as Spenser's actual literary debut and suggests for his poetic career yet another road not taken (at least at that time).

The retrogressiveness of this anthology is also apparent from another perspective in its engagement with an assortment of 'archaic' poetic forms, including beast fable, fabliau, estates satire, dream vision, and of course complaint. A minor medieval genre – or better, *mode* – the complaint underwent something of a revival towards the end of the sixteenth century.[14] Spenser had a part in this revival, and from the beginning complaint played a determinative role in the articulation of his career and his ambitions. That career is begun 'officially' with the plaintive 'Januarye' eclogue of *The Shepheardes Calender* and its broken pipes. It is concluded with the railing complaint of Dame Mutabilitie – a complaint seemingly silenced by the *de facto* verdict of Jove against her, only to be reprised in the final stanzas of the 'Mutabilitie Cantos' by the poet's own uneasy validation of the goddess's allegations:

> When I bethinke me on that speech whyleare,
>> Of *Mutability*, and well it way:
> Me seemes, that though she all vnworthy were
> Of the Heav'ns Rule; yet very sooth to say,
> In all things else she beares the greatest sway.
> Which makes me loath this state of life so tickle,
>> And loue of things so vaine to cast away;
> Whose flowring pride, so fading and so fickle,
> Short *Time* shall soon cut down with his consuming sickle.
>
> (7.8.1)

These expressions of vanity, fickleness, and the devouring appetite of time are recognizable as a return to the concerns of the generically titled *Complaints* volume, in which Spenser gives the complaint form its fullest exposition.[15] Drawing upon a variety of medieval and Henrician sources. Spenser makes complaint something of a master form there, weaving into his book of complaints strands of satire, homily, and elegy; pastoral locales and epic topoi (the latter most fabulously in the Homeric descent of Mercury in *Mother Hubberds Tale*); and the stern morals of *de casibus* tragedy and *contemptus mundi* philosophy. For poetic models, Spenser turns here to an array of plaintive predecessors including Petrarch, Boccaccio, du Bellay, Langland, Lydgate, Skelton, Wyatt, and especially Chaucer, who had engaged the form of complaint in such works as *Anelida and Arcite*, *The Complaint of Venus*, and *The Complaint of Chaucer to his Purse*, as well as significant portions of *The Legend of Good Women*.

I do not mean to suggest here that the 'revised' medievalism of *Complaints* represents an absolute departure in Spenser's poetics. The seminal model of Chaucer, as we have seen, always figured powerfully in Spenser's verse and the shaping of his career. Likewise, both *The Shepheardes Calender* and *The Faerie Queene* regularly touch upon complaint and satire in their generic range. Moreover, there is latent in *The Faerie Queene* an alternative etiology of Spenser's epic, which, running counter to the notion of it as a Virgilian imitation, offers the poem as a sustained effort to finish the unfinished 'Tale of Sir Thopas,' with Prince Arthur in the role of the Thopas figure. Chaucer's romance, abandoned at the insistence of the other pilgrims, features what is probably the first appearance in English literature of the Faery Queen, and to that extent it foretells Spenser's own romance epic. The medievalism of *Complaints* thus represents less a fundamental change of direction than a strategic foregrounding of 'the medieval Spenser' that has been part of the career all along.

At the same time, I see the volume as staging an ostensible public deflection away from Spenser's epic itinerary, as well as much of what that itinerary implies in terms of his role as a poet, his relations to courtly society, and his position towards political power in general. Set aside is the 1590 *Faerie Queene*'s announced agenda of recording and preserving the noble deeds of knights and ladies, not to mention the enshrinement of Elizabeth as the new Augustus. In *The Teares of the Muses*, Spenser now declares, 'Because I nothing noble have to sing' (108). In place of these imperial designs, the poet's abiding concern in his *Complaints* seems to be predicting and documenting the downfall and eventual erasure from cultural memory of the once high and mighty, 'Forgotten quite as they were neuer borne' (*The Ruines of Time*, 182). Ironically, despite this shift in matter and style, one concern that remains constant in many of the *Complaints* is Spenser's continued occupation of the role of amanuensis.

He is still taking down women's words; but instead of recording the queen's praises as he does in *The Faerie Queene*, Spenser is now taking dictation from a ghost in *The Ruines of Time*, 'recording in my troubled brain' (481) the complaints of the deposed Verlame. Similarly, in *The Teares of the Muses* we find him transcribing the 'secret causes' (50) of an unhappy troop of muses.

Underpinning many of the poems gathered in *Complaints* is the medieval philosophical commonplace that everything on earth 'in th'end to nought shall fade' (*Ruines of Rome*, 280). This sobering lesson is typified, and consequently generalized, in the desolation of ancient cities like Verulamium or Rome. But in *The Ruines of Time* Spenser comes close to naming names and applying this hardly savory moral to the fortunes of contemporary English powerbrokers as well. Presumably even less palatable to the powers that be, his *Visions of the Worlds Vanitie* provides a dozen cautionary exempla about how the small and seemingly powerless are able to upstage or even injure their 'betters.' A tiny worm fells a mighty cedar; a wasp wounds and incapacitates a lion; a small fish stalls an entire ship; a goose saves Rome from invasion – and all the while the poet keeps reminding us 'not to despise, / What euer thing seemes small in common eyes' (*Visions*, 69–70).[16]

By publishing these corrosive poems between installments of his epic, and hence interrupting in midcourse his path along the *rota Virgilii*, Spenser is also staging an implicit challenge to the example of Virgil as the normative model for the poetic career.[17] Taking the place of Virgil, the successful imperial poet (placed by Puttenham rather dubiously among the 'cunning Princepleasers')[18] is Chaucer, who is reasserted in *Complaints* as Spenser's major literary propagator. Although in actuality a successful court poet himself, Chaucer had been associated in *The Shepheardes Calender* with the low style and a penchant for personal complaint: 'Well couth he wayle hys Woes,' Spenser writes of him in the 'June' eclogue (85). The strategic reprioritization of Chaucer here in *Complaints* goes hand in hand with Spenser's critical detachment from the court and its values, along with a return to the poetics of lowliness, seemingly set aside in the exchange of pastoral pipes for epic trumpets.

My claims about the restaging of Spenser's career that is enacted by the publication of *Complaints* can be further anchored by returning to *Mother Hubberds Tale*. That poem begins with a rough versed and, after the poems of the 1590 *Faerie Queene*, politically loaded refusal of assistance from any muse: 'No Muses aide me needes heretoo to call; / Base is the style, and matter meane withall' (43–4). Overlaying beast fable with a fierce estates satire, this poem is, as many have noted, Spenser's most Chaucerian performance.[19] In addition to its 'low' style,

Mother Hubberd features self-consciously archaic locutions, an astrological *incipit* and a characteristically Chaucerian sleepless narrator, whose insomnia is relieved only by the round of storytelling provided by his concerned friends:

> They sought my troubled sense how to deceaue
> With talke that might vnquiet fancies reaue
> And sitting all in seates about me round,
> With pleasaunt tales (fit for that idle stound)
> They cast in course to waste the wearie howres:
> Some tolde of Ladies, and their Paramoures;
> Some of braue Knights, and their renowned Squires;
> Some of Faeries and their strange attires;
> And some of Giaunts hard to be beleeued,
> That the delight thereof me much releeued.
>
> (23–32)

Mother Hubberd's frame evokes the serial taletelling structure of the *Canterbury Tales,* and perhaps also that of Boccaccio's *Decameron* (for Spenser's poem is likewise set in a time of 'plague, pestilence, and death' [8]). At the same time, however, the principals of the other tales told in the narrator's bedchamber – ladies, knights, faeries, giants – also foretell (recall?) the epic matter of *The Faerie Queene,* the poem whose production has been forestalled by the publication of *Complaints* and will continue to be forestalled on through the 1595 volume containing the *Amoretti* and the *Epithalamion* Spenser writes in celebration of his own marriage.

The 'faery' tales of knights and ladies are set aside in *Mother Hubberds Tale* for the recounting of the satiric adventures of the Fox and Ape, who begin their pilgrimage disguised as yeoman and soldier – roles selected from a suitably Chaucerian repertoire that also includes pilgrim and limitour among its options (see lines 85–6). As the Fox and Ape rise through the various estates, examples of negligence and corruption are uncovered at every level of society. What's more striking is that Spenser's satiric method refuses to provide – unlike, say, Pope's, or even Chaucer's in the *General Prologue* – a few exemplary models as a contrast to show up the corrupt ones. There is no honest parson in *Mother Hubberds Tale,* for instance, to balance the tale's portrait of the unscrupulous priest who provides detailed instructions on the dissimulative 'arte' of winning benefices. In fact, while the Fox and the Ape may be the poem's chief culprits, no one they encounter in its tour of abuses entirely eludes the wide net of *Mother Hubberd's* satire. Included in its all-fronts indictment is the royal court that so readily receives the imposters and provides a platform for their rapid ascendancy, as well as the sleeping lion/monarch, whose administrative neglect opens the door for his sovereignty to be impersonated and usurped in the first place. The poem even casts doubt on the so-called 'honest' shepherd (259), who responds empathetically, though foolishly, to the complaints of the Fox and the Ape.[20] The point is that there seems to be no position of absolute innocence available in the poem. Even the model courtier, who can appear in the iron age world of *Mother Hubberd* only as a massively idealized abstraction and not as an actual character in its narrative, does not seem very far from the Machiavellian Fox in being himself 'practiz'd well in policie' (783).

Satirists, Puttenham tells us in *The Arte*, are 'spiers out of all secret faults.'[21] And as a satirist, Spenser, rather than keeping secrets – a practice out of which he had forged his careers as secretary and poet – systematically uncovers in *Mother Hubberd* what might be better left covered, even if already widely known. Spenser's practice of exposure is conducted at a level aimed beyond the satirical, however, when the Fox and the Ape set their sights on the court. For in charting their rise to positions of prominence and wealth, *Mother Hubberd* becomes a virtual 'how-to' manual for achieving a place at a competitive and corrupt court – a kind of demonic *Il Cortegiano* – as it provides instruction on dress, manners, wit, and all the necessary accomplishments. Pedagogic pronouncements such as 'This is the way, for one that is vnlern'd / Liuing to get, and not be discern'd' (535–6; cf. 513–14) preface every movement of the Fox and the Ape up the rungs of the social ladder. Even as Spenser satirizes each estate, in other words, he gives away the secrets of the trade.

Not surprisingly, one of the trade 'secrets' for success at court is itself the ability to discover and deploy the secrets of others. In his essay 'Of Simulation and Dissimulation,' Francis Bacon counsels that 'an habit of secrecy is both political and moral.'[22] By this advice Bacon is recommending the safeguarding of one's own enterprises with a strategic cover of secrecy; but he also means that a well-disseminated reputation for closeness often results in a privileged access to the secrets of others:

> But if a man be thought secret, it inviteth discovery [i.e., disclosures], as the more close air sucketh in the more open . . . so secret men come to the knowledge of many things in that kind. In few words, mysteries are due to secrecy.

In this Baconian physics of secrecy, one is more likely to earn a privileged access to the secrets of others when he maintains the appearance (whether actual or not) of keeping his own. Thus, in accounting for the Fox and the Ape's social and economic dominance at court, Mother Hubberd explains that the Fox was 'school'd by kinde in all the skill / Of close conueyance' (855–6) and

vsd' oft to beguile
Poore suters, that in Court did haunt some while:
For he would learne their busines secretly,
And then informe his Master hastely,
That he by meanes might cast them to preuent,
And beg the sute, the which the other ment.

(877–82)

Similarly, the model courtier, who we have already noted is well practiced
in 'policie,' would be himself no stranger to these arts of 'close
conveyaunce.' Like a kind of ambassador/spy (which, we might recall,
is just what Philip Sidney was during his 1577 continental tour), the
courtier attempts to uncover the secret

enterdeale of Princes strange,
To marke th'intent of Counsells, and the change
Of states, and eke of priuate men somewhile,
Supplanted by fine falsehood and faire guile;
Of all the which he gathereth, what is fit
T'enrich the storehouse of his powerfull wit.

(785–90)

Mother Hubberds Tale itself daringly participates in such covert 'policie'
by prying, under the cover of fable, into the internal affairs of the
Elizabethan court. The passage, for example, beginning at line 1151 in
which the Fox is seen to prefer his own cubs for important
administrative offices invites application as an attack on Burghley's
controversial efforts to promote his son Robert Cecil to the Privy Council
– efforts which succeeded in 1591. The appearance of granting access to
court secrets is even more pronounced when the poem turns to the always
volatile question of who is currently 'in' at court and who is 'out': 'But
tell vs (said the Ape) we doo you pray, / Who now in Court doth beare
the greatest sway[?]' (615–16). Although this is an inquiry that would
have had a different answer in 1591 than it might have had in 1579, the
potentially scandalous gesture of retailing inner court gossip was no
doubt of abiding force. For, as the poem goes on to reveal, the status of
a favored 'Liege' has been put in jeopardy by his acquisition of a 'late
chayne' (628) – an unapproved marriage? This new bond is deemed
'vnmeete' by the lion/monarch because it competes, the poem intimates,
with her own claim on that liege, whom she had similarly (and
punningly) attempted to 'Enchaste with chaine and a circulet of golde'
(624).

To a greater extent than any other poem in Spenser's canon, *Mother
Hubberds Tale* has been received as a *roman à clef* – a fact to which the

dozen pages of the *Variorum* devoted to the endeavor of deciphering its allusions amply testify. The gossipy passage we have been examining about the liege and the lion, for instance, has been variously applied to Leicester, Ralegh, and Essex, all one-time favorites of the queen who contracted secret marriages, and with those secret marriages Elizabeth's jealous displeasure. The iterability of a satire (and here I am referring to the poem as a whole) that can be seen to target so many prominent courtiers points to, as Crewe notes, a flip side to the satiric decorum which declines to name names.[23] For by not naming names just about anyone in the appropriate circumstances – Leicester, Burghley, Simier, Alençon, Essex, Robert Cecil, Ralegh, even the queen – becomes a candidate for identification and stands to have his or her 'secret faults' spied out. Furthermore, by establishing the exploitative careers of the Fox and the Ape as constitutive models of what counts as success within the terms of Elizabethan court politics, *Mother Hubberd* threatens to implicate everyone who has ever achieved a measure of success there. To be successful at court, the poem insinuates, is to be like the Fox and the Ape. Even Mercury, eventually sent by Jove to impose order in the animal kingdom and depose the 'impostors,' too closely resembles them to secure the impression at the end of the poem that the court has been wholly purged of what they represent.[24] For like the Fox and the Ape, Mercury is characterized by his 'cunning theeueries' (1287), by his skill at altering his shape (1266: 1289–90), and of course – being the god of secrecy, Hermes – by his ability to pry 'into each secrete part' (1303).

Spenser's systemic indictment of the court was not without consequences. It appears from a number of roughly contemporary sources that the poem not only was controversial, but also occasioned, as Thomas Middleton puts it in his own satiric *Black Book* (1604), the 'calling in' of *Complaints* for *Mother Hubberd*'s 'selling her working bottle-ale to bookbinders, and spurting the froth upon courtiers' noses.'[25] Judging from the testimony of Middleton and others, the suppression of the volume had nothing to do with the by-then long resolved Alençon crisis, a point that further argues for a recontextualization of *Mother Hubberds Tale* in terms of Spenser's career as it stood in the early 1590s. Nor does it seem from these reports that his troubles with the authorities arose from any notion that, in identifying the shortcomings and abuses of the court, Spenser was disclosing something that was previously unknown. More likely, the official disfavor that met the poem stemmed from the fact that he was disclosing at all – that he was seen to be an arrogant malcontent, far out of line in assuming the role of a satiric 'secret agent' uncovering in print what was better left, if not unknown, at least unsaid. (This same 'molish' posture of having uncovered scandalous information about the court from the 'inside' is again assumed by the poet in *Colin Clouts Come Home Againe*.) The notion that Spenser had stepped out of line in *Mother Hubberds Tale* is likewise indicated by Gabriel Harvey in a letter he published in his *Fowre Letters and Certaine Sonnets* (1592). There Harvey remarks that 'Mother Hubberd in the heat of chollar, forgetting the pure sanguine of her sweete Faery Queene, wilfully over-shot her malcontented selfe.'[26] The terms of Harvey's unfriendly public jibe (as Thomas Nashe in his *Strange Newes* [1593] no doubt rightly identified it)[27] also call Spenser to task for having taken a wrong turn *generically*. The poet of *The Faerie Queene*, that is, had no business in abandoning his 'sweete' epic to spew up the 'chollar' of complaint. Similarly, Middleton's account of Mother Hubberd's 'selling her working bottle-ale to bookbinders' suggests that with the publication of *Complaints* Spenser was thought to have turned his back on the court to pander to another audience.

The other poem in *Complaints* that has been singled out in accounts of the volume's difficulties with the censors is *The Ruines of Time*:

> *Colin's* gone home, the glorie of his clime,
> The Muses Mirrour, and the Shepheards Saint:
> *Spencer* is ruin'd of our latter time
> The fairest ruine. Faeries foulest want:
> When his *Time-ruines* did our ruine show,
> Which by his ruine we vntimely know;
> *Spencer* therefore thy *Ruines* were cal'd in,
> Too soone to sorrow least we should begin.

These obituary verses come from the pen of John Weever in 1599, and they suggest that, in satirically uncovering 'our ruine,' Spenser's *Time-ruines*' itself ruined the poet.[28] Once again, the cardinal offense as it is figured here resides in Spenser's turn from *The Faerie Queene* ('Faeries foulest want') to the matter of *Complaints* (which 'did our ruine show'), in the deflection of his task as an imperial epic poet towards the satirist's exposure of abuses.

As the opening poem in the collection, *The Ruines of Time* foretells the structure of the entire volume and embodies many of its querulous concerns. It begins with a highly formalized complaint voiced by the figure of a woman (another gesture that follows a Chaucerian precedent), and it concludes with two sets of pageant-like visions in sonnet form. The first vision illustrates time's ruinous power over the accomplishments of civilization, while the second exemplifies in the apotheosis of Philip Sidney the memorializing power of the poet to preserve what would otherwise be ravaged by time. The appearance of Mercury in the final vision, forecasting his role in *Mother Hubberds Tale*, ends the poem.

In the prefatory dedication of the poem to Sidney's sister, the Countess of Pembroke, Spenser declares *The Ruines of Time* to be an atonement for his truancy from the task of 'renowming' the 'noble race' of his first patrons (p. 471). At the center of the poem is an extended necrology of the Dudley and Bedford families, a virtual 'political party' upon which all of Spenser's early hopes for advancement had been hung. But Sidney had died in 1586, followed by Leicester in 1588, Leicester's brother Ambrose, the Earl of Warwick, in 1589, and Walsingham in 1590. True to the volume's title. Spenser's memorialization slides from obituary towards complaint. Indeed, his elegies for Leicester, Sidney, and Walsingham can be seen to do double duty as hardly concealed elegies for unrealized versions of Spenser's own career and his hopes for preferment which had died along with these powerful patrons. As the poet complains in the dedication, with Sidney's death his own 'hope of anie further fruit was cut off' (p. 471). Beyond a personal loss, however, Spenser is also pointing to a significant alteration in the political landscape of Elizabethan England. For the death of Leicester allowed Burghley to tighten further the reins he held over the Privy Council: 'He now is gone, the whiles the Foxe is crept / Into the hole, the which the Badger swept' (216–17). Burghley was always perceived as an adversary by Spenser (the fulsome dedicatory sonnet appended at the last minute to the 1590 *Faerie Queene* notwithstanding), and these lines presage the gloomy prospects for poets – 'Not honored nor cared for of anie' (*The Teares of the Muses*, 225) – that are the subject of this next poem in *Complaints*. As Richard Schell has remarked cogently of Spenser's position in the early 1590s, 'Old friends and patrons were simply *not there* . . . New circles of power provided less hope: Spenser was not so near to their centers, and he knew he never would be.'[29]

But if on the one hand *The Ruines of Time* re-enacts Spenser's career-long inability to set himself above factional differences in order to claim the position of a national poet, on the other it reveals his developing ambivalence about the whole process of hiring himself out for patronage. In a poem that is putatively intended to eulogize the departed and console the survivors, Spenser's repeated announcement in *The Ruines of Time* of the inglorious circumstances of Leicester's death, for instance, has a rather unsettling effect:

> I saw him die, I saw him die, as one
> Of the meane people, and brought forth on beare.
> I saw him die, and no man left to mone
> His doleful fate, that late him loued deare.
> . . .
> He now is dead, and all is with him dead,

> . . .
> He now is dead, and all his glorie gone.
>
> (190–3; 211; 218)

It is difficult to name the sentiment underwriting these insistent, unflattering declarations. Is it a feeling of loss, coupled with an attempt to awaken militant action among the 'survivors' in the Leicester party? Or is it something approaching satisfaction? Moreover, in the preface and throughout the body of the poem Spenser perhaps too proudly shows off his truancy from the obligation of honoring his departed benefactors. Considered from this perspective, what the poem seems ultimately to enact is Spenser's *refusal* to elegize, his refusal to perform one of the tasks of a patronized poet:

> Ne doth his *Colin*, carelesse *Colin Cloute*,
> Care now his idle bagpipe vp to raise,
> Ne tell his sorrow to the listning rout
> Of shepherd groomes, which wont his songs to praise.
>
> (225–8)

Nor does it help matters that the only sort of memorializing forthcoming for Leicester is put in the mouth of the dubious figure of Verlame, who in *The Ruines of Time* is associated, in addition to her other religious and political encodings, with papism and the Whore of Babylon.

Spenser's ambivalence about 'marketing' his poetic abilities as a kind of hired hand, available for the procurement of those who would patronize him, is likewise signalled in the prefatory letter of the publisher that I have already discussed:

> I haue sithence endeuoured by all good meanes . . . to get into my handes such smale Poemes of the same Authors: as I heard were disperst abroad in sundrie hands, and not easie to bee come by, by himselfe: some of them hauing bene diuerslie imbeziled and purloyned from him, since his departure ouer Sea. (p. 470)

The anxiety expressed in this passage is partly the Orphean anxiety of scattered limbs, a response of poets in this period more regularly associated with the recent practice of anthologization, which presented variously authored small lyric poems in piecemeal miscellanies. But the central concern ventriloquized here on behalf of the poet is the embezzlement and piracy of his poems, the sense that the poems have been 'disperst abroad in sundrie hands' while he is himself exiled overseas. In the attempt to reassemble Spenser's poetic corpus, the first claim in print to his ownership of his poems, as well as, ironically, to

81

poems that are chiefly imitations – copies – of du Bellay and Petrarch, is made on behalf of Spenser. I read these aggressive gestures of authorial possession and literary property – of the desire to 'get into my handes' what had been 'by himselfe 'formerly 'disperst abroad in sundrie hands' – moreover as a revisionary career move made against what we have seen to be the disseminative' many handedness' of *The Shepheardes Calender* and its production. It is also made against the fully elaborated secretarial poetics of the 1590 *Faerie Queene*, in which Spenser writes under the screening conceit of merely taking dictation at the hand of Elizabeth, his queen and his muse.

And what does it mean for a poet/secretary to assert his own hand? To reclaim what he has penned as belonging to himself? to insist upon ownership and autonomy? What these issues underscore is Spenser's thoroughgoing renegotiation in *Complaints* of both his loss of important patrons and his own discrediting of the operations of preferment established at court into a new statement of poetic self-reliance. *Complaints*, that is, inaugurates the turn towards the personal, the 'self-centred,' which, though complicated by the questions above, would more overtly inform the rest of Spenser's career.

Notes

Footnotes have been altered slightly for this volume – Ed.

1. Given that several extant copies of the poem contain only ten sonnets, it has been deduced that these dedications were added to *The Faerie Queene* in two batches. The remaining seven – including, most notably, the one to Lord Burghley – would then have been appended just before printing was completed. See the account offered by JUDSON in his *Variorum* biography of Spenser, 11:142–3.

2. JANE TYLUS, 'Spenser, Virgil, and the Politics of Poetic Labor,' *ELH* 55 (1986): 53–77, at 54.

3. For a related discussion of the relations between Red Crosse, the rustics of *The Shepheardes Calender*, and Immeritô, see JOHN D. BERNARD, *Ceremonies of Innocence: Pastoralism in the Poetry of Edmund Spenser* (Cambridge: Cambridge University Press, 1989), pp. 79–81; 91–2.

4. See, for example, the account offered by THOMAS FULLER in *The History of the Worthies of England* (London, 1662): 'There passeth a story commonly told and believed, that *Spencer* presenting his Poems to Queen *Elizabeth*: She highly affected therewith, commanded the Lord *Cecil* Her Treasurer to give him an hundred pound; and when the Treasurer (a good Steward of the Queens money) alledged that sum was too much, then *give him* (quoth the Queen) *what is reason*; to which the Lord consented, but was so busied, belike, about matters of higher concernment, that *Spenser* received no reward: Whereupon he presented this petition in a small piece of paper to the Queen in her Progress.

I was promis'd on a time,
To have reason for my rhyme:
From that time unto this season,
I receiv'd nor rhyme nor reason.

Hereupon the Queen gave strict order (not without some check to her Treasurer) for the present payment of the hundred pounds [sic], the first intended upon him.' Fuller's account is reproduced in CUMMINGS, *Spenser: The Critical Heritage,* (London: Routledge, 1971), pp. 320–1. While this particular anecdote may very well be apocryphal, Spenser's dissatisfaction with what his poetic endeavors had earned him at Elizabeth's court is evident in nearly every poem of the 1591 *Complaints* volume.

5. See SIMON SHEPHERD, *Spenser* (Hemel Hempstead: Harvester, 1989), p. 105. STEVEN W. MAY notes that annuities from the crown averaged on the short side of twenty pounds. Even so, he reports, Lord Henry Seymour, sewer to the queen, for example, gained an annuity of three hundred pounds, while the countess of Kildare's amounted to seven hundred pounds. See Steven W. May's *The Elizabethan Courtier Poets: Their Poems and Their Contexts* (London and Columbia: University of Missouri Press, 1991), p. 29. For a detailed consideration of Spenser's annuity, see HERBERT BERRY and E. K. TIMINGS, 'Spenser's Pension,' *Review of English Studies* 11 (1960): 254–9.

6. On this unprecedented social flux, see LAWRENCE STONE, *The Crisis of the Aristocracy: 1558–1641* (Oxford: Oxford University Press, 1967), abridged edn., pp. 21–8.

7. This point is discussed by WILLIAM A. ORAM in his informative introduction to *Mother Hubberds Tale* for the *Yale Edition of the Shorter Poems* (New Haven: Yale University Press, 1989), p. 330.

8. It is true that the Fox and the Ape are described at the onset of the poem as 'craftie and unhappie witted' (49), but the moral valences of these terms are not necessarily as one-directional and censorious as the *Yale Edition*'s gloss of 'apt to cause trouble' might suggest.

9. JONATHAN CREWE, *Hidden Designs: The Critical Profession and Renaissance Literature* (New York and London: Methuen, 1986), p. 56.

10. See, for example, GREENLAW's 'Spenser and the Earl of Leicester,' *PMLA* 25 (1910): 535–61; '*The Shepheardes Calender*,' *PMLA* 26 (1911): 419–51; and '*The Shepheardes Calender* II,' *SP* 11 (1913): 3–25.

11. CREWE, *Hidden Designs*, p. 55.

12. Cf. RONALD BOND's introductory remarks on *Complaints* in the *Yale Edition of the Shorter Poems*. JEAN R. BRINK, in 'Who Fashioned Edmund Spenser? The Textual History of *Complaints*,' *SP* 87 (1991): 153–68, however, does dispute the prevailing assumption that Spenser directed the publication of *Complaints*.

13. See BERNARD, *Ceremonies of Innocence*, p. 113, for a similar point. See also BOND's Introduction to *Complaints* in the *Yale Edition*, p. 218.

14. See HALLETT SMITH, *Elizabethan Poetry* (Cambridge, Mass.: Harvard University Press, 1964), p. 103.

15. LINDA VECCHI notes that Spenser's volume is the only book in *The Short-Title Catalog* to appear under the title 'Complaints.' See her essay 'Spenser's *Complaints*: Is the Whole Equal to the Sum of its Parts?' in *Spenser at Kalamazoo* (1984): 127–38, at 130.

16. BERNARD offers the best account I have found of these seldom-discussed poems and the way they figure in Spenser's revisionary appraisal of his career in *Complaints*. See *Ceremonies of Innocence*, pp. 111–13.

17. Significantly, *Virgils Gnat*, the most 'Virgilian' – or more precisely, pseudo-Virgilian – poem in the volume does not represent the high 'canonical' Virgil; nor has it, as a complaint, found a place in the authorized Virgilian progression of pastoral-georgic-epic.

18. PUTTENHAM, *The Arte of English Poesie* (1589), facsimile ed. Baxter Hathaway (Kent, Oh.: Ohio State University Press, 1970), p. 32.

19. See, for example, ORAM's Introduction to *Mother Hubberds Tale* for the *Yale Edition of the Shorter Poems*, p. 329.

20. Cf. CREWE's discussion in *Hidden Designs*, p. 61, of this episode and its implications for the potential insidiousness of any sympathetic response in this poem.

21. PUTTENHAM, *The Arte of English Poesie*, p. 46.

22. BACON, 'Of Simulation and Dissimulation,' in *Essays*, ed. JOHN PITCHER (New York: Penguin, 1987), p. 77.

23. CREWE, *Hidden Designs*, p. 62.

24. Cf. ORAM's discussion of this point in the *Yale Edition of the Shorter Poems*, pp. 332–3.

25. THOMAS MIDDLETON, *The Black Book*, in *The Works of Thomas Middleton*, 8 vols., ed. A. H. BULLEN (London: John C. Nimmo, 1886): 8:31.

26. GABRIEL HARVEY, *Foure Letters and Certeine Sonnets*, in *The Works of Gabriel Harvey*, 3 vols., ed. ALEXANDER B. GROSART (London: Hazel, Watson and Viney, 1884): 1:164.

27. THOMAS NASHE, *Strange Newes*, in *The Works of Thomas Nashe*, 5 vols., ed. R. B. McKERROW (London: Sidgwick and Johnson, 1904–1910): 1:281–2.

28. JOHN WEEVER, *Epigrammes* (London, 1599), sig. G3a, reproduced in facsimile in *John Weever*, ed. E. A. J. HONIGMANN (Manchester: Manchester University Press, 1987).

29. RICHARD SCHELL, Introduction to *The Ruines of Time*, in the *Yale Edition of the Shorter Poems*, p. 227.

5 Spenser's poetics: the poem's two bodies*

David Lee Miller

'The Poem's Two Bodies' attempts to combine post-structural and historicist ways of reading *The Faerie Queene*, using a synthesis of deconstruction, psychoanalysis and Marxism based partly on Roland Barthes' book on Balzac, *S/Z: An Essay* (1970). Miller's essay captures much of the eclectic and assimilative brilliance of its model, especially in its application of Lacanian psychoanalytic theory to Spenser's text. Miller disclaims a critical position as such, suggesting instead that, as Harold Bloom argued, you *are* your method. The critical task is not to *apply* theory but to rediscover its emergence from the literary text. Such rediscoveries are not the product of a 'method' but of a 'practice', the practice of intensive and inventive textual analysis. *The Faerie Queene* opens itself endlessly to such analysis.

Miller's essay explores the poet's and reader's quest for the whole body of the Queen, represented in the poem as Gloriana and destined only to appear as an insubstantial wraith, a process he compares to the impossible goal of historical scholarship. The quest for wholeness and completion can only start to occur if, paradoxically, we abandon such inevitably frustrated desires. In the same way, the allegorical *Faerie Queene* can only speak the truth as fiction.

> How might I that fair wonder know
> That mocks desire with endless No?
>
> John Dowland, *Third Book of Airs*

On the fifteenth of January 1559, a sacred transformation was wrought in the person of Elizabeth Tudor. The ceremony of royal coronation had not technically been classed as a sacrament since the twelfth century, but in many ways it still bore the stamp of its ecclesiastical original, the ordination of a bishop; each smallest detail of word, gesture, and regalia was understood as 'the outward and visible sign of an inward and

*First published in *PMLA* 101 (1986), 170–85.

spiritual grace' (Schramm 6–9; Churchill 20). At the heart of this inwardness, created and sustained by an impressive array of sacred objects and solemn actions, lay the arch-mystery that anchored all others: the investiture of a natural body with the *corpus mysticum* of the realm. Drawn by analogy from Western culture's central religious ceremonies, this 'political sacrament' tended to deify both Elizabeth and the state she governed, converting what was essentially an allegorical personification into mystified or doctrinal form as a species of legal incarnation.[1]

This incarnation of empire is the central 'figure' of Spenser's *Faerie Queene* – its founding trope as well as its title character.[2] Conceived and designed to abet the glorification of the body politic in Elizabeth, Spenser's epic reflects a distinctly imperial and theocentric poetics. In his magisterial study of early Renaissance 'political theology,' Ernst Kantorowicz has written that

> in 16th-century England, by the efforts of jurists to define effectively and accurately the King's Two Bodies, all the Christological problems of the early Church concerning the Two Natures once more were actualized and resuscitated in the early absolute monarchy.
>
> (17)

In much the same way, certain contradictions embedded in Tudor 'Royal Christology' reemerge in the aesthetic theology of *The Faerie Queene*, where an implicit doctrine of 'the poem's two bodies' constitutes the literary self-image of Spenser's epic tribute to early absolute monarchy under Elizabeth.[3]

In centering his artistic vision on Elizabeth, whose various names point outward to the sixteenth century's far-reaching reinscription of the received 'text' of English monarchy, Spenser opens his poesis to the forces of contemporary history. Elizabeth is Gloriana, and she in turn is the ideal form of the poem itself: the Fairy Queen is *The Faerie Queene*, a vision of perfection pursued along parallel lines by Arthur and the reader. We will return to the complexities of this conceit; for the moment it is enough to observe that it represents a prophetic wager on the historical fortunes of the house of Tudor, as well as a singular act of invention, compounding and overgoing such precedents as Vergil's Augustus, Dante's Beatrice, Petrarch's Laura, and Ariosto's house of Este. In this respect *The Faerie Queene* stands out even among Spenser's poems for its willingness to take up the burden of history.

Kantorowicz's remark suggests that the legal problematics of the king's two bodies must be understood as a special case of the body-soul dualism endemic to Christian and Platonic thought. This observation may also apply to key structural features in the broadly Platonized Christianity that informs the medieval tradition of allegorical and philosophical fiction. Beginning with the strange two-bodied monster we meet in constitutional theory, we will follow three motifs – perfect wholeness, secular perpetuity, and the doctrine of 'assimilation' – from political into aesthetic theology, where they emerge as an implicit poetics of two bodies. Our first concern will be to describe the structure of this poetics, especially the role of what I call its negative moment, exemplified in such texts as Boethius's *Consolation of Philosophy*, Petrarch's letter on the ascent of Mount Ventoux, and Spenser's *Fowre Hymnes*, as well as in passages from the 'Legend of Holiness.' Having set forth a structural description and glimpsed it at work in the narrative of *The Faerie Queene*, we will return to the founding conceit of Arthur's quest for Gloriana-Elizabeth, seen as an allegory of the poem's quest for a figure of its own identity; once again we will want to focus on the crucial role of the negative moment in summoning the poem's ideal form into representation. Finally we will take up the image Spenser regularly employs to figure this ideal wholeness: the hermaphrodite. Reading this 'figure' as the trope of catachresis, I suggest an answer to the question asked in the epigraph to this essay. Our quest as readers for the truth of the poem can only proceed as an extension of Spenser's catachresis, with its inveterate tendency to breach the mimetic decorum proper to allegory. At this point we will return to the poem's engagement with history, ending with a brief but (I hope) tendentious sketch of the politics of interpretation we are drawn into by reading Spenser.

Two aspects of the legal fiction known as the king's two bodies will help focus our inquiry into Spenserian poetics. First is the corporate metaphor, a figure of integral wholeness: like Christianity, Spenser's art fantasises its own perfection as full access to a spiritual body replete with truth. 'The Faerie Queene', writes Leonard Barkan, 'is a limitless landscape of the world, a vast number of men who are themselves multiple and subdivided, and finally a simple, perhaps perfect, human being who contains in body and spirit all the virtues of the heroes and all the struggles necessary to gain and keep those virtues' (6). This simple, perhaps perfect human being who figures the complex unity of Spenser's poem is figured in turn by the marriage of Arthur and Gloriana. 'The Faerie Queene,' writes Rosemond Tuve, 'holds that role of shadowy but great importance, the Sovereignty itself, in a sense "the realm" ' (347). Separate quests begin and end at Gloriana's court because all adventures (as Tuve reminds us) belong to the sovereign, who grants them as favors to individual knights and who acts 'through his fellowship as through an extended self' (348). Arthur meanwhile serves 'as a combined figure for the dynasty, the all-inclusive virtue, the spouse-to-be of the personified realm, [and] the royal house through whom divine power flowed into country and people' (350). The mystical union of these two persons in one flesh perfects the image of sovereignty and constitutes the ideal body of Spenser's poem.

This ideal body is diffracted into many signatures, from the 'pressed gras' Arthur finds in the wake of his dream, or the image graven on Guyon's shield, to the numerological patterns that mimic celestial symmetry, the 'golden wall' that surrounds Cleopolis (2.10.72), the name 'Telamond' at the head of book 4, the veiled shapes of Venus and Nature, or the sacramental embrace in which Scudamour and Amoret became one flesh in the first ending to book 3.[4] Ultimately perhaps all the words and things in the poem are synecdochic traces in quest of the wholeness they signify. Even Spenser's figure for his textual source, the 'everlasting scryne' from which the Muse lays forth ancient scrolls telling of Arthur's quest, is a synecdoche for what we might call 'the archive': it represents nothing less than the perpetuity and coherence of Western imperial culture. As synecdoche, it attributes a distinctly global unity to the scattered hoards of documents found, purchased, transported, translated, reread, and otherwise recovered during the late medieval and early modern explosion of *translatio studii* in Western Europe. Thus the gentleman Spenser seeks to fashion pursues an ego ideal that would integrate the private self with an encyclopedia of the culture's symbolic matrices, from literary genres to chronicle histories, from legal fictions to theological doctrines.[5] In Arthur's quest for Gloriana, Spenser recasts the Ur-narrative of his culture's search for this global unity – now in the millennial form of a Protestant world empire.

The second feature of Tudor political theology that is important for our understanding of Spenser's poetics is the relation between the bodies natural and politic. Although the body politic was denied a living soul and acknowledged as an artifact of human policy, it was nevertheless held to be perfect and imperishable, 'utterly void of Infancy, and Old Age, and other natural Defects and Embicilities, which the body natural is subject to.' Most important, this ideal fictive body was held to 'assimilate to its own excellence' all defects and imbecilities in the monarch's natural body (Kantorowicz 7–12).[6] For an aesthetic corollary to these doctrines of perpetuity and assimilation, we may turn to Spenser's *Amoretti* 75:

> One day I wrote her name upon the strand,
> But came the waves and washed it away:
> Agayne I wrote it with a second hand,
> But came the tyde, and made my paynes his pray.
> Vayne man, sayd she, that does in vaine assay
> A mortall thing so to immortalize!
> For I my selve shall lyke to this decay,

And eek my name be wyped out lykewize.
Not so (quod I) let baser things devize
To dy in dust, but you shall live by fame:
My verse your vertues rare shall eternize,
And in the hevens write your glorious name;
    Where, whenas death shall all the world subdew,
    Our love shall live, and later life renew.

(732)

The grandiose gesture of turning away from writing that 'reachest unto dust,' to inscribe the soul as a 'glorious name' in the crystalline substance of heaven – this gesture and its promise depend on the easy confidence with which the poet assimilates *saeculum*, the medium of fame, to eternity, the medium of 'later life.' In this uninterrupted transition from perpetuity to eternity, writing itself undergoes a kind of aesthetic coronation, absorbed into an incorruptible body void of misinterpretation, linguistic drift, and the transvaluations of secular history, which the merely natural letter is subject to.

We can see more clearly how Spenser assimilates the natural body of writing to its perfected form by looking briefly at his idea of poetic inspiration. It is Neoplatonic love that inspires the poet to transcendent inscriptions,

    For love is lord of truth and loialtie,
    Lifting himselfe out of the lowly dust
    On golden plumes up to the purest skie . . .

(HL 176–8)[7]

The 'golden plumes' on which love ascends from dust to the sky also feather the 'golden quill' of poetic inspiration:

    Deepe in the closet of my parts entyre,
    Her worth is written with a golden quill:
    That me with heavenly fury doth inspire,
    And my glad mouth with her sweet prayses fill.

(*Amoretti* 84)

This inner quill writes 'worth,' or sheer value, not merely material letters. The sweet praises we see before us on the page are a secondary and derivative thing, for Spenser projects an idealised image of his own language as the golden paradigm from which his verse proceeds. Assimilating the poet's words to 'it's own excellence,' this immaterial body renders poetry, like love, incorruptible.[8]

In passages like this one Spenser internalises the image of writing in the same way the poet of the proems to *The Faerie Queene* internalises and purifies the image of Elizabeth: through a discipline of erotic meditation whose tradition extends from Plato's *Symposium* to Spenser's *Fowre Hymnes*. This discipline of 'pure regard' (HB 212) works by abstracting from the human body a pure fire and symmetry said to be the essence of heavenly beauty. In the course of this meditative sublimation, a natural body is first transformed into a mystical one by attenuation of its material being. The flesh is then reinvested with the mystical essence derived from its shape and energy. Just as poetic beauty occurs when the poet assimilates mere letters to an idealised, metaphoric version of themselves, so natural beauty occurs when the pristine soul assimilates matter to its own excellence. The ladder of love thus operates by a metaleptic reversal of origins; it might well be called the ladder of the former, turning as it does on a negative moment in which the 'latter' term (in the language-meaning or body-soul sequence) elevates itself by rejecting as ontologically belated the material original from which it was 'formed.'

Some version of this negative moment can be found in any narrative of transcendence, whether it appears as a humiliation of the personal ego, as a mortification of the flesh, as a visionary blindness to nature, or as a revulsion from the things of the natural world. In Spenser's 'Legend of Holiness,' for example, we *expect* to find Heavenly Contemplation blind to nature, just as we expect to find the Redcrosse Knight's illumination accompanied by a parallel blinding of *his* natural eye. An equivalent moment in the affective rhythm of ascent occurs when the visionary pilgrim looks back from the threshold of beatitude in a fit of acute revulsion from the world below. This moment is present, for instance, in *The Consolation of Philosophy* (bk. 4, poem 1) and in Petrarch's 'The Ascent of Mount Ventoux.'

Petrarch's letter shows very well how negation works in the logic of transcendence. Petrarch first describes the 'literal' ascent of Mount Ventoux, although it sounds suspiciously allegorical from the start, given its obvious indebtedness to the opening of the *Inferno*. After much labor with little progress comes a reflective pause: 'My thought quickly turned,' he writes, 'from the material to the spiritual' (47). He proceeds to extract an allegorical tenor from the story as its disembodied simulacrum. But this allegorical or spiritual tenor appears less as something derived from the story of climbing a mountain than as something informing it from the start, like Providence; hence the 'staged' quality of the initial account. Finally there is the moment of revulsion. Having reconciled himself to the steep ascent and attained the top of the mountain, Petrarch lights by sortilege on a passage from Augustine's *Confessions*: 'men go to admire the high mountains . . . and they abandon themselves!' (*Conf.* 10.8.15; Petrarch 49). This triggers in him a recognition that kicks the ladder, as it were, out from under the emergent tenor by repudiating its literal or narrative vehicle: 'How eagerly we should strive,' he reflects, 'to tread beneath our feet, not the world's heights, but the appetites that spring from earthly impulses!' (50).

Versions of the moment of revulsion may be found throughout Spenser's work: in the hermit's irritation when Redcrosse arrives on the Mount of Contemplation, for instance, and in the knight's own later reluctance to descend; in Colin Clout's analogous distress when Calidore turns up on Mount Acidale, and in Calidore's desire to remain there; at the end of the *Mutability Cantos*, when the narrator turns from the vanished epiphany of nature to look on the sublunary world; and, in an especially revealing instance, at the conclusion to each of the heavenly hymns. The *Fowre Hymnes* is so useful an example because it doubles the structure found in Petrarch's letter. This structure occurs once in the internal progress of each hymn, where scripture, the creation, and the human body each form the text of a meditation whose gesture of completion is to turn on the text in revulsion. It occurs a second time in the relation between the two pairs of hymns. The heavenly pair, as I mentioned, end in beatitudes accompanied by the moment of revulsion. But the earthly hymns end in what we might call by contrast moments of *reversion*, or erotic turning back to the pleasures of the embodied soul. Such a reversion is also staged in *Amoretti* 72 ('Oft when my spirit doth spred her bolder winges'), which concludes: 'Hart need not wish none other happinesse, / But here on earth to have such hevens blisse.' Petrarch ends his letter by praying for strength to resist a similar turn, and Boethius's Philosophia warns against such temptations in closing book 3 of the *Consolation*. In her reading, the backward glance that lost Euridice becomes an emblem of reversion: whoever 'turns his eyes to the pit of hell,' she says, 'loses all the excellence he has gained' (74). By 'the pit of hell,' Philosophia means the created world; it is precisely a failure of necessary blindness to this world that would threaten her program for the absolute recuperation of value through religious ascesis.

The contrast between revulsion and reversion is crucial to the *Fowre Hymnes*, for what appears at the close of each heavenly hymn as a moment of revulsion is replayed as a palinode both in the dedication and at the center of the sequence. This gesture has never quite made sense; it seems blind to the integrity of the four poems taken together. The earthly hymns, says Spenser, composed in the greener times of his youth, have proved treacherous reading for others 'of like age and disposition,' who are moved rather to passion than 'honest delight.' Unable to call in the poems 'by reason that many copies thereof were formerly scattered abroad,' Spenser announces his present intention '[a]t least to amend, and by way of retraction to reforme them, making in stead of those two hymnes of earthly or natural love and beautie, two others of heavenly and celestiall' ('Dedication'). The most obvious paradox is simply that Spenser then proceeds to publish all four hymns together. But even had he suppressed the first two in printing the 'latter' pair, we would still have to wonder what it means to reform 'by way of retraction' or to amend by substitution. Such self-contradictory phrasing perfectly expresses the metaleptic relation between the heavenly hymns and the earthly model they purport to imitate, correct, and supplant in a single gesture.

For this reason *Fowre Hymnes* is an especially revealing product of the poetics that informs it. The visionary hermeneutics of Christian Neo-platonism was always a sort of epistemological romance, in which disciplined meditation on a signifying body (whether nature, Scripture, or a beloved) produces the transcendental object of its own desire. Disciplined meditation, what Spenser in the hymn to beauty calls 'pure regard and spotlesse true intent' (HB 212), offers itself as a methodical return from the secondary, derivative, merely apparent object of regard – the body, text, or world – to the source of its form, the logos, which the object is then assumed to signify by the metonymy of effect for cause. Whatever its text, though, this hermeneutic systematically misreads its own procedure, offering as an act of decoding what is in fact the work of production. Soul, says Spenser, 'is forme, and doth the bodie make' (HB 133), but the ladder of the former is a formula for making soul. Beginning where all the ladders start and ascending through prescribed stages of abstraction, it derives the heavenly logos from an image of the human body.

If we turn back now to Redcrosse in his quest for holiness, we can see both metalepsis and negation at work in Spenser's narrative of the knight's ascent. We can also see them at work as hermeneutic principles, for it is in the House of Holiness that Redcrosse learns to read Scripture. Parallel mortifications of the letter and the flesh prepare the knight for his vision of the transcendental city – where all the blood and sorrows of his combative errancy here below will finally be redeemed, and where he will assume the 'glorious name' revealed along with his vision. That name – *Saint George* – contains in miniature the path from dust to heaven the knight's transcendence must follow, for it glances both forward to his canonisation in the city of saints and backward to his 'georgic' beginnings in the *geos*, or earth.[9]

In the House of Holiness Redcrosse meets Fidelia. Like the hermit Contemplation, she personifies a condition to be achieved by the knight as well as a principle latent within him; just as the lover must look with 'pure regard and spotlesse true intent' to perceive the soul of his beloved, so the Christian must awaken the 'inner light' of faith by which to read scripture. Hence Fidelia's beginning gesture is to clear the knight's 'dull eyes, that light mote in them shine.'

That none could reade, except she did them teach,
She unto him disclosed every whitt,
And heavenly documents thereout did preach,
That weaker witt of man could never reach,
Of God, of grace, of justice, of free will,
That wonder was to heare her goodly speach:
For she was hable with her wordes to kill,
And rayse again to life the hart, that she did thrill.

And when she list poure out her larger spright,
She would commaund the hasty sunne to stay,
Or backward turne his course from hevens hight:
Sometimes great hostes of men she could dismay;
Dry-shod to passe, she parts the flouds in tway;
And eke huge mountaines from their native seat
She would commaund, themselves to beare away,
And throw in raging sea with roaring threat:
Almightie God her gave such powre and puissaunce great.

                                                (1.10.19–20)

The mediation of the letter is blood, death and blindness. Transcending the letter is the way to life and 'puissaunce great,' the power Redcrosse will need to triumph in battle.

The passage itself is rhetorically impressive.[10] Since Fidelia stands for the spirit that is prior to the letter, Spenser can take over events recorded in Hebrew Scripture (st. 20, lines 2–5) and represent them together with Matthew's testament to the power of faith (lines 6–8) not as events that occurred in a historical past but as typical or potential effects of the spirit that stands before us. Thus the trope of personification lets Spenser appropriate the New Testament's authoritative metalepsis, its reversal of priority over the Hebrew Scriptures. Meanwhile, although the narrative scene depends on clear distinctions between Fidelia, the book she holds in her hand, and the words she speaks about the book, the language of the passage quoted effaces these distinctions. The word 'documents,' from *docere* 'to teach,' refers to speech rather than writing; and the phrase 'her wordes' at the end of stanza 19 confirms this shift from writing to the speech of the tutor, 'assimilating' to Fidelia's voice the power vested in Scripture. Then at the opening of the next stanza the act of exposition is named directly as an outpouring of spirit, as though the commentary now preceded its text. Through this gradual metalepsis, the sense first of written and then of all verbal mediation is deftly elided from the scene. The passage thus foregrounds the illusion of a release of spirit, a leaping out of the frame of language preparing us for the conversion of recorded miracles into what Wordsworth calls 'something evermore about to be.'

What we see at work in this passage is a local instance of the grand strategy Paul employed in designating the New Testament 'writing on the heart' in contrast to the old law written in clay, 'the ministration of death written with letters.' The difference between letter and spirit is used to privilege the new covenant with respect to the old, although the division is reproduced within each. Spenser's use of the Pauline trope (which actually derives from Jeremiah 31.31–4) similarly stages the text of *The Faerie Queene* as a release of the spirit hidden beneath the letter of Scripture. In one sense his verses clearly depend on the priority of the biblical passages they refer 'back' to; yet they also tacitly assert their own precedence in presuming to represent the scriptural scene of instruction – in presuming access to the originary ground of knowledge about Scripture. The rhetorical figures that produce the illusion of such access are self-occulting, for their success precisely depends on, and consists in, our inadvertence to them as strategy. The illusion succeeds, in other words, because it appears within the shadow of its own effect, a rhetorical sleight of hand that kicks the ladder, or letter, out from under what then presents itself as a pure signified.

Redcrosse's reading lesson, drawn into the pattern of blindness and vision we encounter on the Mount of Contemplation, inevitably produces its own moment of revulsion. The knight's *contemptus mundi* festers into a self-loathing so acute that recuperation comes only through an ascesis made up of fasting, corrosives, the removal of 'superfluous flesh' by means of hot pincers, beatings with an iron whip, lancing of the pericardium, and saline immersion. This regimen of horrors is administered by the medical team of Patience, Penance, Remorse, Repentance – and 'Amendment,' whose name should alert us to the deep structural parallel between this episode and the *Fowre Hymnes*. Redcrosse is being amended in much the same way as the earthly hymns had to be: he is reformed 'by way of retraction,' his guilt displaced into a series of visually spectacular figurative assaults on the integrity of his natural body.[11]

The amendment of Redcrosse is a powerful version of the negative moment intrinsic to Spenser's poetics. It suggests that the poem's vision of its own risen or incorruptible body rests on a pervasively internalised principle of self-renunciation. What we find in *The Faerie Queene* is, after all, romance – the genre of unconstrained fabulation – in love with didactic allegory. The fiction has introjected a powerful cultural demand for truth, a demand it can meet only by striving to differ internally from itself as fiction. In the effort to secure within itself a *decisive representation* of this difference, *The Faerie Queene* becomes allegory, or 'otherwords,' in the most radical sense – generating itself out of internal contradiction in forever divided form, at once the integral body of truth and its repressed or uncanny 'other.' Much as the heavenly hymns depend equally on the informing presence of the earthly pair and on their unqualified renunciation, *The Faerie Queene* is able to summon its ideal form into representation only as a sublimated negative image of itself. This is why in book 1, for instance, the Redcrosse Knight's betrothal to the whole body of Truth can never finally cast out the demons of duplicity and illusion. Superficially the contrast between Una and Duessa could not be clearer: the One, 'Who, in her self-resemblance well beseene, / Did seeme, such as she was, 'versus the Other, declaring just as flatly, 'I, that do seeme not I, Duessa ame' (1.12.8; 5.26). Yet Spenser can represent Una to us only in divided form. Initally she is set apart from us by a veil, recognisable in that she is hidden. But even when she stands revealed in canto 12, Spenser's language can express Una's integrity only as mediated relation, 'self-resemblance.' Like the truth of the heavenly hymns, Una emerges into representation only through a differential repetition that sets her apart from herself and so makes her dependent on what she is not – dividing Truth to assert its self-resemblance in a phrase that echoes, as it opposes, Duessa's counterepiphany. However deeply Spenser may desire to set his own poetic activity in opposition to Archimago's, structurally they are alike, for he can create Una only by doubling her.[12]

In a poem where Truth appears as a romance heroine, we should expect the structure of knowing to coincide with that of desire. The epistemological quandary that identity depends on repetition is venerable enough, and vexing enough in its implications, that it drove Plato to postulate seminal reasons. His doctrine of anamnesis makes all knowledge déjà vu, and every philosopher therefore a kind of sublime Narcissus, striving to resurrect the fragments of a lost self-knowledge into perfect correspondence with their imagined heavenly paradigm and origin. The Protestant doctrine of 'inner light' works in much the same way: for this reason Fidelia and Heavenly Contemplation, as I said before, must represent at once a condition still to be achieved by the knight and a principle already latent within him. Like Boethius's *Philosophia*, they enable the subject's return to a divine source he already contains. Allegory is the literary method appropriate to a recognition theory of knowing because, as Rosemond Tuve remarked, allegorical fictions make us think about what we already know: they seek to awaken and charge with motive force a knowledge that remains latent, passive, or merely implicit in the reader (Roche 30). Accordingly medieval commentaries on the *Consolation* identify Philosophia as 'sapientia Boethiae' and the work itself as a figurative dialogue between two parts of the same person: the introduction to a fifteenth-century manuscript of Chaucer's translation, for instance, refers to the *Consolation* as 'this dialogue in this oon persone as it were too, oon desolate and another full of confortht' (Robertson 358–9). By the end of the dialogue Boethius has embraced his truth and once again coincides with himself – two persons as it were one, in his self-resemblance well beseen.

As a structure of desire, epistemological romance begins in the loss of denial of bodily presence, analogous to the forgetting of truth in Platonic anamnesis. (If the descending soul's forgetfulness is in one sense Plato's image of a tragic fall, in another, equally important sense it figures the massive erasure of precedent by which Plato himself clears the ground of authority for the strenuous *poesis* of his dialectic.) We see an early example of this myth of bodily loss in the April eclogue to *The Shepheardes Calender*, where the Ovidian episode of Pan and Syrinx becomes in Spenser's hands a fable of the poem's two bodies. Ovid tells of a god in pursuit of carnal ecstasy, intent on ravishing a river nymph. The nymph cries out to Diana, and just at the liminal moment – at the edge of the river, as the god's embrace gathers her in and his sigh passes over her lips – she is transformed into water reeds, and the breath of violent passion yields a harmonic chord. For Ovid as for Spenser this is primarily a story not of feminine protest against rape but of masculine consolation, a story of loss made over into renunciation as it is replayed in a ludic register, where mastery and recuperation seem possible after all. 'This union, at least, shall I have with thee,' says Pan to the vanished Syrinx (Ovid 1.710); and he makes the reeds over into another 'syrinx,' a shepherd's pipes – reasserting his baffled will and recovering, in symbolic form, the lost feminine body. Spenser works this narrative into the self-referential symbolism of his pastoral debut, making 'Elisa,' queen of shepherds, the fruit of an immaculate union between Pan and Syrinx. At once pastoral mask for the queen of England and metafictional symbol for Colin's song,[13] 'Elisa' names the sublimated body that comes to occupy the space of loss – the space opened up for Pan by his loss of Syrinx, for Colin by his failure to win Rosalind, and for Spenser, as for his culture generally, by the renunciation of the body as an object of desire.

Elisa is a prototype for Gloriana, who also represents both the English queen and the aesthetic body 'assimilated' to her visionary form. Arthur desires the Fairy Queen first in an adolescent fantasy of sex (1.9.9–15) but wakes to find 'her place devoyd, / And nought but pressed gras where she had lyen.' Since then he has sought out her ideal, displaced form through synecdochic traces like the pressed grass beside him or the image on Sir Guyon's shield. Freud tells a story much like Arthur's in a celebrated passage from *Beyond the Pleasure Principle*. He has observed the game his grandson plays with a string and wooden reel:

What he did was to hold the reel by the string and very skilfully throw it over the edge of his curtained cot, so that it disappeared into it, at the same time uttering an expressive 'o-o-o-o.' [Earlier Freud had remarked, 'His mother and the writer of the present account were agreed in thinking this was not a mere interjection but represented the German word *"fort"* ("gone").] He then pulled the reel out of the cot again by the string and hailed its reappearance with a joyful '*da*.' This, then, was the complete game – disappearance and return.

(???)

Freud may hesitate over the question this anecdote raises for his theory of the instincts, but he has little trouble in reconstructing the primary episode reenacted in the game of *fort-da*: it is the infant's constrained renunciation of his mother's immediate presence. *Da!* is the first in an open series of symbolic substitutions in which he will keep on seeking that lost original. *The Faerie Queene*, we might say, unfolds in the long interval between the *fort!* of Arthur's awakening from erotic reverie into moral consciousness and the terminally postponed *da!* of his nuptial entry into the body of glory. Arthur bears the attendant loss of presence as a 'secret wound' (1.9.7) – the melancholy that persists in the waking aftermath of his dream, signifying his painful renunciation of the carnal immediacy suffusing that fantasy.[14]

The emphasis in this poetics on the wounded renunciation of sexual desire makes it seem inevitable that Gloriana's alter ego should be *la belle dame sans merci* and her avatars: predatory succubae who enervate their victims. Redcrosse melting in Duessa's arms is only the first of many such images in the poem. The most remarkable, surely, is Verdant, preyed on by the witch Acrasia in the Bower of Bliss:

> And all that while, right over him she hong,
> With her false eyes fast fixed in his sight,
> As seeking medicine whence she was stong,
> Or greedily depasturing delight:
> And oft inclining downe, with kisses light,
> For feare of waking him, his lips bedewd,
> And through his humid eyes did sucke his spright,
> Quite molten into lust and pleasures lewd;
> Wherewith she sighed soft, as if his case she rewd.

(2.12.73)

Many readers have testified to the fascination of this passage, with its eerie transfusion of erotic and sadistic frissons. Its special horror lies in its uncanny affinity with the epic's scene of conception, Arthur prostrate and dreaming of Gloriana. In the Bower of Bliss this dream has become a lurid tableau of predatory metaphysical fellatio. Verdant, like Adonis later in the poem, shares Arthur's 'secret wound': his recumbent passivity, his expenses of spirit, and the erasure of his heraldic insignia (st. 80) all testify to his symbolic castration.[15] Meanwhile Acrasia, in a wicked parody of Venus's pietà sorrow over the fallen Adonis, mocks pity for her enervated victim even as she battens on his soul. She is truly Spenser's 'faery quean,' secret sharer of the principle by which the succuba of the superego feeds on bodily energy, summoning desire to ends beyond its knowing.[16]

This reading of Arthur's melancholy as the private wound of Spenserian poetics will seem like neo-Freudian critical fantasy only if we forget the mythic provenance of Arthurian romance. Behind Spenser's Arthur stands the Arthur of medieval romance, and behind him the shadowy image of the Fisher King, whose identity with the realm he governs is powerfully expressed in the mysterious wound or sickness that dries up his organs of increase and renders the land barren. Rosemond Tuve argues persuasively that Arthur's role in *The Faerie Queene* 'is directly in line with what a reader of earlier Arthurian romance expects' (345). There is, however, one major exception: 'Spenser makes no important use of the motif of a land waste through a wound given the ruler, which is the form of a clear identification between king's and country's health most common in Arthurian romances' (351). True enough; Spenser had a different and far more sophisticated form of clear identification closer to hand in the constitutional theory of his age, an extensively rationalised version of the ancient myth. Crown law had evolved a doctrine of incorruptible perpetuity: sovereignty has neither defect nor morality and assimilates the sovereign's nature to its own. Thus what was for Spenser the 'authorised' version of the myth denies the burden of more archaic versions, precisely inverting their symbolism: instead of contaminating his realm, the king is purified by it. We have seen how radically this doctrine depends on a negative moment it can never finally recuperate. In this respect it has something in common with the Arthurian materials Tuve has studied, where the king's mysterious ailment is rationalised in all sorts of unconvincing ways. Beneath the explanations, writes Tuve, we glimpse 'the more primitive conception of a *loss of sovereignty* or [an] unexpected decline of power that cannot be countered in natural ways' and also 'some sense of deep human inadequacy which must be expiated even though it is not understood' (353–4; emphasis added). Looking to still older forms of the legend, we find this inadequacy expressed as impotence or castration – sent down by god, in one version, to punish the king's concupiscence (Weston 20–1).

This loss of sovereignty is just what the doctrine of the king's two bodies was calculated to economise, much as Philosophia teaches Boethius to economise against 'loss of excellence.' Spenser follows legal theory in rejecting the tragic myth of Arthur's wound, but the wound returns to haunt his protagonist in the form of that nostalgia for lost pleasure on which culture is founded, as Freud argued in *Civilisation and Its Discontents*. (No wonder the bedrock virtue of Spenser's knights is sheer persistence.[17] Certainly that is what it takes to read *The Faerie Queene*.) Leigh DeNeef, in a subtle reading of the role of Cupid in book 3, suggests quite accurately that all the poem's heroic lovers must learn to sublimate love's wound into a figurative pregnancy, so that love will inspire them to bring forth worthy deeds (173). Arthur, for instance, rescues Redcrosse 'Nyne monethes' after his dream of Gloriana (1.9.15) – having gestated her image until it matures into an ethical ideal whose parturition is heroic action (cf. 1.5.1). One effect of this half-hidden metaphor is to make Arthur a sort of spiritual hermaphrodite; sexually ambiguous, he anticipates Spenser's grand icons of the marriage of opposites: Scudamour and Amoret, the statue of Venus, Dame Nature of the *Mutability Cantos*. Roche suggests that Scudamour's canceled fusion with Amoret alludes to Ephesians 5.25–32, where man and wife are said to be 'one flesh' (133–6); we are similarly instructed at Galatians 3.27–8 that 'there is neither male nor female' in the *corpus mysticum*, 'for you are all one in Christ Jesus.' The politico-religious symbolism of marriage that is so pervasive in our culture rests partly on these passages, and the projected union of Arthur and Gloriana is no exception. With these associations in mind we may see Arthur's metaphoric femininity as a typological anticipation of his union with Gloriana. The hermaphrodite that emerges from their marriage is Spenser's implicit figure for the perfected spiritual body of his poem.

Imitations of this figure abound in the poem. The metaphor of pregnancy for intellectual work is at least as old as Plato's *Symposium*, and in the Renaissance it became a common figure for the imaginative work of poets, who seem to have borne their reproductive organs in their heads, like snails.[18] Camille A. Paglia has discussed the motifs of hermaphrodism and androgyny in *The Faerie Queene* in terms of 'the classical tradition of *coincidentia oppositorum*, which legitimises the psychosexual level of the poem in its attraction to the androgynous'; she notes that the 'savagely circular world' of violent masculinity-victimised femininity is 'transcended by those higher characters who internally subsume the extremes of masculinity and femininity . . . Both principals who found the line of the British throne, Britomart and Arthegall, are hermaphroditic' (57–8).

This explicitly dialectical model for synthesising genders needs to be supplemented (in the Derridean sense) by a Freudian reading. If we consider Alma's epicene, humanoid castle as an icon of this synthetic sexuality, we may begin to see that the mark of transcendence on signifiers of the body is a confusion of sexual differentia: there are at once none and too many. Our tour of the castle's symbolic anatomy takes in any number of *heimlich* details (nose, lips, beard – even Port Esquiline) but omits all mention of the genitals. Yet because Alma's castle is physically epicene, it can also be metaphysically hermaphroditic, joining an 'imperfect, mortall, foeminine' delta (whose apex marks the bodily lacuna) to the inevitably 'immortall, perfect, masculine' circle (2.9.22).[19] The erasure of this body's reproductive organs thus sets the stage for a recuperation of its sexuality in the Pythagorean geometry of its architecture. The ideal body has a plenitude of sexuality, for it embraces both genders; or it has none at all, castrated by its transgression of the generative difference within human nature.

Hamlet plays on the sexual ambiguity of this body with bitter literal-mindedness when he insists on mocking Claudius as 'My mother – father and mother is man and wife, man and wife is one flesh, and so my mother' (4.3.51–2). Spenser's tone and values could scarcely be further from Hamlet's, yet the mystical body of his poetry bears no less confused an anatomy. Any number of passages might be read for traces of this aesthetic body; consider as one example these lines from *Amoretti* 84, quoted earlier to show that Spenser's poetics of transcendent inscription depends on the implicit fiction of such a body:

> Deepe in the closet of my parts entyre,
> Her worth is written with a golden quill:
> That me with heavenly fury doth inspire,
> And my glad mouth with her sweet prayers fill.

We know that in Petrarchan sonnet sequences writing typically unfolds in the interval of deferred sexual union, taking the place of the body as Elisa and Gloriana do. This passage, while not quite sexual, is certainly erotic. It suggests both hollow space and repletion, most strangely in the phrase 'parts entyre,' which sounds almost like a riddle with 'synecdoche' for its answer. A profound and intimate interior is both hole and whole in these lines, filled by a powerful surge of spirit issuing in a sweet flow. Hallowed by its diction – 'closet' with its connotations of secrecy and interiority, 'entyre' with its mingled sense of completion, perfection, and health[20] – the rhetoric of inspiration is nevertheless underwritten here by a 'former' bodily impression, representing inspired composition as a displaced and idealised consummation of desire. To anatomise body parts – the insides of the breast and mouth or the uterine depths of the mother and the phallic quill of the father – would be awkwardly literal. The poet, who has followed Neoplatonic prescription in idealising the body of his beloved, now synthesises parts and genders in a consummation too devoutly wished.

If it seems in the end that the ideal form into which Spenser recuperates castration can only be sexed as an epicene hermaphrodite – perhaps that should not come as a surprise. Indeed, how except by catachresis could one hope to name a body that transcends the mark of gender, without which never a body could come into being? If with Leonard Barkan we follow the anthropocosmic metaphor back to Plato's *Timaeus*, here is what we find:

> ... he made the world one whole, having every part entire, and being therefore perfect and not liable to old age and disease. And he gave to the world the figure which was suitable and also natural. Now to the animal which was to comprehend all animals, that figure was suitable which comprehends within itself all other figures. Wherefore he made the world in the form of a globe, round as from a lathe, having its extremes in every direction equidistant from the center, the most perfect amd most like itself of all figures; for he considered that the like is infinitely fairer than the unlike. This he finished off, making the surface smooth all around for many reasons: in the first place, because the living being had no need of eyes when there was nothing remaining outside him to be seen, nor of ears when there was nothing to be heard: and there was no surrounding atmosphere to be breathed ...
>
> (Plato 15–16)

And so it goes. The cosmos appears to be a body extensively reformed 'by way of retraction'; eyeless, earless, noseless, mouthless, anusless, limbless, and sexless, 'for there was nothing beside him' (16). And yet this spherical animal, sans organs, apertures, and appendages, is nevertheless *the* perfect figure, the plenum of animal forms, comprehending 'within itself all other figures.' It is also distinctly masculine, despite – or rather, by virtue of – its lack of appendages. As in the design of Alma's castle, the privileged signifier of masculinity is no longer the penis, but the circle, 'immortall, perfect, masculine' – that crown of divine self-sufficiency from which the 'imperfect, mortall, foeminine' body represents a falling away.

Barkan observes that Plato's figure is constructed according to a doctrine of likeness and answers to the nature of its divine creator (9–14). Yet however mimetic of transcendent reality it may claim to be, the erasure of all signs of its relational dependency on an ecosystem renders this creature a sheer anomaly in the world of nature. Perhaps, then, its real 'figure' may be *catachresis*. This term bears two distinct meanings: it is the 'forced,' or unnatural, use of metaphor, and it is the 'extensive' use. Here 'extensive' denotes the transfer of a name from its right object to something otherwise nameless (Miller et al. 106–9). The

difference between a meaningful 'extensive' figure and a flurry of language
signifying nothing is thus made to depend on whether a nameless referent
does in fact wait patiently for its designation, preinscribed as the blank
fourth corner of an analogy that was already in place. A difference of
this kind will always be open to question, which is one reason Derrida,
in his discussion of Aristotelian rhetoric, calls metaphor the 'risk of
mimesis' (*Margins* 241). Displacing names from their conventional referents,
metaphor opens a space of figuration that it does not control; there is no
telling what anomalies may be troped into being through the
constitutive force of language. Arthur and Gloriana, comprehending
within themselves all lesser knights and virtues and combining to form
a transcendental hermaphrodite, type of the Christian apocalypse, may
equally put mimesis at risk.

We saw earlier that the ideal totality sought by epistemological romance
is called forth by an elaborate metaphoric system. Prosopopoeia, or
personification, may be the most prominent trope in this system, but
metalepsis and synecdoche also play important roles. Boethius will
again provide a convenient illustration. As metalepsis, his Philosophia
represents the truth that precedes and authorises true representations,
including the various philosophical schools Boethius thought to
synthesise in the *Consolation*. As synecdoche she represents the whole
body of this truth, grasped only piecemeal (as she herself explains) by
contending schools that have torn fragments from her gown. Finally, as
personification she is a trope for the presence, within Boethius's language,
of the whole body of truth that precedes and authorises all philosophical
discourse. The *Consolation* thus represents itself as having gathered the
diversity of philosophical schools into the total form of their common
divine origin.

Insofar as it tropes into being that super-phenomenal totality which
has been given so many names (the cosmos, the soul, the body politic,
the *corpus mysticum*, Telamond, Arthur plus Gloriana), this metaphoric
system may be seen as an elaborate catachresis, constituting anomalies
under a mimetic alibi and offering them to us as images of the world.
Arthur's quest for Gloriana depends on a curious splice in Spenser's
genealogy of the English throne: the Tudors' mythic progenitor, Arthur,
has been displaced from the 'literal' body of history, Britomart ruling
with Arthegall in his stead. This break in Spenser's mimesis of chronicle
history creates the anomalous space in which his fiction can emerge.
Thomas Roche has observed that

> by his elliptical treatment of Arthur, Spenser is able to imply a
> relationship between the historical Arthur and Elizabeth that he could
> not convey if either were present in the action as historical personages.
> The Arthur of *The Faerie Queene* exists only in his quest for Gloriana.

Elizabeth exists only as a prophecy and in the archetype of her Glory,
Gloriana. But at that point (unrealized) when Arthur finds Gloriana,
England and Faeryland, Elizabeth and Gloriana, become one . . . all
[are] subsumed in the triumph of the Tudor Apocalypse.

(49)

The distance between Arthur and Gloriana is thus the purely negative
space of resistance to the millennial advent, but this resistance is also
the figural space in which the poem has its being, the distance between
Elizabeth and Gloriana. In the terms developed in this essay, it is an interval
of catachresis at the heart of the poem's constitutive metaphor, across
which Spenser tropes conventional signs toward a beyond they artfully
summon to the threshold of recognition.

Spenser tells us he chose the history of Arthur partly because it was
'furthest from the daunger of envy, and suspition of present time'
('Letter to Raleigh,' *Works* 136). Yet his fable departs from the historical
present of Elizabethan England precisely in order to circle back,
elevating romance quest into a typological summons to the Tudor
apocalypse. In this respect the poem, for all its fictive remove from the
present, has something in common with political rhetoric. If we look
outward from Spenser's text to the history it both receives and
reinscribes, we find the same rhetorical structures that organise the poem,
working to shape history as the poem would also do. Consider the
efforts in the lower house of successive Elizabethan parliaments to
establish freedom of speech among the recognised 'privileges of the
house.' Traditionally the prerogatives of the throne had included setting
the agenda for parliamentary debate; when Sir Thomas More succeeded
in getting Parliament's 'freedom of speech' formally instituted, in 1523,
it represented only the right of dutiful opposition to royal bills. In effect,
what was then established was a rule of interpretation: all speeches
delivered in Parliament were to be understood within the assumption
of a loyal intentionality, so that no member's opposition to the crown on
legislative matters could be taken as evidence of treason. Radical
Protestant factions in subsequent parliaments seized on this 'freedom of
speech' as a precedent for insisting on the Commons' right to set its
own legislative agenda, even though royal prerogative comprehended
the power to forbid discussion of certain topics and even though
Elizabeth continued trying to exercise this prerogative throughout her
reign (Neale, *Elizabeth I* 1: 17–28). This creative use of precedent is a
form of metalepsis, a revision of origins; under a shaky mimetic alibi (the
claim to be correctly interpreting constitutional history) it did eventually
trope into being the precedent it claimed merely to preserve.

The mimetic alibi says the use of verbal signs answers to their referents.
Political rhetoric offers easy illustrations of the reverse – that the referent

of a phrase like 'free speech' or 'the privileges of the house' can be altered by the way the words are used. Language is always to some extent 'performative,' generating authority out of misreading, just as community, or the body politic, is always to some extent a project rather than an artifact – forever in the making as particular, strategically motivated utterances compete for authority.[21] The transformation of Elizabeth Tudor into Elizabeth I is a striking example of authority re-creating itself through a massive display of signifiers – for as a contemporary witness of her coronation progress so blandly noted, 'In pompous ceremonies a secret of government doth much consist' (Neale, *Queen Elizabeth* 59). The history of the English coronation, reflected in a series of *ordines*, or protocols, that goes back to the tenth century, may be read as an exemplary tale of the struggle for control over privileged signifiers. One fascinating episode involves an early twelfth-century cleric, the 'Anonymous of York,' who argued for the king's right to interfere in ecclesiastical affairs. What makes his case interesting is not that he anticipated events of the Reformation but that he offered a structural interpretation of the coronation ritual, comparing it point for point with the Church's episcopal confirmations. Initially of course the sacramental character of the royal coronation had served to strengthen the arguments of pope against crown: the ceremonial anointing of the monarch sanctified royal claims to authority at the same time as it helped annex the right of coronation to the pope and his delegates. But as our modern historian of the English coronation relates, the result was a structure of signifiers that could easily be reversed:

> It was . . . possible to draw up out of the old *ordo* a sort of 'Bill of Rights' in favor of the encroachment of the king on the administration of the Church. If in the tenth century the clergy had thoroughly clericalized the coronation, the wheel had come full circle, and the argument of the Anonymous showed how the coronation service supplied the legal title for a regalization of the Church.
>
> (Schramm 35)

Here again the act of interpreting authoritative precedent uses a mimetic alibi to trope its supposed origin into existence in the present, converting the form of ceremony into the force of persuasion.

There is no question that Elizabeth understood the instrumental (as opposed to mimetic or referential) value of language; the hallmark of her political style was its shrewd deployment of ambiguity. Time after time she sought compromise in obscure or even contradictory wording, as in the communion service and 'Ornaments Rubric' that formed part of the Elizabethan settlement (Neale, *Elizabeth I* 1: 78–80). The pattern was established early, when she was confronted in the first year of her

reign with the problem of formulating her royal title; should she revive
the controversial wording 'Supreme Head of the Church,' abandoned by
Mary? Elizabeth finessed the problem by adding an ambiguous '&c'
('etcetering' herself, as Neale puts it [46]). The strategic feel for language
reflected in these and many other incidents is pointed up nicely in the
note she sent to her fifteen-year-old godson, Harrington, along with a
copy of her 1576 address to Parliament: 'Boy Jack,' she began,
'. . . ponder [my words] in thy hours of leisure, and play with them till
they enter thine understanding. So shalt thou hereafter, perchance, find
some good fruits hereof . . .' (Neale, *Elizabeth I* 1: 367–8).

Elizabeth contrived her verbal labyrinths with a shrewd eye to their
deployment in the overdetermined contexts of action. Spenser too returns
from his long detour through fairyland by way of the catachresis we have
examined, exhorting his readers to see the Tudor apocalypse and become
its imperial *figurae*. For modern readers such a response is historically
impossible, not to mention ideologically unacceptable. Yet the poem still
demands from us a catachrestic, and not just a mimetic, reading: as
Spenser overgoes Ariosto, as Troynovant overgoes Rome, so we are
asked to overgo the text we read in the direction of something as yet
nameless.[22]

The traditional name for this something is apocalypse. Perhaps the
biblical Apocalypse, an extended catachresis so authoritative it portends
the destruction of nature, may be thought of as the negative moment of
transcendence writ large. The impulse to self-renunciation we have been
tracing in Spenser's text would then be seen as a continuous mini
apocalypse that releases the revelatory energy of writing. Recalling the
epigraph to this essay, we might say that this revelatory energy depends
on the 'endless No' by which language displaces reading momentum
from the complacent review of a world already known toward glimpses
of a 'fair wonder' that 'mocks desire' because it never *is* but is evermore
about to be. Strictly speaking, a 'world' of that kind, really no world at
all, cannot be known, for it has no repeatable essence. But it can prompt
the energy of reading, if not organise and conserve it. This is why criticism
that comes to rest in a scholarly mimesis of the past, however learned,
falls short of being truly historical. At the heart of the texts whose
influence we cannot escape, beneath the ideological burden of
knowledges, politics, and theologies we *want* to escape, rhetoric displaces
meaning toward recognitions without precedent, recognitions we will
always desire and always have yet to produce. To call them by names
we already know (to produce them as meaning, whether moral,
philosophical, literary, aesthetic, psychoanalytic, or political) is to resume
the work of catachresis, snatching fragments from the gown of Truth.
When we do this work well enough we find, to our relief, that 'The old
poems / In the book have changed value once again' (Ashbery 5).[23]

Edmund Spenser

Notes

Footnotes have been altered slightly for this volume – Ed.

1. Its political importance had always meant that the coronation ritual's form, status, and significance were subject to revision and dispute. Religious controversy surrounding the coronations of Edward, Mary, and Elizabeth appears to have hastened the secularising of the ceremony.

2. Nearly every critic who writes on *The Faerie Queene* speaks to the role of Elizabeth. Early work by FRANCES YATES on contemporary images of Elizabeth opened a rich vein of inquiry, brought to bear on the reading of Spenser's poem most recently by ROBIN HEADLAM WELLS (whose useful study provided the epigraph for this essay [153]). The main focus of work since Yates has been on establishing the historical context of Spenser's celebration of his queen and on analysing specific representations of her in the poem. My emphasis in the present essay on the role of sovereignty in the implicit poetics of *The Faerie Queene* owes a debt to recent studies by GOLDBERG and GREENBLATT.

3. In *The Queene's Two Bodies*, MARIE AXTON demonstrates the importance of the Elizabethan succession controversy and Jacobean unification debates in popularising Edmund Plowden's legal theory. She stresses that the notion of the king's two bodies 'was never a *fact*, nor did it ever attain the status of orthodoxy; it remained a controversial idea' (x). In excellent discussions covering the Inns of Court revels, court entertainments, and popular drama of the period, she explores the development of a complex symbolic vocabulary for implicit exhortation, criticism, and praise of the queen and for veiled debate over the troubled question of the succession. Spenser tends to avoid the succession question in *The Faerie Queene*, but his use of Gloriana to represent the sovereignty both draws on and lends support to the notion that Elizabeth 'beareth two persons, the one of a most royall queene or empresse, the other of a most vertuous and beautiful Lady' ('Letter to Raleigh,' *Works* 136).

4. On the wall of gold as an emblem of the monarchy as protectorate, see AXTON 103–5.

5. A useful survey of the textual history effaced in the figure of the Muses' scryne may be found in REYNOLDS and WILSON's *Scribes and Scholars*. On the human ego as itself derived from bodily wholeness and coordination, see FISHER and CLEVELAND, and for a brief but slightly more recent summary of body-ego theories, see SHONTZ 65–7.

6. AXTON refers to instances of assimilation as 'miracles' and stresses both skeptical resistance to the doctrine and possibilities for using it to criticise the queen. That it had other uses may be seen in NEALE's observation that the body politic could even 'assimilate to its own excellence' defective origins (a version of metalepsis): Elizabeth had been declared illegitimate by statute during her father's reign; Mary, in rehabilitating her own legitimacy, left this statute on the books, but when Elizabeth ascended to the throne 'it remained unrepealed, on the constitutional ground that the crown covered all such flaws' (*Elizabeth* 1 1: 34). It was the sovereignty's legal capacity to absorb flaws that so complicated proceedings against that other Mary, who was at once queen of Scotland and the most dangerous traitor in England.

7. Citations from *Fowre Hymnes* use these abbreviations: 'An Hymne in Honour of Love,' HL; 'An Hymne in Honour of Beautie,' HB.

8. My argument at this point owes a debt to Derrida's remarks on metaphoric writing in *Of Grammatology* (14–16).

9. For the etymological link between *George* and *georgos* see 1.10.52.2 and 66.6–7, together with Hamilton's gloss in the Longman edition.

10. Some of the material in this paragraph and the following one is drawn from my essay 'The Pleasure of the Text'.

11. Among the treasures buried in Nohrnberg's *Analogy* is a discussion of the scriptural and etymological bases for the association of holiness with wholeness (277–82). In *Purity and Danger* Mary Douglas has a suggestive discussion of the Hebrew anthropology of this metaphor. Especially relevant to our analysis of Redcrosse are the following points, which emerge from Douglas's chapter 'The Abominations of Leviticus.' First, holiness combines the idea of *separateness*, or setting apart, with the potentially opposite notion of wholeness (51). Second, 'the idea of holiness [is] given an external, physical expression in the wholeness of the body seen as a perfect container' (52; elsewhere she implies that the idea of holiness may be as much *produced* as expressed through the bodily metaphor). Especially interesting in comparison with the imagery of Redcrosse's bodily 'amendment' is Douglas's comment on the customs governing spiritual purification of warriors about to do battle: 'all bodily discharges disqualified a man from entering the camp as they would disqualify a worshipper from approaching the altar' (52). 'To be holy,' she concludes, 'is to be whole, to be one' (54).

12. My argument comes very close here to that of Leigh DeNeef (esp. 95–6), who stresses the unsettling affinities between Spenser and Archimago. In general, DeNeef's chapter 6 offers an original and persuasive demonstration of Spenser's need for, and dependency on, 'false' versions of his own activity. I would add that the pattern DeNeef observes is another version of Spenser's dependency on a negative moment; Spenser can assimilate his own image making to the spiritual body of truth only by negating, in such figures as Archimago, the instability inherent in representation.

13. On Spenser's use of the Pan-Syrinx myth in 'Aprill,' see Cullen 112–19, Cain 16–17, Montrose 40–3, and D. Miller, 'Authorship' 230–2.

14. Lacan reads the *fort-da* passage as emblematic of the infant's 'birth' at once into language and into 'fully human' desire (ch. 3; Muller and Richardson 9–12, ch. 3). The Lacanian argument that Spenser's poetics is grounded in the essential lack that constitutes human desire has been set forth by Goldberg in *Endlesse Worke* and by Guillory, especially in his provoctive reading of the Acidalian vision as a Spenserian *mise en abŷme* (33–48).

15. My use of the term *castration* in this essay derives from Barthes's Lacanian extension of the Freudian concept (*S/Z*).

16. Cf. Guillory's remarks on the Bower of Bliss and on the relation of desire to 'the approved concept of generation' (35–9).

17. Tuve reads Arthurian magnificence as *Fortitudo*, or perseverance (57–9, 134–40).

18. Halio. The part that 'spiritual gestation' plays in Spenser's poetics is discussed in D. Miller, 'Spenser's Vocation' 201–5.

19. Hamilton's gloss on 2.9.22 calls attention to its hermaphrodite symbolism. In *The Prophetic Moment*, Angus Fletcher observes that this passage 'reduces the marriage trope to its absolute microcosm' (20); he also remarks that in 'the castle of Alma . . . Spenser fully explicates the idea that the human body,

Edmund Spenser

the human soul, the divine "mystical body," and the perfect artifacts of the poet cohere in a vast architectural allegory' (79).

20. *OED* 'closet,' 6a and b. Two anatomical senses were current for Spenser: 'closet' as womb (cf. *FQ* 3.2.11) and as pericardium, for which *OED* cites an example from *The French Academy* (1594, very close to the date of the *Amoretti*). See also FLETCHER, *Allegory*: 'the word "health", suggesting wholeness, suggests the basic allegorical trope of the *whole body*, the untorn garment, the complete paradise, the *hortus conclusus*' (201n). I am suggesting that many of the same connotations are evoked by the word *entyre*. Cf. the beginning of the passage from Plato's *Timaeus* quoted in the next paragraph of this essay, as well as the following lines from *Fowre Hymnes*: 'Therefore he fashions his higher skill / An heavenly beautie to his fancies will, / And it embracing in his mind entyre, / The mirrour of his owne thought doth admyre' (HB 221–4).

21. Among AXTON's most valuable revisions of KANTOROWICZ is her demonstration that the theory of the king's two bodies itself developed out of a strategically motivated misreading of legal precedent, used by Catholic jurists in the *Duchy of Lancaster Case* (1561) to 'minimise the personal impact of the new sovereign' (16), and that the theory was first popularised by supporters of Mary Stuart for the succession (18–20).

22. There can be no question of choosing *between* mimesis and catachresis as if they were alternative critical programs. MAUREEN QUILLIGAN separates the two by labeling deconstructive criticism 'allegoresis,' which she then distinguishes from her own form of allegorical commentary according to a criterion of intentionality: allegoresis rests on 'a huge and ahistorical freedom,' she says, including the freedom to contradict 'the text's manifest intentions,' whereas 'a reading of an allegory' proceeds 'within the limits of the text's surface (generic) intentionality' (25–6). Such a critical prophylaxis appears to me futile, resting on a failure to recognise the implications of Derrida's work in particular. The point is neither to read simply '*against* the text's manifest intentions' nor to read 'within [their] limits' but to situate those intentions – to read *them*. To claim that one reads the text 'in its own terms' simply begs the question. For an extended consideration of this issue in terms of the Derridean-Heideggerean metaphor of 'framing,' see JAY and MILLER, 'The Role of Theory in the Study of Literature?' in *After Strange Texts* (1–28).

23. My work on this essay was supported by a fellowship to the School of Criticism and Theory at Northwestern University in the summer of 1982 and by a stipend from the University of Alabama (RGC Project 1216) in the summer of 1984. For comments on drafts of the essay I would like to thank Dwight Eddins, Jonathan Goldberg, Pat Hermann, William Ulmer, Elizabeth Meese, and especially Greg Jay.

Works Cited

ASHBERY, JOHN. *Houseboat Days: Poems by John Ashbery,* New York: Penguin 1977.

AXTON, MARIE. *The Queen's Two Bodies: Drama and the Elizabethan Succession*. London: Royal Historical Soc., 1977.

BARKAN, LEONARD. *Nature's Work of Art: The Human Body as Image of the World*. New Haven: Yale UP, 1975.

BARTHES, ROLAND. *S/Z: An Essay*. Trans. Richard Miller. New York: Hill, 1974.

BOETHIUS. *The Consolation of Philosophy*. Trans. with introd. and notes by RICHARD GREEN. Indianapolis: Bobbs, 1962.

CAIN, THOMAS H. *Praise in* The Faerie Queene. Lincoln: Nebraska UP, 1978.

CULLEN, PATRICK. *Spenser, Marvell, and Renaissance Pastoral*. Cambridge: Harvard UP, 1970.

DENEEF, A. LEIGH. *Spenser and the Motives of Metaphor*. Durham: Duke UP, 1982.

DERRIDA, JACQUES. *Of Grammatology*. Trans. Gayatri Chakravorty Spivak. Baltimore: Johns Hopkins UP, 1976.

—— *Margins of Philosophy*, Trans. ALAN BASS. Chicago: U of Chicago P, 1982.

DOUGLAS, MARY. *Purity and Danger: An Analysis of the Concepts of Purity and Taboo*. 2nd ed. London: Routledge, 1969.

FISHER, S. and S. E. CLEVELAND. *Body Image and Personality*. Princeton: Van Nostrand, 1958.

FLETCHER, ANGUS. *Allegory: The Theory of a Symbolic Mode*. Ithaca: Cornell UP, 1964.

—— *The Prophetic Moment: An Essay on Spenser*. Chicago: U of Chicago P, 1971.

FREUD, SIGMUND. *Beyond the Pleasure Principle*. Trans. JAMES STRACHEY. New York: Bantam 1959.

—— *Civilisation and Its Discontents*. Trans. James Strachey. New York: Norton, 1961.

GOLDBERG, JONATHAN. *Endlesse Worke: Spenser and the Structures of Discourse*. Baltimore: Johns Hopkins UP, 1981.

—— *James I and the Politics of Literature: Jonson, Shakespeare, Donne, and Their Contemporaries*. Baltimore: Johns Hopkins UP, 1983.

GREENBLATT, STEPHEN J. *Renaissance Self-Fashioning from More to Shakespeare*. Chicago: U of Chicago P, 1980.

GUILLORY, JOHN. *Poetic Authority: Spenser, Milton, and Literary History*. New York: Columbia UP, 1983.

HALIO, JAY L. 'The Metaphor of Conception and Elizabethan Theories of Imagination.' *Neophilologus* 50 (1966): 454–61.

HAMILTON, A. C., ed. *Spenser: The Faerie Queene*. London: Longman, 1977.

JAY, GREGORY S. and DAVID L. MILLER. *After Strange Texts: The Role of Theory in the Study of Literature*. University: U of Alabama P, 1985.

KANTOROWICZ, ERNST. *The King's Two Bodies: A Study of Medieval Political Theology.* Princeton: Princeton UP, 1957.

LACAN, JACQUES. *Ecrits: A Selection.* Trans. ALAN SHERIDAN. New York: Norton, 1977.

MCCOY, RICHARD C. *The Rites of Knighthood: The Literature and Politics of Elizabethan Chivalry.* Berkeley: The University of California Press, 1989.

MILLER, DAVID LEE. 'Authorship, Anonymity, and *The Shepheardes Calender.' Modern Language Quarterly* 40 (1979): 219–36.

—— ' "The Pleasure of the Text," Two Renaissance Versions.' *New Orleans Review* 9 (1982): 50–5.

—— 'Spenser's Vocation, Spenser's Career.' *ELH* 50 (1983): 197–231.

MILLER, JOSEPH M., MICHAEL H. PROSSER and THOMAS W. BENSON, eds. *Readings in Medieval Rhetoric.* Bloomington: Indiana UP, 1973.

MONTROSE, LOUIS ADRIAN, ' "The perfecte paterne of a Poete: The Poetics of Courtship in *The Shepheardes Calender." ' Texas Studies in Literature and Language* (1979): 34–67.

MULLER, JOHN P., and WILLIAM J. RICHARDSON, *Lacan and Language: A Reader's Guide to* Ecrits. New York: International UP, 1982.

NEALE, J. E. *Elizabeth I and Her Parliaments,* Vol. 1, 1559–81. Vol. 2, 1584–1601. London: Cape, 1953, 1957.

—— *Queen Elizabeth.* New York: Harcourt, 1931.

NOHRNBERG, JAMES. *The Analogy of* The Faerie Queene. Princeton: Princeton UP, 1976.

OVID. *Metamorphoses.* Ed. and trans. FRANK JUSTUS MILLER. 2nd ed. Cambridge: Harvard UP, 1921.

PAGLIA, CAMILLE A. 'The Apollonian Androgyne and the *Faerie Queene.' English Literary Renaissance* 9 (1979): 42–63.

PETRARCH. 'The Ascent of Mt. Ventoux.' *De rebus familiaribus* 4.1. *Letters from Petrarch.* Selected and trans. MORRIS BISHOP. Bloomington: Indiana UP, 1966.

PLATO. *Timaeus.* Trans. BENJAMIN JOWETT. Indianapolis: Bobbs, 1949.

QUILLIGAN, MAUREEN. *Milton's Spenser: The Politics of Reading.* Ithaca: Cornell UP, 1983.

REYNOLDS, L. D., and N. G. WILSON. *Scribes and Scholars: A Guide to the Transmission of Greek and Latin Literature.* 2nd ed. Oxford: Clarendon, 1974.

ROBERTSON, D. W., Jr. *A Preface to Chaucer: Studies in Medieval Perspectives.* Princeton: Princeton UP, 1953.

ROCHE, THOMAS P., Jr. *The Kindly Flame: A Study of the Third and Fourth Books of Spenser's* Faerie Queene. Princeton: Princeton UP, 1964.

SCHRAMM, PERCY ERNST. *A History of the English Coronation.* Trans. LEOPOLD G. WICKHAM LEGG. Oxford: Clarendon 1937.

SHONTZ, FRANKLIN C. *Perceptual and Cognitive Aspects of Body Experience.* New York: Academic, 1969.

SPENSER, EDMUND. *The Complete Poetical Works of Spenser.* Ed. R. E. NEIL DODGE. Cambridge: Riverside, 1908.

TUVE, ROSEMOND. *Allegorical Imagery: Some Medieval Books and Their Posterity.* Princeton: Princeton UP, 1966.

WELLS, ROBIN HEADLAM. *Spenser's* Faerie Queene *and the Cult of Elizabeth.* Totowa: Barnes, 1983.

WESTON, JESSIE L. *From Ritual to Romance.* New York: Smith, 1920.

YATES, FRANCES A. 'Queen Elizabeth as Astraea.' *Journal of the Warburg and Courtauld Institutes* 10 (1947): 27–82. Rpt. in *Astraea: The Imperial Theme in the Sixteenth Century.* London: Routledge, 1975. 29–88.

6 To fashion a gentleman: Spenser and the destruction of the Bower of Bliss*

STEPHEN GREENBLATT

The essay reprinted here is part of a much larger project, *Renaissance Self-Fashioning* (1980), which revolutionised attitudes to the study of the early modern period and can be seen as the founding moment of New Historicism. In his book Greenblatt sought to show 'that in sixteenth-century England there were both selves and a sense that they could be fashioned', providing studies of six Renaissance authors – More, Tyndale, Wyatt, Spenser, Marlowe and Shakespeare – in terms of their struggles to articulate their own senses of identity and autonomy. Greenblatt argues that 'in the early modern period there [was] a change in intellectual, social, psychological, and aesthetic structures that govern the generation of identities' (p. 1) and presents his six portraits in terms of three developments: a crisis in representation, a crisis in ideology and a crisis in conceptions of the body (specifically, in the desiring body), all related to crucial changes in the state and the church in sixteenth-century Britain. In the second half of the book, Greenblatt contrasts Spenser to Marlowe, the former regarding 'human identity as conferred by loving service to legitimate authority', the latter 'see[ing] identity established at those moments in which order – political, theological, sexual – is violated' (p. 222), and then both to Shakespeare as a writer who 'relentlessly *explores* the relations of power in a given culture'. Greenblatt's version of Spenser has often been challenged, particularly in terms of its unproblematic affirmation of Spenser's absolutism, but no other reading has made such an impact.

It is to a culture so engaged in the shaping of identity, in dissimulation and the preservation of moral idealism, that Spenser addresses himself in defining 'the general intention and meaning' of the entire *Faerie Queene*: the end of all the book, he writes to Ralegh, 'is to fashion a gentleman or noble person in vertuous and gentle discipline.'[1] The poem rests on the

*Reprinted from STEPHEN GREENBLATT, *Renaissance Self-Fashioning: From More to Shakespeare* (Chicago: University of Chicago Press, 1980 pp. 169–92, 285–9).

obvious but by no means universal assumption that a gentleman can
be so fashioned, not simply in art but in life. We will consider the
implications of one episode in this educative discipline, the destruction
of the Bower of Bliss in book 2, canto 12. After a perilous voyage, as
readers of *The Faerie Queene* will recall, Guyon, the knight of Temperance,
arrives with his companion, the aged Palmer, at the realm of the beautiful
and dangerous witch Acrasia. After quelling the threats of Acrasia's
monstrous guards, they enter the witch's exquisite Bower where, aided
by the Palmer's sober counsel, Guyon resists a series of sensual
temptations. At the Bower's center they spy the witch, bending over a
young man, and, rushing in upon her, they manage to capture her in a net.
Guyon then systematically destroys the Bower and leads the tightly
bound Acrasia away.

[. . .]

We are told that after an initial attractiveness the Bower becomes
stultifying, perverted, and frustrating or that the reader's task, like the
hero's, is to interpret the images correctly, that is, to recognise the danger
of 'lewd loves, and wasteful luxury' embodied in the Bower. I believe that
one easily perceives that danger from the beginning and that much of
the power of the episode derives precisely from the fact that his
perception has little or no effect on the Bower's continued sensual power:

> Upon a bed of roses she was layd,
> As faint through heat, or dight to pleasant sin,
> And was arayd, or rather disarayd,
> All in a vele of silke and silver thin,
> That hid no whit her alablaster skin,
> But rather shewd more white if more might bee.
>
> (2.12.77)

'Pleasant sin' – the moral judgment is not avoided or suspended but
neither does it establish its dominion over the stanza; rather, for a
moment it is absorbed into a world in which the normal conceptual
boundaries are blurred: languor and energy, opacity and transparency,
flesh and stone all merge. Similarly, the close of the famous rose song –

> Gather the rose of love, whilest yet is time,
> Whilest loving thou mayst loved be with equall crime –

invites us momentarily to transvalue the word 'crime,' reading it as the
equivalent of 'passion' or 'intensity,' even as we continue to know that
'crime' cannot be so transvalued. We can master the iconography, read
all the signs correctly, and still respond to the allure of the Bower. It is,
as we shall see, the threat of this absorption that triggers Guyon's

climactic violence. Temperance – the avoidance of extremes, the 'sober government' of the body, the achievement of the Golden Mean – must be constituted paradoxically by a supreme act of destructive excess.

[...]

In the Bower of Bliss, Guyon's 'stubborne brest gan secret pleasaunce to embrace' (2.12.45), and he does not merely depart from the place of temptation but reduces it to ruins. To help us understand more fully why he must do so in order to play his part in Spenser's fashioning of a gentleman, we may invoke an observation made in *Civilization and Its Discontents*: 'It is impossible,' writes Freud, 'to overlook the extent to which civilisation is built up upon a renunciation of instinct, how much it presupposes precisely the nonsatisfaction (by suppression, repression, or some other means?) of powerful instincts. . . . Civilisation behaves toward sexuality as a people or a stratum of its population does which has subjected another one to its exploitation.'[2] Modern criticism would make the destruction of the Bower easy by labelling Acrasia's realm sick, stagnant, futile, and joyless, but Spenser, who participates with Freud in a venerable and profoundly significant intertwining of sexual and colonial discourse, accepts sexual colonialism only with a near-tragic sense of the cost. If he had wished, he could have unmasked Acrasia as a deformed hag, as he had exposed Duessa or as Ariosto had exposed (though more ambiguously) the enchantress Alcina, but instead Acrasia remains enticingly seductive to the end. She offers not simply sexual pleasure – 'long wanton joys' – but self-abandonment, erotic aestheticism, the melting of the will, the end of all quests; and Spenser understands, at the deepest level of his being, the appeal of such an end. Again and again his knights reach out longingly for resolution, closure, or release only to have it snatched from them or deferred; the whole of *The Faerie Queene* is the expression of an intense craving for release, which is overmastered only by a still more intense fear of release.

The Bower of Bliss must be destroyed not because its gratifications are unreal but because they threaten 'civility' – civilisation – which for Spenser is achieved only through renunciation and the constant exercise of power. If this power inevitably entails loss, it is also richly, essentially creative; power is the guarantor of value, the shaper of all knowledge, the pledge of human redemption. Power may, as Bacon claimed, prohibit desire, but it is in its own way a version of the erotic: the violence directed against Acrasia's sensual paradise is both in itself an equivalent of erotic excess and a pledge of loving service to the royal mistress. Even when he most bitterly criticises its abuses or records its brutalities, Spenser loves power and attempts to link his own art ever more closely with its symbolic and literal embodiment. *The Faerie Queene* is, as he insists again and again, wholly wedded to the autocratic ruler of the English state; the rich complexities of Spenser's art, its exquisite ethical discriminations in pursuit of the divine in man, are not achieved in spite of what is for us a repellent political ideology – the passionate worship of imperialism – but are inseparably linked to that ideology.

To say that Spenser worships power, that he is our originating and preeminent poet of empire, is not, in the heady manner of the late '60s, to condemn his work as shallow, craven, or timeserving. Rather, his work, like Freud's, bears witness to the deep complicity of our moral imagination even in its noblest and most hauntingly beautiful manifestations in the great Western celebration of power. Alongside Freud, we may invoke Virgil, whose profound faith in Aeneas's personal and world-historical mission and whose adoration of Augustus are tempered but never broken by a bitter sense of all that empire forces man to renounce, to flee from, to destroy. The example of Freud is useful, however, because it helps us to grasp the relation of our response to the Bower to our own contemporary preoccupations, to perceive as well those qualities in Renaissance culture which we are at this moment in our history uniquely situated to appreciate.

If all of civilisation rests, as Freud argues, upon repression, nevertheless the particular civilisation we produce and inhabit rests upon a complex technology of control whose origins we trace back to the Renaissance. We are no longer inclined to celebrate this period as the lifting of a veil of childish illusion, nor are we concerned to attack it in the name of a nostalgic vision of lost religious unity. The great syncretic structures of the Renaissance humanists no longer seem as intellectually compelling or as adequate to the period's major works of art as they once did, and even the imposition upon nature of an abstract mathematical logic, which Cassirer celebrates so eloquently as the birth of modern science, seems an equivocal achievement. We continue to see in the Renaissance the shaping of crucial aspects of our sense of self and society and the natural world, but we have become uneasy about our whole way of constituting reality. Above all, perhaps, we sense that the culture to which we are as profoundly attached as our face is to our skull is nonetheless a construct, a thing made, as temporary, time-conditioned, and contingent as those vast European empires from whose power Freud drew his image of repression. We sense too that we are situated at the close of the cultural movement initiated in the Renaissance and that the places in which our social and psychological world seems to be cracking apart are those structural joints visible when it was first constructed. In the midst of the anxieties and contradictions attendant upon the threatened collapse of this phase of our civilisation, we respond with passionate curiosity and poignancy to the anxieties and contradictions attendant upon its rise. To experience Renaissance culture is to feel what it was like to form our own identity, and we are at once more rooted and more estranged by the experience.

If it is true that we are highly sensitive to those aspects of the Renaissance that mark the early, tentative, conflict-ridden fashioning of modern consciousness, then *The Faerie Queene* is of quite exceptional significance, for Spenser's stated intention is precisely 'to fashion a gentleman or noble person in vertuous and gentle discipline.' This mirroring – the conscious purpose of the work seeming to enact the larger cultural movement – may help to account for the reader's sense of encountering in Spenser's poem the process of self-fashioning itself. In the Bower of Bliss that process is depicted as involving a painful sexual renunciation: in Guyon's destructive act we are invited to experience the ontogeny of our culture's violent resistance to a sensuous release for which it nevertheless yearns with a new intensity. The resistance is necessary for Spenser because what is threatened is 'our Selfe, whom though we do not see, / Yet each doth in him selfe it well perceiue to bee' (2.12.47). We can secure that self only through a restraint that involves the destruction of something intensely beautiful; to succumb to that beauty is to lose the shape of manhood and be transformed into a beast.[3]

The pleasure offered by Acrasia must be rejected with brutal decisiveness, but how exactly does one distinguish between inordinate or excessive sexual pleasure and temperate sexual pleasure? Spenser does not, after all, wish to reject pleasure entirely: if Guyon's destruction of the Bower of Bliss suggests 'the extent to which civilisation is built upon a renunciation of instinct,' Scudamour's seizure of Amoret in the Temple of Venus, recounted in book 4, canto 10, suggests the extent to which civilisation is built upon the controlled satisfaction of instinct, upon the ability to direct and profit from the 'kindly rage' of desire. Pleasure can even be celebrated, as in the nameless supplicant's hymn to Venus, provided that its legitimating function, its 'end' both in the sense of purpose and termination, be properly understood:

> So all things else, that nourish vitall blood,
> Soone as with fury thou doest them inspire,
> In generation seeke to quench their inward fire.
>
> (4.10.46)

Spenser cannot deny pleasure, even the extreme pleasure suggested by 'rage', 'fury', and 'fire', a legitimate function in sexuality. Quite apart from the poet's own experience and observation, it may have been extremely difficult even for figures far more suspicious of the body than Spenser to imagine an entirely pleasureless generation of children (though, as we shall see later, such a doctrine found occasional expression), for there seems to have been widespread medical belief in early modern Europe that for conception to take place, both the male and the female had to experience orgasm.[4] Virtually all of Spenser's representations of sexual fulfillment, including those he fully sanctions, seem close to excess and risk the breakdown of the carefully fashioned identity:

> Lightly he clipt her twixt his armes twaine,
> And streightly did embrace her body bright,
> Her body, late the prison of sad paine,
> Now the sweet lodge of loue and deare delight:
> But she faire Lady ouercommen quight
> Of huge affection, did in pleasure melt,
> And in sweete rauishment pourd out her spright:
> No word they spake, nor earthly thing they felt,
> But like two senceles stocks in long embracement dwelt.
>
> (3.12.45 [1590])

The distinction upon which self-definition rests at the close of book 2 – between temperate pleasure and inordinate pleasure – can only be understood in terms of a further distinction between a pleasure that serves some useful purpose, some virtuous end, and a pleasure that does not. Thus the denizens of the Bower acknowledge time solely as an inducement to the eager satisfaction of desire here and now, before the body's decay, and not as the agency of purposeful direction. That direction – expressed in *The Faerie Queene* as a whole by the idea of the *quest* – is for sexuality found in the power of love to inspire virtuous action and ultimately, with the sanctification of marriage, in the generation of offspring. Generation restores the sense of linear progression to an experience that threatens to turn in upon itself, reveling in its own exquisite beauty. A pleasure that serves as its own end, that claims to be self-justifying rather than instrumental, purposeless rather than generative, is immoderate and must be destroyed, lest it undermine the power that Spenser worships.

But this way of distinguishing temperate and inordinate pleasure is less stable than it first appears, for desire may be 'quenched' in generation but not itself temperate. On the contrary, generation only takes place because all living beings – men and beasts – are 'priuily pricked with' Venus's 'lustful powres' (4.10.45). All attempts to restrain these powers must be overcome for fruitful sexual union to occur: thus Scudamour must seize Amoret from the restraining and moderating figures – Womanhood, Shamefastness, Modesty, Silence, Obedience, and the like – who sit at the feet of Venus's image. The fashioning of a gentleman then depends upon the imposition of control over inescapably immoderate sexual impulses that, for the survival of the race, must constantly recur: the discriminations upon which a virtuous and gentle discipline is based are forever in danger of collapsing. Hence, I suggest, the paradox of the Knight of Temperance's seemingly intemperate attack upon the Bower of Bliss: Guyon destroys the Bower and ties Acrasia 'in chaines of adamant' – 'For nothing else might keepe her safe and sound' – in a violent attempt to secure that principle of difference necessary to fashion the self. 'Excess' is defined not by some inherent imbalance or impropriety, but by the mechanism of control, the exercise of restraining power. And if excess is virtually invented by this power, so too, paradoxically, power is invented by excess: this is why Acrasia cannot be destroyed, why she and what she is made to represent must continue to exist, forever the object of the destructive quest. For were she not to exist as a constant threat, the power Guyon embodies would also cease to exist. After all, we can assume that the number of people who actually suffer in any period from *melt-down* as a result of sexual excess is quite small (comparable to the number of cases of that spontaneous combustion depicted by Dickens), small enough to raise questions about the motives behind the elaborate moral weaponry designed to combat the supposed danger. The perception of the threat of excess enables institutional power to have a legitimate 'protective' and 'healing' interest in sexuality, to exercise its constitutive control over the inner life of the individual.

Self-fashioning, the project of Spenser's poem and of the culture in which it participates, requires both an enabling institution, a source of power and communal values – in *The Faerie Queene*, the court of Gloriana – and a perception of the not-self, of all that lies outside, or resists, or threatens identity. The destruction of the Bower is the fulfillment of the knight's quest – the institution has been glorified, the demonic other at once identified and destroyed – but the inherent contradictions in the relations between temperance and pleasure, restraint and gratification have been deferred rather than resolved. What appears for a moment as decisive closure gives way to renewed efforts, other quests, which, as we have already glimpsed in Scudamour, attempt to compensate for the limitations, the sacrifice of essential values, implicit in the earlier resolution.

[...]

It is not possible within the scope of this chapter to outline the dense network of analogies, repetitions, correspondences, and homologies within which even this one episode of Spenser's immense poem is embedded. But I can point briefly to three reiterations by the culture of important elements of the destruction of the Bower of Bliss: the European response to the native cultures of the New World, the English colonial struggle in Ireland, and the Reformation attack on images. The examples suggest the diversity of such reiterations – from the general culture of Europe, to the national policy of England, to the ideology of a small segment of the nation's population – while their shared elements seem to bear out

Freud's master analogy: 'Civilisation behaves towards sexuality as a people or a stratum of its population does which has subjected another one to its exploitation.'

In the texts written by early explorers of the New World, a long, arduous voyage, fraught with fabulous dangers and trials, brings the band of soldiers, sailors, and religious fathers – knight, boatman, and palmer – to a world of riches and menace. The adventurer's morality is the morality of the ship, where order, discipline, and constant labor are essential for survival, and they are further united by their explicit religious faith and by an unspoken but powerful male bond. The lands they encounter are often achingly beautiful: 'I am completely persuaded in my own mind,' writes Columbus in 1498, 'that the Terrestrial Paradise is in the place I have described.'[5] So Spenser likens the Bower of Bliss to Eden itself, 'if ought with Eden mote compayre,' and lingers over its landscape of wish fulfillment, a landscape at once lavish and moderate, rich in abundant vegetation and yet 'steadfast,' 'attempred,' and well 'disposed.' If these descriptive terms are shared in the Renaissance by literary romance and travelers' accounts, it is because the two modes of vision are mutually reinforcing: Spenser, like Tasso before him, makes frequent allusion to the New World – to 'all that now America men call' (2.10.72) – while when Cortes and his men looked down upon the valley of Mexico, they thought, says a participant, of Amadis of Gaule.[6] The American landscape has to European eyes the mysterious intimations of a hidden art, as Ralegh's description of the Orinoco suggests: 'On both sides of this river, we passed the most beautiful country that ever mine eyes beheld: and whereas all that we had seen before was nothing but woods, prickles, bushes, and thorns, here we beheld plains of twenty miles in length, the grass short and green, and in diverse parts groves of trees by themselves, as if they had been by all the art and labor in the world so made of purpose: and still as we rowed, the Deer came down feeding by the water's side, as if they had been used to a keeper's call.'[7]

Spenser, to be sure, has no need of the 'as if' – he credits art as well as nature with the making of the paradisal landscape – but this difference should not suggest too sharp a contrast between an 'artless' world described by the early voyagers and the poet's 'artificial' Bower. The Europeans again and again record their astonishment at the Indians' artistic brilliance: 'Surely I marvel not at the gold and precious stones, but wonder with astonishment with what industry and laborious art the curious workmanship exceedeth the matter and substance. I beheld a thousand shapes, and a thousand forms, which I cannot express in writing; so that in my judgment I never saw anything which might more allure the eyes of men with the beauty thereof.'[8]

But all of this seductive beauty harbors danger, danger not only in the works of art which are obviously idolatrous but in the Edenic landscape itself. The voyagers to the New World are treated, like Guyon and the Palmer, to mild air that 'breathed forth sweet spirit and holesom smell' (2.12.51), and they react with mingled wonder and resistance: 'Smooth and pleasing words might be spoken of the sweet odors, and perfumes of these countries,' writes Peter Martyr, 'which we purposely omit, because they make rather for the effeminating of men's minds, than for the maintenance of good behavior.'⁹ Similarly, if the New World could be portrayed as a place 'In which all pleasures plenteously abownd, / And none does others happiness envye' (2.10.58), a Golden World, it could also serve – often in the same text and by virtue of the same set of perceptions – as a screen onto which Europeans projected their darkest and yet most compelling fantasies: 'These folk live like beasts without any reasonableness, and the women be also as common. And the men hath conversation with the women who that they been or who they first meet, is she his sister, his mother, his daughter, or any other kindred. And the women be very hot and disposed to lecherdness. And they eat also one another. The man eateth his wife, his children. . . . And that land is right full of folk, for they live commonly 300 year and more as with sickness they die not.'¹⁰ In 1582 Richard Madox, in Sierra Leone with Edward Fenton's expedition, heard from a Portuguese trader comparable stories of African customs: 'He reported that near the mountains of the moon there is a queen, an empress of all these Amazons, a witch and a cannibal who daily has intercourse with a great number of men by whom she begets offspring. The kingdom, however, remains hereditary to the daughters, not to the sons.'¹¹

Virtually all the essential elements of the travel narratives recur in Spenser's episode: the sea voyage, the strange, menacing creatures, the paradisal landscape with its invisible art, the gold and silver carved with 'curious imagery,' the threat of effeminacy checked by the male bond, the generosity and wantonness of the inhabitants, the arousal of a longing at once to enter and to destroy. Even cannibalism and incest which are the extreme manifestations of the disordered and licentious life attributed to the Indians are both subtly suggested in the picture of Acrasia hanging over her adolescent lover:

> And oft inclining downe with kisses light,
> For fear of waking him, his lips bedewed,
> And through his humid eyes did sucke his spright,
> Quite molten into lust and pleasure lewd.

> (2.12.73)

In book 6 of *The Faerie Queene* Spenser offers a more explicit version of these dark imaginings;¹² here in book 2 the violation of the taboos is carefully displaced, so that the major threat is not pollution but the very attractiveness of the vision. Sexual excess has caused in Verdant a melting of the soul,[13] and this internal pathology is matched by an external disgrace:

> His warlike armes, the idle instruments
> Of sleeping praise, were hong vpon a tree,
> And his braue shield, full of old moniments,
> Was fowly ra'st, that none the signes might see.
>
> (2.12.80)

The entire fulfillment of desire leads to the effacement of signs and hence to the loss both of memory, depicted in canto 10, and of the capacity for heroic effort, depicted in the figure of the boatman who ferries Guyon and the Palmer to the Bower:

> Forward they passe, and strongly he then rowes,
> Vntill they nigh vnto that gulfe arryve,
> Where streame more violent and greedy growes:
> Then he with all his puisaunce doth stryve
> To strike his oares, and mightily doth dryve
> The hollow vessell through the threatfull wave,
> Which, gaping wide, to swallow them alyve
> In th'huge abysse of his engulfing grave,
> Doth rore at them in vaine, and with great terrour rave.
>
> (2.12.5)

The threat of being engulfed that is successfully resisted here is encountered again at the heart of the Bower in the form not of cannibalistic violence but of erotic absorption. Verdant, his head in Acrasia's lap, has sunk into a narcotic slumber: all 'manly' energy, all purposeful direction, all sense of difference upon which 'civil' order is founded have been erased. This slumber corresponds to what the Europeans perceived as the *pointlessness* of native cultures. It was as if millions of souls had become unmoored, just as their ancestors had, it was thought, somehow lost their way and wandered out of sight of the civilised world. Absorbed into a vast wilderness, they lost all memory of the true history of their race and of the one God and sank into a spiritual and physical lethargy. It is difficult to recover the immense force which this charge of idleness carried; some sense may be gauged perhaps from the extraordinary harshness with which vagabonds were treated.[14]

That the Indians were idle, that they lacked all work discipline, was proved, to the satisfaction of the Europeans, by the demonstrable fact that they made wretched slaves, dying afer a few weeks or even days of hard labor. And if they were freed from servitude, they merely slid back into their old customs: 'For being idle and slothful, they wander up and down, and return to their old rites and ceremonies and foul and mischievous acts.'[15] That the European voyagers of the sixteenth century, surely among the world's most restless and uprooted generations, should accuse the Indians of 'wandering up and down' is bitterly ironic, but the accusation served as a kind of rudder, an assurance of stability and direction. And this assurance is confirmed by the vast projects undertaken to fix and enclose the native populations in the mines, in encomiendas, in fortified hamlets, and ultimately, in mass graves. A whole civilisation was caught in a net and, like Acrasia, bound in chains of adamant; their gods were melted down, their palaces and temples razed, their groves felled. 'And of the fairest late, now made the fowlest place.'[16]

Guyon, it will be recalled, makes no attempt to destroy the Cave of Mammon; he simply declines its evil invitations which leave him exhausted but otherwise unmoved. But the Bower of Bliss he destroys with a rigor rendered the more pitiless by the fact that his stubborn breast, we are told, embraced 'secret pleasance.' In just this way, Europeans destroyed Indian culture not despite those aspects of it that attracted them but in part at least because of them. The violence of the destruction was regenerative; they found in it a sense of identity, discipline, and holy faith.[17] In tearing down what both appealed to them and sickened them, they strengthened their power to resist their dangerous longings, to repress antisocial impulses, to conquer the powerful desire for release. And the conquest of desire had the more power because it contained within itself a version of that which it destroyed: the power of Acrasia's sensuality to erase signs and upset temperate order is simultaneously attacked and imitated in Guyon's destruction of the exquisite Bower, while European 'civility' and Christianity were never more ferociously assaulted than in the colonial destruction of a culture that was accused of mounting just such an assault.

One measure of European complicity in what they destroyed is the occurrence of apostasy or at least fantasies of apostasy. Bernal Diaz del Castillo tells one such story about a common seaman named Gonzalo Guerrero who had survived a shipwreck in the Yucatan and refused to rejoin his compatriots when, eight years later, Cortes managed to send word to him: 'I am married and have three children, and they look on me as a *Cacique* here, and a captain in time of war. Go, and God's blessing be with you. But my face is tattooed and my ears are pierced. What would the Spaniards say if they saw me like this? And look how handsome these children of mine are!'[18] The emissary reminded him that he was a Christian and 'should not destroy his soul for the sake of an Indian woman', but Guerrero clearly regarded his situation as an improvement in his lot. Indeed Cortes learned that it was at Guerrero's instigation that the Indians had, three years before, attacked an earlier Spanish expedition to the Yucatan.

We have, in the tattooed Spanish seaman, encountered an analogue to those disfigured beasts who try to defend the Bower against Guyon and, in particular, to Gryll, who, having been metamorphosed by Acrasia into a hog, 'repyned greatly' at his restoration. Such creatures give a local habitation and a name to those vague feelings of longing and complicity that permeate accounts of sensuous life that must be rejected and destroyed. And if the Yucatan seems too remote from Spenser's world, we need only turn to our second frame of reference, Elizabethan rule in Ireland, to encounter similar stories. In Spenser's own *View of the Present State of Ireland*, probably written in 1596, Eudoxius asks, 'is it possible that an Englishman brought up naturally in such sweet civility as England affords could find such liking in that barbarous rudeness that he should forget that any should so far grow out of frame that they should in so short space quite forget their country and their own names? . . . Could they ever conceive any such devilish dislike of their own natural country as that they would be ashamed of her name, and bite off her dug from which they sucked life?'[19] In reply, Spenser's spokesman, Irenius, speaks bitterly of those Englishmen who are 'degenerated and grown almost mere Irish, yea and more malicious to the English than the very Irish themselves' (48); these metamorphosed wretches even prefer to speak Irish, although, as Eudoxius observes, 'they should (methinks) rather take scorn to acquaint their tongues thereto, for it hath been ever the use of the conqueror to despise the language of the conquered, and to force him by all means to learn his.'[20] Irenius locates the source of this unnatural linguistic betrayal, this effacement of signs, in the subversive power of Irish women. The rebel Englishmen will 'bite off her dug from which they sucked life' because another breast has intervened: 'the child that sucketh the milk of the nurse must of necessity learn his first speech of her, the which being the first that is enured to his tongue is ever after most pleasing unto him,' and 'the speech being Irish, the heart must needs be Irish.'[21] The evil metamorphosis caused by Irish wetnurses is completed by miscegenation: 'the child taketh most of his nature of the mother . . . for by them they are first framed and fashioned' (68). As the fashioning of a gentleman is threatened in book 2 of *The Faerie Queene* by Acrasia, so it is threatened in Ireland by the native women.

It is often remarked that the *View,* which Spenser wrote after his completion of *The Faerie Queene*, expresses a hardening of attitude, a harsh and bitter note brought on by years of tension and frustration. It may well reflect such a change in tone, but its colonial policies are consistent with those with which Spenser had been associated from his arrival in Ireland as Lord Grey's secretary in 1580, that is, from the time in which *The Faerie Queene* was in the early stages of its composition. When Spenser 'wrote of Ireland,' Yeats comments, 'he wrote as an official, and out of thoughts and emotions that had been organized by the State.'[22] It was not only in his capacity as an official that Spenser did so: in art and in life, his conception of identity, as we have seen, is wedded to his conception of power, and after 1580, of colonial power. For all Spenser's claims of relation to the noble Spencers of Wormleighton and Althorp, he remains a 'poor boy,' as he is designated in the Merchant Taylor's School and at Cambridge, until Ireland. It is there that he is fashioned a gentleman, there that he is transformed from the former denizen of East Smithfield to the 'undertaker' – the grim pun unintended but profoundly appropriate – of 3,028 acres of Munster land. From his first acquisition in 1582, this land is at once the assurance of his status – the 'Gent.' next to his name – and of his insecurity: ruined abbeys, friaries expropriated by the crown, plow lands rendered vacant by famine and execution, property forfeited by those whom Spenser's superiors declared traitors.

For what services, we ask, was Spenser being rewarded? And we answer, blandly, for being a colonial administrator. But the answer, which implies pushing papers in a Dublin office through endless days of tedium, is an evasion. Spenser's own account presses in upon us the fact that he was involved intimately, on an almost daily basis, throughout the island, in the destruction of Hiberno-Norman civilisation, the exercise of a brutal force that had few if any of the romantic trappings with which Elizabeth contrived to soften it at home.[23] Here, on the periphery, Spenser was an agent of and an apologist for massacre, the burning of mean hovels and of crops with the deliberate intention of starving the inhabitants, forced relocation of peoples, the manipulation of treason charges so as to facilitate the seizure of lands, the endless repetition of acts of military 'justice' calculated to intimidate and break the spirit. We may wish to tell ourselves that a man of Spenser's sensitivity and gifts may have mitigated the extreme policies of ruthless men, but it appears that he did not recoil in the slightest from this horror, did not even feel himself, like his colleague Geoffrey Fenton, in mild opposition to it.[24] Ireland is not only in book 5 of *The Faerie Queene*; it pervades the poem. Civility is won through the exercise of violence over what is deemed barbarous and evil, and the passages of love and leisure are not moments set apart from this process but its rewards.

'Every detail of the huge resettlement project' in Munster, writes Spenser's biographer Judson, 'was known to him as it unfolded, including its intricate legal aspects, and hence his final acquisition of thousands of acres of forfeited lands was entirely natural.'[25] Natural perhaps, but equally natural that his imagination is haunted by the nightmares of savage attack – the 'outrageous dreadfull yelling cry' of Maleger, 'His body leane and meagre as a rake' and yet seemingly

impossible to kill[26] – and of absorption. The latter fear may strike us as
less compelling than the former – there is much talk, after all, of the
'savage brutishness and loathly filthiness' of native customs – but the
Elizabethans were well aware, as we have already seen, that many of
their most dangerous enemies were Englishmen who had been
metamorphosed into 'mere Irish.' Spenser's own career is marked by
conflicting desires to turn his back on Ireland forever and to plant
himself ever more firmly in Munster;[27] if the latter course scarcely
represented an abandonment of English civility, it may nonetheless have
felt like the beginning of the threatened transformation. I do not propose
that Spenser feared such a metamorphosis on his own behalf – he may,
for all we know, have been obscurely attracted to some of the very things
he worked to destroy, though of this attraction our only record is his
poetry's fascination with the excess against which it struggles – only that
he was haunted by the fact that it had occurred over generations to so
many of his countrymen. The enemy for Spenser then is as much a
tenacious and surprisingly seductive way of life as it is a military force,
and thus alongside a ruthless policy of mass starvation and massacre, he
advocates the destruction of native Irish identity.

Spenser is one of the first English writers to have what we may call a
field theory of culture, that is, the conception of a nation not simply as an
institutional structure or a common race, but as a complex network of
beliefs, folk customs, forms of dress, kinship relations, religious
mythology, aesthetic norms, and specialised modes of production.
Therefore, to *reform* a people one must not simply conquer it – though
conquest is an absolute necessity – but eradicate the native culture: in the
case of Ireland, eliminate (by force, wherever needed) the carrows,
horseboys, jesters, and other 'idlers'; transform the mass of the rural
population from cowherds with their dangerous freedom of movement to
husbandmen; break up the clans or sects; prohibit public meetings,
councils, and assemblies; transform Irish art, prohibiting the subversive
epics of the bards; make schoolchildren ashamed of their parents'
backwardness; discourage English settlers from speaking Irish; prohibit
traditional Irish dress; eliminate elections of chiefs, divisible inheritance,
and the payment of fines to avoid capital punishment. And always in
this immense undertaking, there is the need for constant vigilance and
unrelenting pressure, exercised not only upon the wild Irish but upon
the civilising English themselves. 'So much,' writes Spenser, 'can liberty
and ill example do' (63) that the threat of seduction is always present,
and the first inroad of this seduction is misguided compassion: 'Therefore,
by all means it must be foreseen and assured that after once entering
into this course of reformation, there be afterwards no remorse or drawing
back' (110). Pitiless destruction is here not a stain but a virtue; after all,
the English themselves had to be brought from barbarism to civility by

a similar conquest centuries before, a conquest that must be ever renewed lest the craving for 'liberty and natural freedom' (12) erupt again. The colonial violence inflicted upon the Irish is at the same time the force that fashions the identity of the English.

We have returned then to the principle of regenerative violence and thus to the destruction of the Bower of Bliss. The act of tearing down is the act of fashioning; the promise of the opening stanza of canto 12 – 'Now gins this goodly frame of Temperance / Fairely to rise' – is fulfilled at the close in the inventory of violence:

> But all those pleasant bowres and Pallace braue,
> *Guyon* broke downe, with rigour pittilesse;
> Ne ought their goodly workmanship might saue
> Them from the tempest of his wrathfulnesse,
> But that their blisse he turn'd to balefulnesse;
> Their groues he feld, their gardins did deface,
> Their arbers spoyle, their Cabinets suppresse,
> Their banket houses burne, their buildings race,
> And of the fairest late, now made the fowlest place.
>
> (2.12.83)

If the totality of the destruction, the calculated absence of 'remorse or drawing back,' links this episode to the colonial policy of Lord Grey which Spenser undertook to defend, the language of the stanza recalls yet another government policy, our third 'restoration' of the narrative: the destruction of Catholic Church furnishings. In the *Inventarium monumentorum superstitionis* of 1566, for example, we may hear repeated echoes of Guyon's acts:

> Imprimis one rood with Mary and John and the rest of the painted pictures – burnt. . . .

> Item our rood loft – pulled down, sold and defaced . . .

> Item our mass books with the rest of such feigned fables and peltering popish books – burnt. . . .

> Item 3 altar stones – broken in pieces. . . . [28]

In 1572 Spenser, a student at Pembroke, could have witnessed a similar scene at nearby Gonville and Caius where the authorities licensed the destruction of 'much popish trumpery'. Books and vestments, holy water stoops and images were 'mangled, torn to pieces, and mutilated' – *discerpta dissecta et lacerata* – before being consigned to the bonfire.[29]

There is about the Bower of Bliss the taint of a graven image designed
to appeal to the sensual as opposed to the spiritual nature, to turn the
wonder and admiration of men away from the mystery of divine love.
In the Bower the love survives only in the uncanny parody of the Pietà
suggested by Verdant cradled in Acrasia's arms. It is not surprising then
to find a close parallel between the evils of the Bower and the evils ·
attributed to the misuse of religious images. Devotion to the
representations of the Madonna and saints deflected men from the vigorous
pursuit of the good, enticed them into idleness and effeminacy. With their
destruction, as Hugh Latimer writes, men could turn 'from ladyness to
Godliness'.[30] Statues of the virgin were dismembered by unruly crowds,
frescoes were whitewashed over and carvings in 'Lady Chapels' were
smashed, in order to free men from thralldom to what an Elizabethan
lawyer calls, in describing the pope, 'the witch of the world'.[31]

But the art destroyed by Guyon does not pretend to image holy things;
it is designed to grace its surroundings, to delight its viewers with its
exquisite workmanship. Against such art there could be no charge of
idolatry, no invocation of the Deuteronomic injunctions against graven
images, unless art itself were idolatrous. And it is precisely this possibility
that is suggested by Guyon's iconoclasm, for Acrasia's realm is lavishly
described in just those terms which the defenders of poetry in the
Renaissance reserved for imagination's noblest achievements. The
Bower's art imitates nature, but is privileged to choose only those aspects
of nature that correspond to man's ideal visions; its music is so perfectly
melodious and 'attempred' that it blends with all of nature in one
harmony, so that the whole world seems transformed into a musical
'consort'; above all, the calculation and effort that lie behind the
manifestation of such perfect beauty are entirely concealed:

> And that which all faire workes doth most aggrace,
> The art, which all that wrought, appeared in no place.

'Aggrace' has virtually a technical significance here; Castiglione had
suggested in *The Courtier* that the elusive quality of 'grace' could be
acquired through the practice of *sprezzatura*, 'so as to conceal all art and
make whatever is done or said appear to be without effort and almost
without any thought about it.'[32]

Spenser deeply distrusts this aesthetic, even as he seems to pay homage
to its central tenets; indeed the concealment of art, its imposition upon
an unsuspecting observer, is one of the great recurring evils in *The Faerie
Queene*. Acrasia as demonic artist and whore combines the attributes of
those other masters of disguise, Archimago and Duessa.[33] Their evil
depends upon the ability to mask and forge, to conceal their satanic
artistry; their defeat depends upon the power to unmask, the strength to

turn from magic to strenuous virtue. Keith Thomas notes that in the sixteenth and seventeenth centuries the Protestant 'emphasis upon the virtues of hard work and application . . . both reflected and helped to create a frame of mind which spurned the cheap solutions offered by magic, not just because they were wicked, but because they were too easy.'[34] *Sprezzatura*, which sets out to efface all signs of 'hard work and application,' is a cult of the 'too easy,' a kind of aesthetic magic.

But what can Spenser offer in place of this discredited aesthetic? The answer lies in an art that constantly calls attention to its own processes, that includes within itself framing devices and signs of its own createdness. Far from hiding its traces, *The Faerie Queene* announces its status as art object at every turn, in the archaic diction, the use of set pieces, the elaborate sound effects, the very characters and plots of romance. For the allegorical romance is a mode that virtually by definition abjures all concealment; the artist who wishes to hide the fact that he is making a fiction would be ill-advised to write about the Faerie Queene.

If you fear that images may make a blasphemous claim to reality, that they may become idols that you will be compelled to worship, you may smash all images or you may create images that announce themselves at every moment as things made. Thus did the sixteenth-century kabbalists of Safed circumvent the Hebraic injunction against images of the Godhead;[35] their visions are punctuated by reminders that these are merely metaphors, not to be confused with divine reality itself. So too did the more moderate Protestant Reformers retain a version of the Communion, reminding the participants that the ceremony was a symbol and not a celebration of the real presence of God's body. And so does Spenser, in the face of deep anxiety about the impure claims of art, save art for himself and his readers by making its createdness explicit. Images, to be sure, retain their power, as the sensuous description of the Bower of Bliss attests, and Spenser can respond to the charge that his 'famous antique history' is merely 'th'aboundance of an idle braine . . . and painted forgery' by reminding his readers of the recent discoveries, of 'The Indian *Peru*,' 'The *Amazons* huge riuer,' and 'fruitfullest *Virginia*':

> Yet all these were, when no man did them know;
> Yet haue from wisest ages hidden beene:
> And later times things more vnknowne shall show.
> When then should witlesse man so much misweene
> That nothing is, but that which he hath seene?
> What if within the Moones faire shining spheare?
> What if in euery other starre vnseene

Of other worldes he happily should heare?
He wonder would much more: yet such to some appeare.

(2 Proem 3)

For a moment the work hovers on the brink of asserting its status as a newfound land, but Spenser immediately shatters such an assertion by invoking the gaze of royal power:

And thou, O fairest Princesse vnder sky,
In this faire mirrhour maist behold thy face,
And thine owne realmes in lond of Faery,
And in this antique Image thy great auncestry.

(2 Proem 4)

In an instant the 'other world' has been transformed into a mirror; the queen turns her gaze upon a shining sphere hitherto hidden from view and sees her own face, her own realms, her own ancestry. That which threatens to exist independent of religious and secular ideology, that is, of what we believe – 'Yet all these were, when no man did them know' – is revealed to be the ideal image of that ideology. And hence it need not be feared or destroyed: iconoclasm gives way to appropriation, violence to colonisation. J. H. Elliot remarks that the most significant aspect of the impact of the new world upon the old is its insignificance: men looked at things unseen before, things alien to their own culture, and saw only themselves.[36] Spenser asserts that Faerie Land is a new world, another Peru or Virginia, only so that he may colonise it in the very moment of its discovery. The 'other world' becomes mirror becomes aesthetic image, and this transformation of the poem from a thing discovered to a thing made, from existence to the representation of existence is completed with the poet's turn from 'vaunt' to apology:

The which O pardon me thus to enfold
In couert vele, and wrap in shadowes light,
That feeble eyes your glory may behold,
Which else could not endure those beames bright,
But would be dazled with exceeding light.

(2 Proem 5)

The queen is deified precisely in the act of denying art's claim to ontological dignity, to the possession or embodiment of reality.

Such embodiment is the characteristic achievement of great drama, of Marlowe and supremely of Shakespeare, whose constant allusions to the fictionality of his creations only serve paradoxically to question the status of everything outside themselves. By contrast, Spenser's profoundly *undramatic* art, in the same movement by which it wards off idolatry, wards off this radical questioning of everything that exists. That is, if art like Shakespeare's realises the power we glimpsed in Wyatt, the power of Althusser's words, to 'make us "perceive" . . . from *the inside*, by an *internal distance*, the very ideology' in which it is held, Spenserean allegory may be understood as a countermeasure: it opens up an internal distance within art itself by continually referring the reader out to a fixed authority beyond the poem. Spenser's art does not lead us to perceive ideology critically, but rather affirms the existence and inescapable moral power of ideology as that principle of truth toward which art forever yearns. It is art whose status is questioned in Spenser, not ideology; indeed, art is questioned precisely to spare ideology that internal distantiation it undergoes in the work of Shakespeare or Marlowe. In *The Faerie Queene* reality as given by ideology always lies safely outside the bounds of art, in a different realm, distant, infinitely powerful, perfectly good. 'The hallmark of Spenserean narration,' Paul Alpers acutely observes, 'is confidence in locutions which are at the same time understood to be provisional.'[37] Both the confidence and the provisionality stem from the externality of true value, order, meaning. For Spenser this is the final colonialism, the colonialism of language, yoked to the service of a reality forever outside itself, dedicated to 'the Most High, Mightie, and Magnificent Empresse . . . Elizabeth by the Grace of God Queene of England Fraunce and Ireland and of Virginia, Defendour of the Faith.'

Notes

1. We may note that in 1589 (the date of the letter), Ralegh is perhaps the supreme example in England of a gentleman not born but fashioned.

2. SIGMUND FREUD, *Civilization and Its Discontents*, trans JAMES STRACHEY (New York: Norton, 1962), pp. 44, 51.

3. For modern versions, see SAMUEL Z. KLAUSNER, 'A Collocation of Concepts of Self-Control,' in *The Quest for Self-Control: Classical Philosophies and Scientific Research*, ed. Klausner (New York: Free Press, 1965), pp. 9–48.

4. NATALIE ZEMON DAVIS, ' "Women's History" in Transition: The European Case,' *Feminist Studies* 3 (1976), p. 89 and the refs. in note 31.

5. CHRISTOPHER COLUMBUS, *Journals and Other Documents on the Life and Voyages of Christopher Columbus*, trans. and ed. Samuel Eliot Monson (New York: Heritage Press, 1963), p. 287.

6. TASSO, *Gerusalemme Liberata* (book 15, stanzas 28ff.), relates the quest for the realm of Armida to Columbus's voyages. Spenser's Maleger carries arrows 'Such as the *Indians* in their quiuers hide' (2.11.21). BERNAL DIAZ DEL CASTILLO recalls the first reaction to the sight of the Aztec capital in *The Conquest of New Spain*, trans. J. M. COHEN (Baltimore: Penguin, 1963), p. 214. On Spenser and the New

World, see ROY HARVEY PEARCE, 'Primitivistic Ideas in the *Faerie Queene'*, *Journal of English and Germanic Philology* 45 (1945), pp. 139–51; A. BARTLETT GIAMATTI, 'Primitivism and the Process of Civility in Spenser's Faerie Queene', in *First Images of America: The Impact of the New World on the Old*, ed. FREDI CHIAPPELLI, 2 vols. (Berkeley: University of California Press, 1976), 1:71–82.

7. RALEGH, *The Discovery of Guiana*, ed. V. T. HARLOW (London: Argonaut Press, 1928), p. 42.

8. PETER MARTYR, *The Decades of the New World*, trans. MICHAEL LOK, in *A Selection of Curious, Rare, and Early Voyages and Histories of Interesting Discoveries chiefly published by Hakluyt . . .* (London: R. H. Evans and R. Priestly, 1812), p. 539.

9. Ibid., p. 530.

10. *Of the newe landes*, in *The First Three English Books on America*, ed. EDWARD ARBER (Birmingham: Turnbull and Spears, 1885), p. xxvii; cf. WILBERFORCE EAMES, 'Description of a Wood Engraving Illustrating the South American Indians (1505)', *Bulletin of the New York Public Library* 26 (1922), pp. 755–60.

11. ELIZABETH STORY DONNO, ed., *An Elizabethan in 1582: The Diary of Richard Madox, Fellow of All Souls*, Hakluyt Society, Second Series, No. 147 (London: Hakluyt Society, 1977), p. 183. The editor notes that 'in the older maps the mountains of the moon figure as a range extending across the continent from Abyssinia to the Gulf of Guinea.'

12. At 6.8.43, the cannibals who capture Serena consider raping her, but they are stopped by their priests.

13. Compare Redcrosse who, when he dallies with Duessa, is described as 'Pourd out in loosnesse on the grassy grownd, / Both carelesse of his health, and of his fame' (1.7.7).

14. On vagabonds, see FRANK AYDELOTTE, *Elizabethan Rogues and Vagabonds* (London: Frank Cass & Co., 1913).

15. MARTYR, *Decades*, p. 628. On charges of idleness, see EDMUND S. MORGAN, *American Slavery, American Freedom: The Ordeal of Colonial Virginia* (New York: Norton, 1975).

16. Cortes 'had ordered that all houses should be pulled down and burnt and the bridged channels filled up; and what he gained each day was thus consolidated. He sent an order to Pedro de Alvarado to be sure that we never crossed a bridge or gap in the causeway without first blocking it up, and to pull down and burn every house' (BERNAL DIAZ, *Conquest*, p. 369).

17. I am indebted here to RICHARD SLOTKIN, *Regeneration through Violence: The Mythology of the American Frontier, 1600–1860* (Middletown, Conn.: Wesleyan University Press, 1973).

18. BERNAL DIAZ, *Conquest*, p. 60.

19. *A View of the Present State of Ireland*, ed. W. L. RENWICK (Oxford: Clarendon, 1970), pp. 48, 64, 65. Our primary purpose is to explore aspects of Elizabethan policy in Ireland as a reiteration of a characteristic cultural pattern rather than to detail the direct influence of Ireland upon *The Faerie Queene*; for the latter, see M. M. GRAY, 'The Influence of Spenser's Irish Experiences on *The Faerie Queene*', *Review of English Studies* 6 (1930), pp. 413–28; PAULINE HENLEY, *Spenser in Ireland* (Folcroft, Pa.: Folcroft Press, 1920).

20. Ibid., p. 67. Cf. LOUIS-JEAN CALVET, *Linguistique et colonialisme: Petit traité de glottophagie* (Paris: Payot, 1974) and STEPHEN J. GREENBLATT, 'Learning to

Curse: Aspects of Linguistic Colonialism in the Sixteenth Century', in *First Images of America* 2:561–80.

21. *View*, pp. 67–8. Children 'draweth into themselves together with their suck, even the nature and disposition of their nurses, for the mind followeth much the temperature of the body; and also the words are the image of the mind, so as they proceeding from the mind, the mind must be needs effected with the words' (p. 68).

22. YEATS, *Essays and Introductions* (London: Macmillan & Co., 1961), p. 372.

23. R. DUDLEY EDWARDS, *Ireland in the Age of the Tudors: The Destruction of Hiberno-Norman Civilization* (London: Croom Helm, 1977); NICHOLAS P. CANNY, *The Elizabethan Conquest of Ireland: A Pattern Established, 1565–76* (Hassocks, Sussex: Harvester Press, 1976); DAVID BEERS QUINN, *The Elizabethans and the Irish* (Ithaca, NY: Cornell University Press, 1966). For an apologetic account of Spenser's involvement, see PAULINE HENLEY, *Spenser in Ireland*; for an enigmatic indication of Spenser's personal profit from the Smerwick massacre, see ANNA MARIA CRINÒ, 'La Relazione Barducci-Ubaldini sull'Impresa d'Irlanda (1579–1581),' *English Miscellany* 19 (1968), pp. 339–67.

24. ALEXANDER C. JUDSON, *The Life of Edmund Spenser* (Baltimore: Johns Hopkins University Press, 1945), pp. 107–8.

25. Ibid., p. 116. The reference to the 'fennes of Allan' in 2.9.16 indicates that it was written after Spenser acquired New Abbey, a ruined Franciscan Friary in County Kildare, in 1582 (see JOSEPHINE WATERS BENNETT, *The Evolution of 'The Faerie Queene'* [Chicago: University of Chicago Press, 1942], p. 131n.).

26. It has been frequently noted that Maleger and his band resemble accounts in Spenser's *View* and in other reports on Ireland of Irish kerns.

27. We should perhaps note in this connection that Guyon leaves the Bower immediately after its destruction: 'But let vs hence depart,' says the Palmer, 'whilest wether serues and wind' (2.12.87).

28. Quoted in PHILIP HUGHES, *The Reformation in England*, 3 vols. (New York: Macmillan, 1954), 3:408.

29. JOHN VENN, *John Caius* (Cambridge: Cambridge University Press, 1910), p. 37. In a letter of the vice-chancellor, Dr. Byng, to the chancellor, Lord Burghley, dated 14 December 1572, the 'trumpery' is catalogued: 'vestments, albes, tunicles, stoles, manicles, corporas clothes, with the pix and sindon, and canopie, besides holy water stoppes, with sprinkles, pax, sensars, superaltaries, tables of idolles, masse bookes, portuises, and grailles, with other such stuffe as might have furnished divers massers at one instant.' The Latin account is from JOHN CAIUS, *The Annals of Gonville and Caius College*, ed. JOHN VENN, Cambridge Antiquarian Society Octavo Series no. 40 (Cambridge, 1904), p. 185. Caius adds that iconoclasts used hammers to smash certain objects.

30. Quoted in JOHN PHILLIPS, *The Reformation of Images: Destruction of Art in England, 1535–1660* (Berkeley: University of California Press, 1973), p. 80.

31. KEITH THOMAS, *Religion and the Decline of Magic* (London: Weidenfeld and Nicolson, 1971), p. 69.

32. *The Book of the Courtier*, trans. Singleton, p. 43. On *sprezzatura*, see WAYNE A. REBHORN, *Courtly Performances: Masking and Festivity in Castiglione's 'Book of the Courtier'* (Detroit: Wayne State University Press, 1978), pp. 33–40.

33. On demonic artists, see A. BARTLETT GIAMATTI: *Play of Double Senses: Spenser's Faerie Queene* (Englewood Cliffs, NJ: Prentice-Hall, 1975), pp. 106–33. We may

observe that Spenser seems on occasion to invoke positive versions of self-concealing art:

> Then came the Bride, the louely *Medua* came,
> Clad in a vesture of vnknowen geare,
> And vncouth fashion, yet her well became;
> That seem'd like siluer, sprinckled here and theare
> With glittering spangs, that did like starres appeare,
> And wau'd vpon, like water Chamelot,
> To hide the metall, which yet euery where
> Bewrayd it selfe, to let men plainely wot,
> It was no mortall worke, that seem'd and yet was not.
>
> (4.11.45)

Spenser's suspicions of aesthetic concealment can be allayed by its use in a virtuous context, but we might also note that in this instance the device both hides and does not hide its own artifice. The art is designed to seem natural and yet at the same time to let men plainly know, through a kind of 'self-betrayal,' that it is not natural. For conflicting arguments on the status of artifice in Spenser, see C. S. LEWIS, *The Allegory of Love* (New York: Oxford University Press 1979 [first published 1936]), pp. 326–33, and HANS P. GUTH, 'Allegorical Implications of Artifice in Spenser's *Faerie Queene*', *Publication of the Modern Language Association* 76 (1961), pp. 474–9.

34. KEITH THOMAS, *Religion and the Decline of Magic*, p. 275.

35. See GERSHOM SCHOLEM, *Sabbatai Sevi* (Princeton: Princeton University Press, 1973).

36. J. H. ELLIOTT, *The Old World and the New, 1492–1650* (Cambridge: Cambridge University Press, 1970).

37. PAUL ALPERS, 'Narration in *The Faerie Queene*,' *English Literary History* 44 (1977), p. 27.

Singing unsung heroines: androgynous
      discourse in Book III of *The Faerie Queene**

      LAUREN SILBERMAN

'Singing Unsung Heroines' is taken from a collection of essays which
attempted to use the insights of Marxism, psychoanalysis and decon-
struction in order to break new ground for early modern women's
studies, focusing on 'the structures of patriarchy that organized
power relations both in the state and in the family'. Silberman's essay
brings the perspectives of feminism and gender studies to bear on
the question of how sexuality informs both the politics and poetics
of literature. In contrast to many more orthodox deconstructionists,
Silberman suggests that the troubling androgynous representations
in *The Faerie Queene* are consciously controlled by Spenser and that
the poem itself is far more critical of Elizabethan sexual politics than
many feminist readings of Spenser allow. The reader, according to
Silberman, is forced to confront the partiality and oppression of male
society, resisting its forms of hierarchy and exclusion.

In the beginning of the second canto of Book 3 of *The Faerie Queene*,
Spenser transforms Ariosto's encomium of unsung heroines in the
Orlando Furioso (20.1–3, 37.1.24) into a compliment for Elizabeth, the
acknowledged mistress of 'artes and policy.' But masquerading as a
conventional compliment to the monarch is, I think, a statement of
genuine iconoclasm. Ariosto pays women a rather backhanded
compliment. He poses as the honest historian of their achievements while
calling attention to his own invention as a poet. The warrior maids
Marfisa and Bradamante never existed outside his poem. There have been
many renowned women, Ariosto assures us; it is just that somehow or
other no one has ever heard of them. Spenser is after something very

---

*Reprinted from MARGARET W. FERGUSON, MAUREEN QUILLIGAN and NANCY J.
VICKERS, eds, *Rewriting the Renaissance: The Discourses of Sexual Difference in Early
Modern Europe* (Chicago and London: University of Chicago Press, 1987),
pp. 259–71, 383–6.

different. In revising Ariosto, he shifts emphasis from fictitious heroines
to the false men who have suppressed the exploits of heroic women:

> Here haue I cause, in men just blame to find,
> That in their proper prayse too partiall bee,
> And not indifferent to woman kind,
> To whom no share in armes and cheualrie
> They do impart, ne maken memorie
> Of their braue gestes and prowesse martiall;
> Scarse do they spare to one or two or three,
> Rowme in their writs; yet the same writing small
> Does all their deeds deface, and dims their glories all.
>
> But by record of antique times I find,
> That women wont in warres to beare most sway,
> And to all great exploits them selues inclind:
> Of which they still the girlond bore away,
> Till enuious Men fearing their rules decay,
> Gan coyne streight lawes to curb their liberty;
> Yet sith they warlike armes haue layd away,
> They haue exceld in artes and pollicy,
> That now we foolish men that prayse gin eke t'enuy.[1]
>
> (3.2.1–2)

The complex pun, that men 'in their proper prayse too partiall bee,'
suggests that the improper partiality that leads men to disregard women
produces only incomplete, partial praise of themselves. Spenser admits
that sexuality affects the way people look at the world, which is radical
enough; characteristic of male *parti pris* is the assumption of universality.[2]
'Man and wife are one person under the law, and that person is the
man.' More than that, however, Spenser considers the *topos* of the unsung
heroine not simply as an opportunity for irony but as a standing
challenge to language itself. How does one write about a reality for which
men have made no room in their writs? How does one challenge the
assumptions of one's own culture? We who find ourselves faced with
the latter problem have, I think, much to learn from Spenser's
willingness and ability to be genuinely revisionary.[3]

When Spenser sets the 'record of antique times' against men's 'writing
small,' he taxes his poetic invention in both senses of the word *invention*.
It requires great creative power to rediscover a world excluded from
written records. Spenser fashions the *Legend of Britomart* in response to
Platonic hierarchical dualism and Petrarchan poetics. Petrarchan poetry,
which is based on the hierarchy of male poet and female love object,
represents the quintessence of partial praise: it parts men and women

and it enshrines male subjectivity in a specious transcendence.[4] The Petrarchan poet writes of a mistress who is unattainable so that his own perpetual longing provides subject matter for his poetry and the occasion for his assuming the vocation of poet. As the woman's active participation in the love relationship is denied, she is removed to the margins of the lyric, allowing the poet ample scope for expatiating on his own ability to make the absent beloved present in his verse. Britomart, who takes a very active role in a loving relationship, is an anti-Petrarchan heroine. Her warmth and vulnerability expose the essential sterility and self-absorption of Petrarchan lovesickness. And her uncertainty, as she falls in love with Artegall having seen nothing more than his image, about whether her love is true and destined to be fulfilled or whether it is a perverse and cruel delusion, shows up the too-pat Petrarchan strategy of making of the poet's own mental state the primary, objective reality.

Consider Spenser's famous image of artifice, Merlin's mirror: 'For thy it round and hollow shaped was, / Like to the world it selfe, and seem'd a world of glas' (3.2.19, ll. 8–9).[5] This is generally considered a model of Spenser's own poetic enterprise, but what is less often remarked is that the world of glass is offered as an alternative model that Spenser goes on, in the next stanza, to contrast with a more conventional version of poetic enterprise:

> Who wonders not, that reades so wonderous worke?
> But who does wonder, that has red the Towre,
> Wherein th' Ægyptian *Phao* long did lurke
> From all mens vew, that none might her discoure,
> Yet she might all men vew out of her bowre?
> Great *Ptolomæe* it for his lemans sake
> Ybuilded all of glasse, by Magicke powre,
> And also it impregnable did make;
> Yet when his loue was false, he with a peaze it brake.
>
> (3.2.20)

Here Spenser suggests that, although the universal, androgynous poetics figured by the mirror seems unusual, is it not equally strange to accept without question a phallic image of artistic creation that will not stand up against woman's autonomy?

Spenser's world of glass and Ptolemy's tower differ, not only in shape but in the epistemology each embodies as well. The unexpectedly fragile tower reveals the hidden inconsistency of a dualistic world view; the world of glass offers a better model, based on the principle of *discordia concors*. Ptolemy's glass tower offers a virtual parody of the epistemological categories *subject* and *object*, and of the sexual values tacitly given those categories: the male subject and the female object. With his artifice, Ptolemy makes Phao a subject of perception – she can see from within her tower but cannot be seen – in order to make of her a private sexual object. Ptolemy obstructs the process of social interaction, where people are objects of others' perception and subjects of their own, in order to exercise power over Phao. Although she gets to be both subject and object, the categories are manipulated for Ptolemy's sexual advantage. In contrast, when Britomart looks into the magic mirror, Spenser gives us an image of woman-as-subject that is not a bad joke. And, in place of the epistemological shell game, where mutually exclusive categories of subject and object are switched around to serve the will to power, Spenser offers a model of subjective participation in the object. In Merlin's looking glass, the interdependence of subject and object effects a kind of truce: as the categories are not entirely separable, it is impossible to accord one or the other primacy:

> It vertue had, to shew in perfect sight,
>> What euer thing was in the world contaynd,
>> Betwixt the lowest earth and heauens hight,
> So that it to the looker appertaynd . . .
>
> (3.2.19 ll. 1–4)

The phrase *so that* is deliberately ambiguous: it is both the introduction of a result clause – the mirror could show sights in such a way that they pertained to the looker – and the equivalent of 'provided that' – the mirror will reveal any sight, provided that it pertains to the looker. The double meaning keeps unclear to what extent the vision in the mirror is a subjective transformation of the object – that whatever appears in the mirror is distorted to pertain to the looker – and to what extent the pertinence of the object to the subject is a necessary precondition for the magic vision – that you can see anything you want, just as long as it pertains to you. The former is accounted a bad kind of subjectivity in Western culture when it is opposed to the virtue of objectivity or, if one has a Romantic sensibility, it is accounted a good kind for the freedom it gives.[6] Spenser's epistemology does not permit the reductive confidence of either idealized objectivity or of Romantic subjectivity. He proposes an engaged subjectivity in which admitting the danger of illusion is the price of vision. Spenser teases the reader about the traditional pejorative judgment of subjectivity when he describes Britomart's encounter with the magic mirror:

> One day it fortuned, faire *Britomart*
>> Into her fathers closet to repayre;
>> For nothing he from her reseru'd apart,

> Being his onely daughter and his hayre:
> Where when she had espyde that mirrhour fayre,
> Her selfe a while therein she vewd in vaine;
> Tho her auizing of the vertues rare,
> Which thereof spoken were, she gan againe
> Her to bethink of, that mote to her selfe pertaine.
>
> (3.2.22)

The word *vaine* raises the specter that Britomart may be guilty of a morally dangerous vanity. She engages in a long dialogue with Glauce about whether or not she is worse than Narcissus to have fallen in love with the image of a handsome knight shown to her by the mirror as soon as she began innocently to speculate about her future husband. Spenser's joke is that 'vanity, self-love' is not the primary meaning of *vaine* in context. As long as Britomart sees her own face in the looking glass, its magic is vain: it does not work. She cannot be content to be the objective observer with no prior interest in what she sees; that is what is truly vain.

Britomart's very uncertainty about what she sees in the mirror supplies the *tertium quid*, the third term, the distributed middle, that mediates between subject and object and transforms binary opposition into the ternary form of *discordia concors*.[7] Britomart cannot know for sure whether Artegall is real or is, in fact, a subjective, Narcissistic fantasy. By seeking after the knight whose image she has seen in the mirror, as her nurse Glauce urges her to do, she risks being in love with a mere fantasy; this risk is the *discordia* of *discordia concors*. And the wounding that forms a recurring motif in Book 3 attests to this risk. Spenser's poetics are based on a theory of reading as an act of courage – braving the gap between subject and object – with both sexual and moral connotations of *courage* equally relevant.

For the rest of this paper, I shall focus on the two major episodes in Book 3 that most clearly and directly express Spenser's critique of Petrarchan poetics and Platonic metaphysics. First, I shall consider the House of Busirane, that master of Petrarchan sexual poetics. Then, I shall discuss the Gardens of Adonis, where Spenser develops his poetics of harmonious discord as a genuine revision rather than an expedient transformation of Platonic dualism of spirit and matter. Just as Spenser restores active female participation, excluded by Petrarchanism from love poetry, so he restores the female and the physical components of procreation in his version of the Gardens of Adonis. The Gardens of Adonis are an erotic parody of Plato's myth of spiritual origins set out in the *Meno* and *Phaedo*, which offers an image of evolving plenitude to replace the Platonic metaphysics of full presence.[8] Spenser criticises Platonic dualism for substituting a will to power for genuine effort at understanding. Busirane's anti-Spenserian poetics exploits the Platonic model of dualism in that it depends on establishing binary oppositions – of reader and text, signifier and signified, subject and object, form and matter – that he can collapse for his own ends. He manipulates dualism in order to reap the benefits of duplicity, making a spurious object of Amoret the better to violate her integrity.

There is a kind of introduction to the House of Busirane in which Britomart comes upon Scudamore lying on the ground crying. She asks him what the problem is, and he explains what Busirane has done to his lady.[9] In many respects, Scudamore's problem is the key to what is wrong in the House of Busirane: the failure of courtly language to do justice to intersubjective reality. As Scudamore chivalrously blames himself for the injustice done his virtuous and innocent lady, his language betrays his failure to understand his own personal engagement in Amoret's plight. In his speech to Britomart, Scudamore admits more than he explicitly acknowledges:

> My Lady and my loue is cruelly pend
> In dolefull darkenesse from the view of day,
> Whilest deadly torments do her chast brest rend,
> And the sharpe steele doth riue her hart in tway,
> All for she *Scudamore* will not denay.
> Yet thou vile man, vile *Scudamore* art sound,
> Ne canst her ayde, ne canst her foe dismay;
> Vnworthy wretch to tread upon the ground,
> For whom so faire a Lady feeles so sore a wound.
>
> (3.11.11)

Scudamore's castigation of himself 'for whom so faire a lady feeles so sore a wound' is a complex judgment. By punning on the preposition *for*, Spenser indicates the ambiguity of the relationship between Amoret's suffering and Scudamore. She feels a wound for his sake – because she will not betray him – and she feels a wound because of him – because of his failure to protect her. Scudamore acknowledges these two meanings, but there is yet a third significance of which he does not seem to be aware; namely, that Amoret feels a wound of desire for Scudamore. Here, again, wounding confirms the engagement of subject and object. Scudamore is blind to this because as a conventional lover, he appropriates all of the active role for himself. In so doing, he connives at Amoret's enforced passivity and, because he has assumed an impossible role, he prevents himself from acting at all. That Busirane's particular villainy – he has 'pend' Amoret by imprisoning her and by penning her in language – has been permitted by Scudamore's misguided view of love suggests the dependence of Busirane's poetic strategy on psychological bias, specifically on Scudamore's characteristically male illusion of objectivity, which ironically blinds him to his own status as a sex object.

If it is Scudamore's own bias that aids Busirane, neither is it an accident that Amoret falls into Busirane's clutches: Busirane and Amoret are natural enemies. Scudamore reveals more about Amoret's role in her own predicament than he himself is able to acknowledge with his explanation, 'All for she Scudamore will not denay.' In context, the primary sense of *denay* is 'abjure, say no to the claims of.' That is, Busirane continues to torment Amoret because she will not deny her commitment to Scudamore. However, the secondary meaning, 'say no to, withhold anything desired' suggests that Amoret is tormented because she will not deny Scudamore anything, not quite Scudamore's picture of wronged, passive innocence. Critics often want to interpret Amoret's problem as her own fear of marriage, but it makes much more sense to see her as the lady who says 'yes' and thereby incurs the animosity of the Petrarchan poet.[10]

But even more is revealed about the source of Busirane's hostility. *Denay* is a special kind of word; one denays by uttering 'nay.' Word and meaning coincide, but only because the referent is so purely a speech act, is so completely defined by social interaction.[11] Busirane seeks to sequester Amoret from any social context in order to impose his own forms on her. He has 'pend' her in both senses of the word. Geographic dislocation and rhetorical manipulation combine strategically in his assault on Amoret's chastity. That is to say, Busirane exploits and confounds dualities of form and content and of speaker and audience in order to disguise the place where the masque is occurring. Is it in Britomart's mind? Amoret's mind? Busirane's castle? The page of Spenser's text?

The masque of Cupid pits form against content in a double assault on both the audience and Amoret. After Ease disappears, twelve paired figures march out, each figure an allegorical representation of a word: Fancy, Desire, Doubt, Daunger, Dissemblaunce, Suspect, Griefe, Fury, Displeasure, and Pleasaunce. The apparent formal coherence of the masque persuades us that the pageant expresses a coherent meaning, but we are being invited to yield to force and call it understanding. If one looks closely at the individual figures, how each expresses its meaning, and how each relates to its companion figure, one sees a picture of extreme incoherence, systematic discontinuity masquerading as continuous allegory. For example, Doubt exemplifies doubt; Hope does not exemplify hope, but provokes it in others. Fancy is linked to its companion Desire through moralised genealogy: Fancy begets Desire. Suspect is defined in relationship to his partner Dissemblaunce: she laughs at him; he lowers at her. But, although Dissemblaunce dissembles, she does not fool Suspect; she just teases him. The iconography of those figures seems rich and complex, but the real poetic point of the masque lies in how the language comes to life the moment Amoret enters. The appearance of a flesh-and-blood woman among the walking allegories gives a genuine shock.

> After all these there marcht a most faire Dame,
>   Led of two grysie villeins, th'one *Despight*,
>   The other cleped *Cruelty* by name:
>   She dolefull Lady, like a dreary Spright,
>   Cald by strong charmes out of eternall night,
>   Had deathes owne image figurd in her face,
>   Full of sad signes, fearfull of liuing sight;
>   Yet in that horror shewd a seemely grace,
> And with her feeble feet did moue a comely pace.
>
> Her brest all naked, as net iuory,
>   Without adorne of gold or siluer bright,
>   Wherewith the Craftesman wonts it beautify,
>   Of her dew honour was despoyled quight,
>   And a wide wound therein (O ruefull sight)
>   Entrenched deepe with knife accursed keene,
>   Yet freshly bleeding forth her fainting spright,
>   (The worke of cruell hand) was to be seene,
> That dyde in sanguine red her skin all snowy cleene.
>
> At that wide orifice her trembling hart
>   Was drawne forth, and in siluer basin layd,
>   Quite through transfixed with a deadly dart,
>   And in her blood yet steeming fresh embayd . . .
>   (3.12.19–21)

Busirane's attempt to impose upon Amoret the conventions of courtly love is a forcible troping: he forces her to embody a metaphor, a profane version of the sacred heart, in order to alienate Amoret's chaste affection for Scudamore. Busirane assaults her integrity with those Petrarchan conventions that identify a woman with a heart and mind of her own as Cruel and Despiteous.[12] He uses the masque both to imprison Amoret among alien forms and to intrude foreign content into her mind. The motif of spoils plays on the metaphor of form as a garment: Amoret's breast is despoiled so that she may become the spoil of Cupid, his *objet trouvé*, the free floating sign of his power. At the opposite extreme, Busirane resorts to psychological warfare as the masque degenerates to a phantasmagoria:

> There were full many moe like maladies,
>   Whose names and natures I note readen well;
>   So many moe, as there be phantasies
>   In wauering womens wit, that none can tell,
>   Or paines in loue, or punishments in hell . . .
>
> (3.12.26, ll. 1–5)

The near-pun on the preposition *in* raises a genuine question about the location of the masque. Is the pageant the product of Amoret's sexual fears: does it represent the pain that naturally accompanies love? Or is the masque torture inflicted from without, like the punishments in hell?[13] Busirane abuses poetry in passing off his own cruelty as both an objective statement about love and as a representation of Amoret's subjective fears.

Busirane's duplicity will not withstand a second look, however, because language cannot be contained by his reductive categories. When the masque appears the next night, Britomart follows the figures back into the room from which they came and sees Amoret chained to a pillar and Busirane 'figuring straunge characters of his art,' (3.12.31, l. 2). The masque has been demystified, but not because its characters turn out to be nothing but a pack of tropes; the transformation of the masque into marks on the page is just another of Busirane's tricks. It is the continued presence of Amoret, her wounded heart still in her breast, that gives the lie to Busirane's dualism. All the signifieds turn into signifiers, all the masque figures are displaced, deferred, by Busirane's writing, with the exception of Amoret. Busirane's limited, phallic poetics can only pen Amoret. He can only confine her; he cannot move her psychologically. 'A thousand charmes her formerly did proue; / Yet thousand charmes could not her stedfast heart remoue' (3.12.31, ll. 8–9). Busirane's charmes are merely incantations; they have no power to move the heart. Spenser's figure, Amoret, eludes Busirane because Spenser shows language eluding dualism. Spenser describes the weapon used by Busirane on Amoret as 'The cruell steele which thrild her dying hart,' (3.12.38.1). The word *thrild* can be taken in three separate senses, 'pierced,' 'made thrall of,' or 'moved emotionally,' Busirane can marshall only the first two of the three senses because his poetics make no allowance for another subjective consciousness, independent yet engaged. Spenser's exclamation, 'Ah, who can loue the worker of her smart?' (3.12.31, l. 7) points up Busirane's failure both as lover and as poet, for the question is both rhetorical and real.[14] The rhetorical answer is, 'no one.' Amoret cannot love Busirane for his abuse of her; mere sadomasochism, the archetypal dualism, is rejected. An alternative to simple sadomasochism is suggested in the other answer to Spenser's question, 'Ah, who can loue the worker of her smart?' The answer is

Britomart. She loves Artegall, the worker of her smart.[15] She risks wounding to receive love. With her, subjective engagement transcends sadomasochism.

The transformation of dualism to *discordia concors* is mapped out in the Gardens of Adonis. Spenser's basic strategy is to rewrite Plato, specifically Plato's theory of recollection propounded in the *Meno* and *Phaedo*; he takes the Platonic myth of spiritual origins and makes it erotic, turning Plato's own terms against Plato in order to challenge the Platonic distinction between abstract ideas and concrete manifestation. Plato's theory of the heavenly origin of ideas is transformed in Spenser's myth to the image of heavenly influence, which combines austere astrophysics with extremely physical eroticism. Belphoebe and Amoret were conceived 'through influence of th'heauens fruitful ray'; literal inflowing as well as spiritual emanation or action at a distance.

By positing immutable origins, Plato achieves a metaphysics of full presence. He opposes abstract and concrete, spirit and flesh, immortal and mortal in order to exalt the ideal over the mutable.[16] In shifting focus from heavenly origins to heavenly influence, Spenser emphasises process and relationship over presence. Spenser seeks intellectual stability by examining the principles of mutability and the nature of the relationship between abstract principles and concrete reality. He revises Plato's binary opposition of abstract and concrete into paradox. Heavenly influence insures the purity of Belphoebe's conception, 'vnspotted from all loathly crime / That is ingenerate in fleshly slime' (3.6.3, ll. 4–5); her conception has the purity of an intellectual idea. At the same time, the entire cosmos is shown to be sexual, which makes spiritual purity and fastidiousness seem a bit beside the point.

The Gardens of Adonis reveal the origins of Belphoebe's virtue, not by reproducing the Platonic myth of an immutable origin but by showing the reconciliation of abstract ideas to what is sensible, concrete, and mutable. Spenser transforms Plato's epistemological puzzle – how can we know something we do not already know – into a playful show of simultaneous ignorance and knowledge of the garden's geography. The narrator pretends to be uncertain whether Venus's particular *pied-à-terre* is Paphos, Cythera, or Gnidus while admitting, 'But well I wote by tryall, that this same / All other pleasant places doth excell,' (3.6.29, ll. 6–7). Delicate hints of physiological punning and feminine geography bring Platonic idealism down to earth. The garden is a seminary – 'the first seminarie / Of all things, that are borne to liue and die,' (3.6.30, ll. 4–5) – in both senses of the word. It is both a seed plot and a place of education. In examining the principle of natural change, Spenser will not deny the possibility of learning. For Plato's metaphysics of full presence, which must reject learning as a sign of lack, Spenser substitutes an evolving plenitude, which allows active, complementary roles to both intellect and nature.

Spenser presents the essential harmony of intellect and nature, abstract and concrete in three contradictory descriptions of the garden, which together enact the maxim *harmonia est discordia concors*. As Donald Cheney observes, the garden appears, first as the womb of the natural world, then as the image of the natural world, and finally, as 'a grove located on top of a "stately Mount." '[17] That can be taken further, however. The first version of the garden, metaphorical womb, represents the idea of generation that underlies the appearance of earthly mutability; the second version is the world as it appears to us; and the third version reconciles stable, intelligible form and changeable appearance in *discordia concors*.[18]

The first version of the Gardens of Adonis offers an allegory of generation in which the principle of earthly generation is expressed in cyclical metaphors of cosmic fecundity. This is a telling parody of Plato's myth of the origin of ideas because in it a generation myth explains the idea of generation and avoids the embarrassment of epistemology. The first version of the garden represents nature considered in the abstract without provision made for the constructing human mind. This is a garden that needs no gardener. The only shortcoming of this version of the garden is that its permanence, dispossessed of human consciousness, degenerates to the bloomin' buzzin' confusion of *Chaos*. The philosophical system grows more complicated and self-contradictory as the language becomes choked with arid abstractions. The decay, both of the poetry and the cosmology, is embodied in the decay of those curious 'formes' that grow in the garden:

> The substance is not changed, nor altered,
> But th'only forme and outward fashion;
> For euery substance is conditioned
> To change her hew, and sundry formes to don,
> Meet for her temper and complexion:
> For formes are variable and decay,
> By course of kind, and by occasion;
> And that faire flowre of beautie fades away,
> As doth the lilly fresh before the sunny ray.

(3.6.38)

A number of critics have made extensive efforts to sort out the metaphysical ground of this passage.[19] Spenser's basic strategy seems to be to cross Plato with Aristotle, but, as in the Masque of Cupid, the real point is not philosophical but poetic, namely our aesthetic surprise and relief as that flower metaphor springs from the philosophical compost.

The welcome metaphor of the flower makes the transition to the second version of the garden. What follows is the same cycle of decay and regeneration given in the first version but this time seen from below, from the human perspective, where the pain of mortality accompanies aesthetic pleasure. Lovely things die and this saddens us. The problem with this version is that nature considered strictly as the world of appearances yields nothing of permanence unless one is prepared to lie about it. The only vision of eternity possible from this perspective is perpetuity, a spurious extension of familiar nature compounded of wishful thinking and rhetorical epanorthosis, or correction:

> All things decay in time, and to their end do draw.

> But were it not, that *Time* their troubler is,
>   All that in this delightful Gardin growes,
>   Should happie be, and haue immortall bliss:
>   For here all plentie, and all pleasure flowes,
>   . . .
> There is continuall spring, and haruest there
>   Continuall, both meeting at one time:
>   (3.6.40, l. 9; 41, ll. 1–4; 42, ll. 1–2)

Plenty is naïvely linked with pleasure, and the mutability that underlies the earthly process of generation is wished away.

The final version, the more circumscribed 'stately Mount' within the garden proper, offers a poetic resolution to the problem of mutability. Here, the Spenserian version of the Venus and Adonis myth reconciles the mutable world of the senses with the peculiarly pliant form of poetry. As the father of all forms, Adonis figures the Platonic myth of origins. But the overt sexuality of Venus and Adonis subverts the neat, bloodless hierarchy of male-form, female-matter that those figures purport to represent. That Adonis is eterne in mutabilitie suggests both that he embodies the idea of change and that, as Venus's consort, he is sexually durable. The point of Spenser's revision of Ovid is just this reinclusion of banished sexuality in order to liberate poetic form. In Ovid, the myth of Venus and Adonis is a cautionary tale about poetic repression.[20] In warning Adonis to forgo hunting fierce beasts in favor of cony-catching, Ovid's decorative, fearful Venus dooms her lover by her own inadequacy as a love goddess. The boar as well as the rabbit belongs in the entourage of the true goddess of love. But, having been excluded from his rightful place, the boar returns as the agent of castration as well as the emblem of a repressed sexuality. Spenser transforms Ovid's paradox into one that is no less ferocious but is liberating in its ferocity. His Venus imprisons the boar 'in a strong rocky Caue, which is they say / Hewen underneath that Mount' (3.6.48, ll. 8–9). The image promises Adonis's safety while figuring forth the *vagina dentata*, ultimate expression of Venus's fearsome power. The interchangeable hierarchies of male/female, form/matter, are resolved by the reader's courage in facing the threat to which hierarchy and exclusion attest. The text itself creates a reader who is anything but partial, who by a courage that is moral as well as sexual transcends the partiality Spenser attributes to men, who, when they write and when they read, praise only themselves.

Notes

1. All quotations from SPENSER are taken from *The Poetical Works of Edmund Spenser*, ed. J. C. SMITH (Oxford: Clarendon Press, 1909).
2. For example, consider PAUL DE MAN's characterization of the ontological self in 'Ludwig Binswanger and the Sublimation of the Self,' in *Blindness and Insight: Essays in the Rhetoric of Contemporary Criticism* (New York: Oxford University Press, 1971), pp. 36–50. For a discussion of the role of gender in interpretation, see ANNETTE KOLODNY, 'A Map for Rereading: Or Gender and the Interpretation of Literary Texts,' *New Literary History* 11 (1980): 451–67.
3. Spenser is revising the patriarchal practice of relegating the female to the margins of culture and, with her, all those aspects of the human condition – emotion, physicality, mortality, subjectivity, vulnerability – that the culture did not, at a given moment, want to confront. An important part of Spenser's interest in chronicling the legend of Britomart and developing an anatomy of love in Book 3 is to restore wholeness to men and to language. The political implications of these discursive practices are well beyond the scope of this paper. Certainly (the highly problematic) Book 5 provides a very different view of female rule in regard to all women who are not Elizabeth.
4. See JOHN FRECCERO, 'The Fig Tree and the Laurel: Petrarch's Poetics,' *Diacritics* 5 (Spring 1975): 34–40; and GIUSEPPE MAZZOTTA, 'The *Canzoniere* and the Language of the Self,' *SP* 75 (1978): 271–6.
5. KATHLEEN WILLIAMS has an extended discussion of Merlin's mirror in *Spenser's Faerie Queene: The World of Glass* (London: Routledge & Kegan Paul, 1966), pp. 93–6.
6. GERALD GRAFF considers this issue in *Literature against Itself: Literary Ideas in Modern Society* (Chicago: University of Chicago Press, 1979), esp. pp. 31–62.
7. For a discussion of Renaissance notions of *discordia concors*, see EDGAR WIND, *Pagan Mysteries in the Renaissance* (1958; 2d ed., New York: W. W. Norton, 1968), pp. 81–96.
8. I borrow terms such as 'Platonic metaphysics of full presence' from Derridean criticism without meaning to ally myself with any particular critical school and certainly without claiming that Spenser's poetic practice illustrates the theories of Jacques Derrida or anyone else. Discussion of linguistic self-

consciousness – how an author's text reflects on the nature of its own language – in earlier texts, particularly in allegorical ones, sometimes seems tantalizing like deconstructive criticism. For a particularly felicitous application of contemporary literary theory to Ovid, the reader is urged to see JOHN BRENKMAN, 'Narcissus in the Text,' *Georgia Review* 30 (1976): 293–327. Such a consideration of literary theory is well beyond the scope of this paper. I suspect, however, that the differences between the deconstructionist project and Spenser's undertaking are apt to be as interesting as the similarities. In particular, unlike the deconstructionists, Spenser is willing to risk mystification in order to construct the subject.

9. KATHLEEN WILLIAMS analyzes Scudamore's personal culpability at some length in *Spenser's World of Glass*. See esp. pp. 105–7, 134–7.

10. See, for example, JAMES NOHRNBERG, *The Analogy of* The Faerie Queene (Princeton, NJ: Princeton University Press, 1976), pp. 474–8.

11. The notion of the speech act comes from J. L. AUSTIN, *How To Do Things with Words* (1962; 2d ed., Cambridge, Mass.: Harvard University Press, 1975). BARBARA JOHNSON discusses the ambiguous role of performative language in 'Poetry and Performative Language: Mallarme and Austin,' in *The Critical Difference: Essays in the Contemporary Rhetoric of Reading* (Baltimore: Johns Hopkins University Press, 1980), pp. 52–66.

12. In *Heroic Love: Studies in Sidney and Spenser* (Cambridge: Harvard University Press, 1968), p. 123, MARK ROSE observes that 'Cruelty' and 'Despight' refer to the role Amoret is made to play.

13. Critics who locate the pageant inside Amoret's head tend to see Busirane as trying to frighten Amoret with a distorted or reductive vision of sexuality that plays on her fears of marriage. Versions of this interpretation are given by JANET SPENS, *Spenser's* Faerie Queene: *An Interpretation* (1934: reprint, New York: Russell, 1967), p. 105; A. C. HAMILTON, *The Structure of Allegory in* The Faerie Queene (Oxford: Clarendon Press, 1961), pp. 145–6; WILLIAM NELSON, *The Poetry of Edmund Spenser* (New York: Columbia University Press, 1963), p. 230; THOMAS P. ROCHE, *The Kindly Flame: A Study of the Third and Fourth Books of Spenser's* Faerie Queene (Princeton, NJ: Princeton University Press, 1976), pp. 473–5. HARRY BERGER, Jr., in 'Busirane and the War Between the Sexes: An Interpretation of *The Faerie Queene* III. xi.xii,' *ELR* 1 (1971): 99–121, shows a much greater appreciation of the role of the imagination in Amoret's plight. For a discussion of the element of fictionmaking in the Masque of Cupid, see ISABEL MACCAFFREY, *Spenser's Allegory: The Anatomy of Imagination* (Princeton, NJ: Princeton University Press, 1975), pp. 107–17.

14. PAUL DE MAN, 'Semiology and Rhetoric,' in *Textual Strategies: Perspectives in Post-Structuralist Criticism*, ed. JOSUÉ HARARI (Ithaca, NY: Cornell University Press, 1979), pp. 121–40.

15. ALPERS makes a similar point, p. 402.

16. JOHN BRENKMAN considers the issue of Platonic hierarchies in relation to the *Symposium* in 'The Other and the One: Psychoanalysis, Reading, the Symposium,' in *Literature and Psychoanalysis. The Question of Reading: Otherwise*, ed. SHOSHANA FELMAN, Yale French Studies, Nos. 55–6 (New Haven: Yale University Press, 1977), pp. 396–456.

17. DONALD CHENEY, *Spenser's Images of Nature: Wild Man and Shepherd in 'The Faerie Queene,'* (New York: Yale University Press, 1966), pp. 126–30.

18. OWEN BARFIELD treats the issue of familiar vs. inferred nature in *Worlds Apart* (Middletown, Conn.: Wesleyan University Press, 1963), esp. in the mock-Platonic dialogue, pp. 65–8. See also HARRY BERGER, Jr., 'Spenser's Gardens of Adonis: Forces and Form in the Renaissance Imagination,' *University of Toronto Quarterly* 30 (1961): 128–49.

19. On the philosophical background of the Gardens of Adonis, see FRANK KERMODE, *The Sense of an Ending: Studies in the Theory of Fiction* (London: Oxford University Press, 1966), pp. 67–89; ROSALIE COLIE, *Paradoxica Epidemica: The Renaissance Tradition of Paradox* (Princeton, NJ: Princeton University Press, 1966), pp. 335–49; HUMPHREY TONKIN, 'Spenser's Garden of Adonis and Britomart's Quest,' *PMLA* 88 (1973): 408–17; FRED L. MILNE, 'The Doctrine of Act and Potency: A Metaphysical Ground for Interpretation of Spenser's Garden of Adonis Passages,' *SP* 70 (1973): 279–87. In *The Kindly Flame*, THOMAS ROCHE makes some judicious comments about the difficulties of assigning a piece of poetry to any particular philosophy.

20. OVID, *Metamorphoses*, (10. 503–59).

8 'Endlesse worke'*

JONATHAN GOLDBERG

Jonathan Goldberg's book *Endlesse Worke* deserves mention – among other things – as the first sustained application of deconstructionist criticism to *The Faerie Queene*. Goldberg argues that the second edition of *The Faerie Queene* (Books I–VI) resists the certainties and confident conclusions of the first edition (Books I–III), and in doing so, brings pleasures of its own, the pleasures of the text, which refuse to end. If the first edition of the poem sought to lead the reader out of the wood of error to safety, the second acknowledged that error has its own appeal, empowering the reader at the expense of the author, as Roland Barthes recognised in his attempt to distinguish between the readerly and the writerly text.

Goldberg's analysis is one of the few to make much of Book IV, traditionally the most neglected part of *The Faerie Queene*, and also possesses the merits of more traditional narrative analyses of the poem like Paul Alpers's or Isabel MacCaffrey's studies. His more recent work – for example, the chapter on Spenser in *Sodometries* – whilst still indebted to deconstructionist theory, now derives its terms from a variety of histories: of literary form, of social formation, and especially of gender and sexuality.

In 1596, the second half of *The Faerie Queene*, books IV to VI, appeared for the first time, preceded by a new edition of books I to III. Some minor textual changes had been made in the first half of the poem, and one major one: the final stanzas of book III had been canceled and, in their place, three new stanzas were provided. Displaced were the five stanzas leading to the union of Scudamour and Amoret; replacing them were stanzas in which Amoret discovered no lover awaiting her, in which Scudamour, 'misdeeming' (III. xii. 45.5) her situation and his own, had abandoned her, and in which Britomart, instead of witnessing their union,

---

*Reprinted from JONATHAN GOLDBERG, *Endlesse Worke: Spenser and the Structures of Discourse* (Baltimore and London: Johns Hopkins University Press, 1981) pp. 1–12.

149

discovered their loss and failed meeting; 'thereat her noble hart was stonisht sore' (44.5).[1] This major revision, this moment of sore astonishment, although it is unique in the textual history of the poem, highlights central tendencies of narration in *The Faerie Queene*. The deliberate cancelation of an ending carries with it an implicit assumption: that narration cannot progress beyond an ending – any ending. What this means, in a broad sense, is easily recognised by any reader of *The Faerie Queene*, for the poem is not merely finally unfinished, but frustratingly incomplete and inconclusive throughout, even when it encourages its readers to expect conclusions. This is characteristic of Spenserian narration, and it is characteristically problematic. How, then, does narration progress in *The Faerie Queene*, and what are the virtues of, the pleasures offered by, a broken text? Raising these questions, the revisionary juncture between books III and IV seems to call into question the very nature of Spenser's narrative.

The new ending – in which Scudamour, Amoret, and Britomart are each at a loss – evidently links narrative progress, or the possibility of going forward, to frustration. It thereby exaggerates one aspect of the original ending. For in the first edition, although Amoret and Scudamour shared a 'long embracement' in which they virtually had 'growne together quite,' Britomart, standing aside, 'halfe envying ther blesse,' remained as far from her own love, Arthegall, as she had ever been. Book III appears to be organised around Britomart's quest (it opens and closes the book), and many readers share her feelings when it arrives at its only partly satisfactory conclusion. They, too, want more satisfaction, with a firmer and fuller ending. The reader has been led to believe that Britomart will reach her goal (books I and II offer strong precedents for that expectation), and the minor felicities of the original conclusion do not really compensate for the anticipated meeting of Britomart and Arthegall. The 1596 ending, however, refuses us even the partial and displaced satisfaction of the first ending and draws all the characters, and the reader too, into a situation of general frustration that appears to be necessary to generate further narration. It seems arguable, and I will want to maintain the point, that this revision clarifies the nature of narrative progress throughout the poem and suggests the peculiar pleasures this text offers.

For one thing, the new ending makes demands upon the reader to revaluate notions of narrative satisfaction, to defer or even to deny the pleasures of conclusions for those of expectations, and to recognise as well that failed endings are part of the design of the poem.[2] Even in the first version, Britomart's position, solitary and half envious, had been a disturbing element, perhaps a blot on an otherwise happy ending. Yet, in fact, Britomart's plight fulfills a pattern in the text: Britomart begins and ends book III in the same situation, and a pair of parallel wounds in her first and last adventures might be said to symbolise her career of frustrated love. Britomart's first adventure concludes with a wound received from Gardante (III. i. 65) , and her final victory, the rescue of Amoret, culminates with the same wound again, this time inflicted by Busyrane (III. xii. 33). Repetition makes it clear that it is the same wound a second time. The first wound is 'not deepe' (65.6), the latter equally superficial; 'nothing deepe imprest' (33.7). In the first instance, the arrow is 'seene/To gore her side' (65.5–6), the second wound 'empurpled her faire brest' (33.5). Drops of blood at the beginning vermeil 'her lilly smocke' (65.9) and 'silken skin' (65.7), and at the end 'her snowie chest' (33.4) is 'empurpled' (33.5). If Britomart's final situation, however much it may disappoint a reader's expectations, nonetheless represents, in these repetitions, a kind of closure, Amoret's revised position – alone, and abandoned – echoes Britomart's. The principle of repetition thus offers a different kind of completion from the original hermaphroditic embrace, but one that also clearly satisfies a demand of the text. Furthermore, Amoret is now not merely doubling Britomart but also exemplifying another of the poem's structural precepts. At the moment of Britomart's victory over Busyrane, Amoret's riven heart had been restored to her, and she was once again, Spenser's text says, 'perfect hole' (xii. 38.9). In the new ending, the ambivalence of 'hole' is more fully taken into account. Instead of the complicated mixture of resolution and frustration that had once ended book III, the reader is being asked to take as the pleasure of the text this moment of doubled loss, fulfillment through want, 'perfect hole' – a paradox that nonetheless satisfies continuing structural demands in the text's language, imagery, and theme.

The new ending, I would argue, gives a taste of the kind of narrative that lies ahead, and most readers, I suspect, would agree that the final installment of *The Faerie Queene* does not include the pleasures of resolution that characterise the opening books. I will want to suggest that those failed pleasures *are* the pleasures of this text. Furthermore, I would venture to say that the revised ending of book III does not merely fulfill the patterns of repeated wounds and 'perfect hole' that have been pointed out. It also draws attention to all the erosions of the quest structure in book III that keep Britomart from seeming to be the kind of hero that the Red Crosse knight and Guyon appear to be. No matter how compellingly human Britomart appears (and most readers find her more dramatic than the heroes of the first two books), hers is in fact a less completely sustained presence in the text than either the Red Crosse knight's or Guyon's. True, these two heroes are both occasionally – at times, quite perplexingly – absent from their books, but never for long; Britomart, on the other hand, disappears for four consecutive cantos at the center of book II, and she disappears, moreover, just after a moment of triumph, her defeat of Marinell, when, we are told, 'all was in her powre' (iv. 18.9).

Here is the passage describing her departure; Cymoent is lamenting her wounded son:

> But none of all those curses overtooke
> The warlike Maid, th'ensample of that might,
> But fairely well she thriv'd, and well did brooke
> Her noble deeds, ne her right course for ought forsooke.

> Yet did false *Archimage* her still pursew,
> To bring to passe his mischievous intent,
> Now that he had her singled from the crew
> Of courteous knights, the Prince, and Faery gent,
> Whom late in chace of beautie excellent
> She left, pursewing that same foster strong;
> Of whose foule outrage they impatient,
> And full of fiery zeale, him followed long,
> To reskew her from shame, and to revenge her wrong.
>
> (III. iv. 44.6–9; 45)

The syntax and shifting pronoun references confuse Britomart here, 'her' in 44.9, with a 'her' in the next line, which does not refer to Britomart but to an as yet unnamed maiden, Florimell; to add to the reader's confusion the name of Archimago is suddenly, but only momentarily and virtually inexplicably, present: he is mentioned nowhere else in book III. Britomart disappears here, merging into a surrogate; she reappears four cantos later, after book III has passed through its symbolic center, the garden of Adonis, and after Britomart has been repeatedly replaced by surrogates – Florimell, Belphoebe, Amoret, and Hellenore. When she once again becomes the protagonist, she journeys on but fails to reach her goal. Finally, the new ending doubles her frustration with Amoret's and thereby robs Britomart's rescue of Amoret of its conclusive force; nonetheless, this episode represents a fitting end to a career that has been consistently eroded by the very structures of narration in book III. Although we may finish the book in expectation of a happy ending, the new conclusion must focus our attention on all the signs that the narrative has been offering that urge readers to give up these expectations: the disappearance of the heroine, her failure to be present at the center of the book, her insubstantial victory, her repeated wounds. This undermining of the hero, and with it, the weakening of the quest as a principle of narrative structure, are, however, minimal when compared with what happens in the next book of *The Faerie Queene*. We scarcely need to get past the opening to see that the erosions of narration highlighted by the new ending of book III have become the central features of narration in book IV.

In its title, 'The Legend of Cambel and Telamond, Or of Friendship,' book IV promises familiar narrative strategies: the book is about a virtue and its hero (the pair of heroes is unique, but appropriate enough for exemplifying the virtue of friendship). But in the name of one of these heroes, Telamond, the title presents a puzzle that is a complement to the new ending of book III, for Telamond appears nowhere in the poem, and his name is merely a word on the title page. The implications for narration seem even more radical than the disappearance of the hero or the frustrated resolution in book III. In *The Kindly Flame*, Thomas Roche addresses this problem when he deciphers Telamond to mean 'perfect world,' and, without much difficulty, attaches the name to the cosmic implications of the three brothers, Priamond, Diamond, and Triamond, and their curious battle with Cambel for the hand of his sister, Canacee.[3] Telamond, in that case, is nothing more than a slip of the pen, a mere substitute name for Triamond, the hero who does appear in the poem. But what might such a slip or substitution actually mean?

If we go back once again to the previous book, we can perhaps see, by means of a small example, where narration seems to be heading in this slip, for there is a similar one early in book III. As Britomart travels with the Red Crosse knight after their departure from Malecasta's castle, she converses with him; as the versicle to canto ii puts it: '*The Redcrosse knight to Britomart / describeth Artegall.*' Four stanzas later, however, the text reports her not with the Red Crosse knight but 'travelling with *Guyon* by the way' (ii. 4.l), and it is not until the end of a long flashback that the name of her original companion reappears: 'through speaches with the *Redcrosse* knight, / She learned had th'estate of *Arthegall*' (iv. 4. 1–2). Whatever readers make of this shuffling of names – the replacement of Guyon for the Red Crosse knight – it seems at the time a very minor disturbance, although retrospectively it may undermine the stability of the identities of the heroes in the first two books of the poem. The implication seems to be that any hero is all heroes, that all heroes are the same hero. When this event is followed, as it is almost immediately, by Britomart's disappearance, we may as well be led to consider the possibility that the true structure of narration in *The Faerie Queene*, even in its opening books, is not described by the quest centered on the career of a single figure. Hence, when book IV opens with its error, the naming of a hero who fails to appear at all – at least under that name – it may be making, however obliquely, a statement about the overall nature of narration in *The Faerie Queene*.

What would the implications of this statement be? Telamond, the 'perfect world,' is announced but fails to appear. On one side of this name (a signifier without a signified) we have Britomart joined to Amoret in loss, 'perfect hole'; on the other side, at the very close of book IV, we face an ultimate act of deferred narration in the story of Florimell and Marinell, 'which,' Spenser's narrator says, 'to another place I leave to be perfected' (IV. xii. 35.9). That final line, like the new ending of book III, indicates that narrative structure in *The Faerie Queene* is not closed, and complete, but instead describes a kind of loop, moving here from 'perfect' to 'to be perfected,' from closure ('tela' derives from *telos*, end) to openness, from the world ('-mond') to 'another place.' This is a structure of undoing or destructuring, a loop threading the void, moving from Telamond, the 'perfect world' that is not present in the text, to the admission that perfection lies elsewhere, in 'another place' that is also not in this text. The text moves from absence to absence, doubling back upon itself and yet never ending at all. Book IV thus concludes with an explicit statement about deferred closure that sums up what narrative structure, with its erosion of the stability of character and its undermining of the conclusive quest, seemed to be preparing. The shape of book IV, to put it briefly, would seem to be this: Telamond is the name of an absence; Triamond, the name given in place of and as a substitute for this one, is itself not a narrative entity – first, because his is a substitute name, but also because he is one of a triad with his brothers, Priamond and Diamond, and because he is paired with his alter ego, Cambel. Triamond and Cambel, the joint heroes of book IV, appear, moreover, in only four cantos of the book, mainly in a long flashback. And by the fifth canto, Triamond and Cambel, the presumed heroes of the book, have disappeared from the poem – forever. With their absence, book IV would seem to have abandoned entirely the assumption that plot moves character towards a goal, or that the protagonists embody theme. These radical disturbances of narration, I would argue, lay bare the nature of narration throughout *The Faerie Queene*.

Book IV calls into question definitions of Spenserian narration that are centered on the questing hero. Even in its most idiosyncratic feature, the pair of disappearing heroes, it bears implications for the entire poem, undermining the notion of the single and singular protagonist. True, in every other book there is nominally only one hero. Yet the pairing in book IV draws attention to how these single heroes are regularly presented – paired, like Guyon and the Palmer, or Arthegall and Talus; or replaced, like Calidore by Calepine, or Britomart by half a dozen maidens. Look, for instance, at how the Red Crosse knight enters the poem:

> A Gentle Knight was pricking on the plaine,
>   Y cladd in mightie armes and silver shielde,
>   Wherein old dints of deepe wounds did remaine,
>   The cruell markes of many' a bloudy fielde;
>   Yet armes till that time did he never wield:

His angry steede did chide his foming bitt,
As much disdayning to the curbe to yield:
Full iolly knight he seemd, and faire did sitt,
As one for knightly giusts and fierce encounters fitt.

(I. i. 1)

Even in this opening stanza, in which he is a knight riding alone, the
Red Crosse knight comes clad in arms that bear the 'cruell markes' of
many battles, though we are told that he has never fought before. In
other words, the Red Crosse knight enters the poem clothed as another;
the 'bloudie Crosse he bore' (2.1) names him only through a sign – as the
Red Crosse knight – and it is a sign of someone else. Furthermore,
the quest he is on provides him with a companion, Una, who, despite
her name, is hardly single in appearance. She is a veiled lady, and the veil
serves as an indication that there is more to her than meets the eye,
offering an invitation to think of her in terms of surface and depth.
Moreover, she does not travel alone; as first presented, she is accompanied
by a dwarf and, briefly, by a symbolic lamb. In other words, from the
start, the single knight has a double identity, or no identity of his own,
while his companion, who is both his truth, the object of his troth, and
Truth itself, seems endlessly decipherable. Una's 'oneness' serves as a
reflection of and an index to the unity of the Red Crosse knight; it is
manifested multiply and represented as external to himself. The end of
the quest, endlessly deferred, promises the marriage of the knight to
Una. Only in a conclusion to *The Faerie Queene* that the poem never
provides will the Red Crosse knight, marrying his unity, truly be one.
Until then, the knight's identity – his singleness – is only the product of
his relationship with, and differentiation from, others. Hence,
throughout book I, the Red Crosse knight is set against the images of
himself that populate the poem; images that he is at times mistaken for,
just as he himself, from the start of his adventure, mistakes images, or
just as Una comes clear only against the various forms of Duessa.
Narration in book I is negotiated within these margins of difference,
between deferred unity and seeming to be one: 'Full iolly knight he
seemd, and faire did sitt,/As one for knightly giusts and fierce encounters
fitt': how he seems, what he is like, not who or what he is, are, from
the first, how the Red Crosse knight is identified. When *The Faerie Queene*
begins again in book IV, the meaning of this differential characterisation
and this condition for knightly action is at last defined openly in the
twinned heroes of the book.

If even the condition of being single and having an identity involves a
relationship with another, then we can see that the central concerns of
book IV reveal crucial facts about the structures of discourse in *The Faerie
Queene*. For book IV is explicitly about groups and regroupings, and the

155

meanings it considers are those that involve relationships. Here, for instance, is how Cambel and Triamond are described when they undergo the wondrous transformation that makes them friends instead of professed enemies: 'Wonder it is that sudden change to see: / Instead of strokes, each other kissed glad, / And lovely haulst from feare of treason free, / And plighted hands for ever friends to be' (IV. iii. 49.2–5). Their change is measured physically as a movement in place and of replacement, 'instead' being the crucial word to mark their differentiation. Instead of blows, kisses are exchanged, instead of raising hands against 'each other,' hands are joined; fear of each other turns into friendship with another, and the new binding is one that takes place in an embrace free 'from feare of treason.' Their sudden and momentary reconciliation in these lines is determined by psychological forces and social demands. Cultural values *situate* and *move* them to replace their antagonism with friendship. They are re-placed. Indeed, throughout book IV, the figures move in groups in ways that resemble the trajectory of some unknown, mapped by an algebraic formula onto a functional grid. In these equations X is the individual, placed and replaced in relational matrices. In its groups and its motion, book IV reveals that narration in *The Faerie Queene* functions as a grid on which different positions and relationships define an actor from moment to moment.

To summarise. The fundamental quality of narration in book IV, that book whose place in the poem is made by the displacement of an ending, is, then, not a progression toward a conclusion, but a deferral, leaving an ending 'to be perfected' in 'another place'; the fundamental quality, as the narrator calls it, is 'endlesse worke' (xii. 1.9).[4] Such work involves seemingly endless acts of undoing, denial, and frustration. Because of it, narration is being measured in losses, the loss of a definitive ending or the loss of an individual hero. 'Instead' of the pleasures of the text that come from completion and stability, this is a text populated with faceless knights (as C. S. Lewis called them) and their ladies moving in flux, constantly resituated, momentarily lodged in relationships from which they are as quickly dislodged, inevitably undone. Here, for instance, is what happens to that perfect pair of friends, the heroes of book IV, Triamond and Cambel cemented 'for ever' (iii. 49.5) in the lines we just looked at. Hardly a canto later, they have become simply two names in a list: 'first *Cambello* brought . . . / His faire *Cambina* . . . / Next did Sir *Triamond* . . . / The face of his dear *Canacee* unheale . . . / And after her did *Paridell* produce / His false *Duessa*' (v. 10–11). They are now merely elements in a formulaic situation in which distinctions and differences have disappeared, the presentation of a series of ladies in the beauty contest given by Satyrane. Heroism and distinct individuality are eroded by these matrices, for they allow endless shifting and substitution. Hence, at the beauty contest, the names of the heroes are in no way different from the names of Paridell or Sir Ferramont – the latter, a knight whose name appears only twice in the whole of *The Faerie Queene*, once in this set of stanzas. And the ladies, listed as beloved objects, possessions, *productions*, soon converge as well; 'And after these an hundred Ladies moe / Appear'd in place, in which each other did outgoe' (v. 11. 8–9). A hundred ladies pass through a place, a site on a map, a location on a functional grid; when they pass through this place they 'appear'd in place' of 'each other,' different only by replacing one another in a virtually endless sequence of substitutions.

The features of narration in *The Faerie Queene* that are so crucial to book IV are strikingly elucidated by the critical terminology provided by Roland Barthes in *S/Z*.[5] Barthes opposes what he calls the readerly and the writerly text; in his terms, *The Faerie Queene* would fall within the latter category. The writerly text, as Barthes describes it, demands and produces readings that go counter to the conventions of narration found in what he calls Classical texts, those texts that are based on the mimesis of such supposedly ordinary and natural processes as sequentiality (opening followed by closure, beginning by ending) or that depend upon empirical commonplaces about a fixed locus of activity and a stable actor therein.

The writerly text, on the other hand, calls these assumptions into question. Unlike the readerly text, which is enslaved to sequence, the writerly text, which is also the text produced by writerly reading, is open, endless, and reversible, a 'galaxy of signifiers, not a structure of signifieds' (p. 5). In other words, whereas the readerly text aims at representation (signifieds), the writerly text is committed to what Derrida describes as play in a centerless void, or, in his word, *freeplay*. The readerly text drives toward signification, and its words mean to name things. The writerly text plays with signifiers, and its names are the names of names linked in the endless chain of words (in Spenser: Telamond is replaced by Triamond; Priamond and Diamond are regenerated as Triamond; Triamond is joined to Cambel – he can wear his arms, take his name, stand in his place). The readerly text offers its reader the word as a product, an object; the name as a thing, an object of communication. The writerly text defers, demands the 'endlesse worke' of play, the discovery of and the dissolving of differences into deferred identity and unity. The readerly text is single, solid, the author's work; the writerly text is infinite, replete, broken, empty, arbitrary, structured and deconstructed in its reading, which is its rewriting, produced by reader and author at once. The writerly text is an 'endlesse worke' of substitution, sequences of names in place of other names, structures of difference, deferred identities. It plays upon a void: it occupies the place of loss – where Britomart's wound is extended to Amoret, where Amoret is 'perfect hole.' This is the space of the text.

The new ending to book III carries these meanings for narration in *The Faerie Queene,* and book IV is the place in the text where its narrative principles are most fully revealed. From its vantage point the nature of *The Faerie Queene* as a writerly text comes clear. From the critical site of book IV, the entire text can be reviewed.

Notes

1. All citations from Spenser are drawn from *The Poetical Works of Edmund Spenser,* ed. J. C. SMITH and E. DE SELINCOURT (London: Oxford University Press, 1912).
2. The ending of book I is the first strong instance of narrative disturbance, both in the deferral of the marriage of Una and the Red Crosse knight (perfectly plausible thematically, but not fully satisfactory in terms of the romance conventions of the narration) and, more strongly, in the way in which the knight's departure returns Una to the state of mourning in which she was first found (cf. I. xii. 41.9 and I. i. 4.6). Book II ends with Guyon at his goal; but some readers have been disturbed by his ruthless destructivity: does it exemplify temperance? In *Renaissance Self-Fashioning* (Chicago: University of Chicago Press, 1980), pp. 157–92, STEPHEN GREENBLATT reviews the discussion of this issue. The questioning of what Greenblatt calls 'virtuous violence' and the ways in which 'each self-constituting act is haunted by inadequacy and loss' (p. 179), occurs throughout *The Faerie Queene.* When book III opens, Britomart's defeat of Guyon may, retrospectively, be putting Guyon in his place, undoing that overreaction to the pleasures of the flesh. Finally, the new ending to book III may serve to highlight the defects even in the happy ending originally provided. HARRY BERGER, Jr., has argued this point, noting that there is something cloyingly unnatural in an embrace that renders Scudamour and Amoret 'like two senceles stocks' (see 'Busirane and the War Between the Sexes: An Interpretation of *The Faerie Queene* III. xi–xii,' *English Literary Renaissance* 1 [1971]: 99–121).
3. THOMAS P. ROCHE, Jr., *The Kindly Flame* (Princeton: Princeton University Press, 1964), pp. 16–31. / 'The legend of Cambell and Telamond is in one allegorical sense a metaphysics of friendship and in another the symbolic statement of the metaphysics of *discordia concors*' (p. 17).
4. This quality of narrative is related to what HARRY BERGER, Jr., terms 'The Spenserian Dynamics,' *Studies in English Literature* 8 (1968): 1–18, and I am indebted to his emphasis on the need to go beyond resolution, to maintain differences. We part company on the notion of an 'evolutionary model' (p. 10) as the motor in this dynamism and in viewing the process almost entirely in psychological terms, although his idea of a horizontal vector, problematising the boundary between in and out, is one that informs my reading of Spenser throughout.
5. All citations from ROLAND BARTHES, *S/Z,* trans. RICHARD MILLER (New York: Hill & Wang, 1974 [1970]). *S/Z* presents a reading of Balzac's *Sarrasine* to demonstrate the readerly/writerly opposition. Like most structuralist literary

criticism, Barthes's *S/Z* is concerned with deconstructing the illusion that the so-called Classical text simply reproduces reality. A writerly reading aims both at revealing that the text is one that the reader produces, and at restoring to a text its primacy as language. The definition of language that Barthes employs is structuralist and is indebted to FERDINAND DE SAUSSURE's *Course in General Linguistics*, trans. WADE BASKIN (New York: McGraw Hill, 1966 [1915]), especially to two key notions: (1) that the relationship between signifier and signified, which taken together constitute the sign, is arbitrary, not referential; and (2) that what separates one signifier from another is a difference (see, e.g., p. 118, 'a segment of language can never in the final analysis be based on anything except its noncoincidence with the rest. *Arbitrary* and *differential* are two correlative qualities,' and p. 120, with its crucial statement, 'in language there are only differences . . . differences *without positive terms*.') These ideas have been the founding principles in structuralism, influencing Claude Lévi-Strauss, Jacques Derrida, and Jacques Lacan. In *S/Z*, Barthes depends on Derrida's ideas about what he calls *différance*, a term that contains at once identity and difference.

In seeing Spenser as the poet of deferred endings and the creator of characters who are paired differentials, I use this crucial Derridean concept (it is elucidated in *Of Grammatology*, trans. GAYATRI SPIVAK [Baltimore: Johns Hopkins University Press, 1974], pp. 44ff., in the course of a discussion of Saussure, and at greater length in the essay entitled 'Differance' in *Speech and Phenomena and Other Essays on Husserl's Theory of Signs*, trans. DAVID B. ALLISON [Evanston, Ill.: Northwestern University Press, 1973]: pp. 129–60). Another crucial term that Barthes and I use is the *supplement*. Again, *Of Grammatology*, esp. pp. 269ff. offers the fullest discussion. It is also briefly, but cogently, explained in DERRIDA's essay, 'Structure, Sign and Play in the Discourse of the Human Sciences,' in *The Structuralist Controversy*, ed. RICHARD MACKSEY and EUGENIO DONATO (Baltimore: Johns Hopkins Press, 1970, p. 260), as an excess that covers a lack. The chain of signifiers endlessly generates itself; in doing so it both replaces a lost center and adds to it. That lost center can be called *presence, fullness* – any term that conveys the notion of a closed and centered structure. Derridean deconstruction takes place when there is no center, or by decentering structures that claim to have centers. (Barthes, it should be added, also uses the Lacanian notion that the central lack is castration; and Barthes's economic analyses make use of Lévi-Straussian notions about exchange; these also have a place in my analysis of Spenser).

Although structuralist criticism has aimed at deconstructing certain privileged notions about representation in classical and postclassical texts, its suitability to preclassical texts is intimated by Barthes in the opening pages of his essay 'To Write: An Intransitive Verb?' (in *The Structuralist Controversy*, pp. 134–45). Before the eighteenth century, literature is frankly rhetorical, and interpretation arrives at describing the moral effect of a text by beginning with its verbal techniques. Think, for instance, of one reader of Spenser that we know about, E. K., the editor/commentator supplied for *The Shepheardes Calender*. E. K. is concerned mainly with the linguistic value of the text; he notes with pleasure rhetorical niceties; he elucidates the text by citing other texts, classical antecedents, contemporary handbooks and dictionaries. Moral meanings follow rhetorical ones. These features of Renaissance culture have been described briefly but acutely in MICHEL FOUCAULT's *The Order of Things* (New York: Random

House, Vintage Books, 1970 [1966]), pp. 17–44. Foucault describes the ways in which the entire world was seen as a text (*liber creaturae*), which could only be elucidated by reference to other texts. Knowledge was endless and endlessly verbal, and some categories that we would erect – boundaries, for instance, between fact and fiction – do not hold in the Renaissance. The features that I consider in Spenser's text, what I refer to as his undoings and deferrals, might be called deconstructions, too; indeed, as Foucault shows, the very shape of knowledge in the Renaissance is deconstructive, an endless work of supplementarity, the provision of lists that fail to exhaust the prose of the world. If words can be endlessly replaced, then none is adequate, and none is final. Ends can never be reached in the universe that Foucault describes; no category is ever filled or is entirely discrete.

In order to deconstruct the classical text, Barthes stars (cuts and splices) *Sarrasine*, breaking up the text into units that are arbitrary in length and in content; the 'naturalness' of the text, its mimetic quality, is thereby disturbed *The Faerie Queene* breaks itself; written in predetermined stanzaic units that shape each piece of narration to fit this arbitrary unit, the text cannot use its textual space to provide emphases; indeed, as PAUL ALPERS shows in *The Poetry of 'The Faerie Queene'* (Princeton: Princeton University Press, 1967), the text subordinates mimesis to rhetoric: 'The lines are organised not by the narrative events that give rise to them (and that, in another poem, they would be imitating), but by the groupings imposed by various verbal means' (p. 37).

Although Alpers correctly emphasises the dynamics of Spenserian narration, he also points to ways in which the stanza form functions almost as a static object. In book I, for instance, the stanzas are so homologous that the fifth line of many stanzas provides a pivotal paradox. No matter how variously stanzas are constructed, narration cannot be felt to progress 'naturally' when every ninth line is a cumulative alexandrine or when a (literal) margin must be traversed by the reader in order to read the following stanza. Hence, Alpers argues, *The Faerie Queene* is not a world or a set of moral judgments, but an ongoing engagement with the reader's responsiveness to the rhetorical organisation and verbal structures of the poem.

9 Praise and defence of the Queen in *The Faerie Queene*, Book V*

PAMELA JOSEPH BENSON

This essay forms part of the second of two chapters on Spenser in *The Invention of the Renaissance Woman*. The book as a whole crosses traditional scholarly boundaries between major authors and their principal texts, minor genres (paradox, dialogue) and works, and the non-literary, in order to examine a body of texts which are united in their common concern to redefine the nature of woman. The author explores how such texts – long poems, didactic treatises, prose fictions – devise common strategies for simultaneously defending womankind's capacity for political virtue and denigrating women for the exercise of such virtue. Benson argues that, for Spenser, chastity was the private expression of a virtue which expressed itself publicly as justice, and thus provided women with a capacity for action in the political as well as the domestic and moral spheres, a subject explored in Books III–V of *The Faerie Queene*. In the chapter from which this extract is taken, she sets the poem in the specific context of the tracts written in defence of Elizabeth's right to rule as a woman, and suggests that learning the vocabulary and premises of the controversy makes it possible to understand the political delicacy of Spenser's handling of the problem of female government.

Benson employs no particular branch of literary theory to argue this case, but her essay is an important contribution to cultural history, a significant piece of archival research and comparative literary analysis which forcefully argues that all texts need to be read in terms of the interests and anxieties of the cultures that produce them – recovering a history of gender representation being a case in point.

In Book III it is possible to use the language of humanist praise and defense of womankind to connect the Queen with a tradition of female

---

*Reprinted from PAMELA JOSEPH BENSON, *The Invention of the Renaissance Woman: The Challenge of Female Independence in the Literature and Thought of Italy and England* (Philadelphia: Pennsylvania University Press, 1993), pp. 291–305.

greatness and to suggest that she is superior to other women because of her 'goodly deeds,' while hinting that some other mysterious superiority inheres in her. In Book V there is no mystery about the source of her superiority, and the language of Aylmer, even Calvin, is heard; Elizabeth was chosen by God. This does not mean, however, that the poem's commitment to feminine virtue and to the defense of womankind has no place in Book V. The book gives affirmative answers to two of the central questions of the defenses of Elizabeth: 'Are there circumstances under which a woman may legitimately hold power?' and 'Can rule by a woman ever be beneficial to a nation; can a woman be a good ruler?' It bases these answers on the case developed for womankind and the feminine in Books III and IV, especially the representation of Britomart and the particular kind of lady knight she is, rather than on the exclusive principles developed by Calvin, Aylmer, and others.

The two most powerful enemies to justice in Book V are women who abuse their power: Radigund and Duessa. Each is conquered by a woman of power: Britomart and Mercilla. In each case the kind of justice represented by Artegall, the titular hero of the Book of Justice, is inadequate to the situation; he actively supports Radigund's abuse, and he wishes for revenge against Duessa. Many critics have noted Artegall needs to be supplemented or controlled by a kind of justice learned by Britomart, embodied in Isis, and exercised by Mercilla: equity.[1] As this list shows, Spenser represents equity as a feminine virtue.[2] This is not mere sentimentality or deference to tradition; it is a logical consequence of his representation of chastity and womanhood in the earlier books. Isis and Mercilla reveal that, when given the authority it deserves, equity, like chaste female sexuality, is characterised by the power to restrain masculine force and turn it to productive use. Book V is a fulfillment of Book III; it unfolds the political benefits of chastity.

By its very nature chastity is a conservative virtue, and, in practice in Book V, the realisation of the social benefits that it contributes depends on a hierarchical model of society in which the female is naturally politically inferior to the male. In the best tradition of all the defenders of womankind whose works we have examined, Spenser uses praise as a method of political containment. He represents the rejection of the Amazonian model of queenship as praiseworthy; he suggests, by means of allegory, that Elizabeth's behavior toward Mary Stuart can be read as just such a rejection of paths she herself might have chosen; thus, he simultaneously advises Elizabeth on how she ought to behave and defends his fictional world and his nation from the notion that acceptance of the legitimacy of Elizabeth's power makes an inversion of the sexual hierarchy inevitable. Only inasmuch as Elizabeth has fitted and continues to fit the pattern of the virtuous woman who is raised to authority but does not seek it, is she and will she be worthy of praise.

Radigund

Radigund represents the kind of female monarch that misogynists predicted, that Aylmer defended his nation and his text against, and that even Britomart, at times, seems to be. The queen of an artificially constructed matriarchy, she subverts male authority and strength; she is politically and sexually corrupt. She makes all the men she conquers with 'force or guile' dress in female clothes, perform feminine domestic occupations, and subsist on a diet of bread and water to keep them 'from reuenge aduenturing' (V. iv). When Artegall makes war against her, she guilefully conquers him, keeps him prisoner, and attempts to seduce him. She is a tyrannical ruler; like a Petrarchist lover, he is 'a womans slave' and 'her vassall' (V. v. 23). Britomart's defeat of Radigund definitively distinguishes the good powerful woman from the Amazon in both the political and the interpersonal spheres.

Artegall's capitulation to Radigund represents the danger of submitting to female authority without demanding that it have natural, legal, and divine sanctions. He conceives of his public relationship to a woman in private terms and literalises the situation of a Petrarchist lover. When he first attacks her city, the fighting is general; at sunset when they call a temporary truce, he is winning and accomplishing the just revenge that is his goal. When Radigund's emissary brings to him the proposal that the terms of the battle be changed to single combat between the two leaders of the forces, however, he responds to the seductive atmosphere, abandons his clear advantage, and agrees, even though her terms ought to be unappealing. They make a mockery of justice because they leave the result to fortune and because they do not address the issue that prompted Artegall to fight her in the first place: the cruel, unnatural nature of her form of government.[3]

At the end of their duel, Artegall errs in assuming that a female opponent is necessarily a special case; he applies the doctrine of equity inappropriately. He knows the evil nature of his opponent, and in the heat of the battle he feels indignation at her 'vaunting vaine'; yet, when her face is revealed, he is so touched with pity that he discards all reason and is paralyzed in front of her, as though Perseus had looked at Medusa. Unable to distinguish between women, he is willing to make exceptions of all of them on the basis of their beauty and their sex rather than on the basis of their deserts.[4] Britomart has a right to have that effect on him as she is not only a gallant knight and a good woman, but his destined bride; she demonstrates her goodness by relinquishing her authority in the course of the courtship. Radigund has no such claims to merit: she is full of unchivalric guile, and he feels no love for her.[5]

Indeed, even though Artegall does not love Radigund, troubling erotic overtones accompany the Narrator's account of the hero's assumption of female clothing and duties. A reference to Hercules stresses his erotic and unheroic aspect: when he spent time spinning and dressed as a woman he forgot war and 'onely joyed in combats of sweet loue' (V v. 24).[6] This suggests that infidelity to one's duty and to one's love are the inevitable results of political submission to a woman. The woman's power may include complete control of the male will.

This possibility is elevated to a political truism by the Narrator in the next stanza when he cites what happens to Artegall as exemplary of what happens when women are elevated above men:

> Such is the crueltie of womenkynd,
>> When they haue shaken off the shamefast band,
>> With which wise Nature did them strongly bynd,
>> T'obay the heasts of mans well ruling hand,
>> That then all rule and reason they withstand,
>> To purchase a licentious libertie.
>> But vertuous women wisely vnderstand,
>> That they were born to base humilitie,
> Vnlesse the heauens them lift to lawfull soueraintie.
>
> (V. v. 25)

Although I once argued that 'so strong is the sense of revulsion for female rule in this episode that Spenser's concession to Elizabeth's right to rule seems almost an afterthought' ('Rule Virginia' 280), I now suggest that this last line is not a 'concession,' but rather the encomiastic point toward which the entire episode has been moving: we must know Radigund to appreciate Elizabeth.

By this strategy Spenser emphasises Elizabeth's divine authority. God does at times sanction female monarchs, and the validity of their governments is recognisable from their conduct. A female governor who behaves like Radigund (or Mary Stuart) is clearly not one of the chosen. Inasmuch as Elizabeth's government does not resemble Radigund's in the oppression of men and in vanity, it can be recognised as legitimate and praiseworthy.[7] Elizabeth's strength lies in her virtue, in her legitimate claim to the throne, and in her divine elevation to it; these points are made repeatedly in the formal defenses of her sovereignty. With these lines Spenser celebrates Elizabeth's position and her virtue, and the proviso is not merely an accommodation to the times.

It is also important not to allow this passage more scope than it claims as a pronouncement on womankind. The stanza is narrowly restricted to a statement of woman's place in the political hierarchy. Although the emphasis on the necessity of divine intervention to produce a queen aligns this passage with the strictest Calvinist pronouncements on gynecocracy, there is no Calvinist disdain for women present here to make it a contradiction of the proems to cantos 2 and 4 in Book III or of the characterisation of Britomart. It is not antifeminist in moral or spiritual terms. It assumes that women can be virtuous and that they can recognise the claims of the political order. Force is not necessary to keep them in their subordinate position. They usually 'wisely understand.'

By this logic, Radigund is a necessary figure in Spenser's profeminist case as the Queen's antithesis. Given the traditional and Calvinist arguments against woman rule, Spenser must admit that there can be bad female monarchs (just as there are bad male monarchs), if his praise of female monarchy is to be taken seriously instead of being discounted as mere courtier's flattery. Radigund is a cautionary figure who demonstrates that feminine qualities misused result in misrule, and she does everything that conventional wisdom said a woman monarch would do, only she does it literally: the danger of male effeminacy is realised in the dressing of male captives in female clothing and in the expectation that they will do female domestic labor. The danger that the monarch will destabilize personal sexual hierarchies as well as political ones and will become the sexual aggressor comes true in the Amazon's passion for Artegall. But the real horror of her reign is its restriction of male freedom of movement and decision. In such a realm nothing gets done. If a woman rules by taking advantage of the weaknesses of men and by appealing to their allegiance to her private person rather than to her public person, then the result is bad government.[8]

This is, of course, a typically Amazonian way of going about ruling, and Radigund shares qualities with other Amazonian figures in *The Faerie Queene*. Sexually aggressive Malecasta, for example, is comically defeated by the prior 'effeminacy' of the male she believes she has conquered. The Amazonian figure with whom Radigund has the most in common, however, is Belphoebe, even though Spenser's descriptions of Belphoebe in Book III evoke the huntress Diana rather than the military Amazon. Like her, Radigund has made a lifetime commitment to carrying arms (unlike Britomart, who took them up for an express purpose) and, although she wears armor, her dress is a corrupt version of the nymph's feminine outfit (Hamilton ed., note to V. v. 2–3), whereas Britomart appears to be a man. Like Belphoebe and Britomart, she conquers by her suddenly seen beauty, but like Belphoebe alone she does not relinquish government to the male. They are both feminine in appearance and masculine in conduct.

Beneath these similarities there lie profound differences, of course. Belphoebe has no interest in sex, Radigund does. Belphoebe does not rule a nation; Radigund does. These differences make it possible for Belphoebe to be a positive figure while her counterpart is negative, but they do not entirely erase the feature that the characters share: their retention of the government of conquered men.[9] Both are figures of the

Petrarchist mistress. In the Belphoebe and Timias episode the Petrarchist problem of lack of sexual satisfaction is solved by Timias's willingness to maintain the relationship on a nonsexual plane, and the problems caused by the hierarchical reversal are avoided. Timias sacrifices his freedom to act in the political world that lies outside Belphoebe's woods, but in exchange he gets emotional satisfaction and spiritual advancement through love. Although a sense of loss in regard to Timias's heroic role in the poem permeates the episode, this solution is adequate in the domestic territory of Book IV, on the margins of the private and the public. An exception can be made for Belphoebe because she is virtuous and virginal and private; she does not rule a kingdom, just one man's heart. When her behavior is projected as a political principle in Book V, however, the result is tyranny and social chaos. The Petrarchist mistress is not a positive political model because, as public policy, restriction of the male sphere does not work.[10]

If Radigund's similarity to Belphoebe implies a criticism of Petrarchism as a model for female rule, then it may also imply criticism of Elizabeth's famed public application of Petrarchist principles, her method of rule, as opposed to her right to rule.[11] She is famous for having tempered the discomfort that courtiers felt at being ruled by a woman by presenting herself as their lady. That is, she offered them the opportunity to perceive themselves as Petrarchist lovers, ever longing, ever her vassals. Her wrath when they turned to other women for satisfaction is well known; the personal pain caused by this strategy is, of course, directly allegorised in the Belphoebe and Timias episodes.

The possibility that the Petrarchism of Radigund's queenship is a critique of Elizabeth's style is reinforced by Simon Shepherd's reading of Artegall as Raleigh and Radigund as Elizabeth in *Amazons and Warrior Women*; Book V urges Elizabeth to follow a more aggressively Protestant foreign policy and to free Raleigh to act: let him go and look what you will achieve, it says. It follows from this interpretation that the distinction between Radigund and Elizabeth in stanza 25 is not just a nod in the direction of praise, but rather a reminder to the Queen that she is queen by God's choice. Therefore, the episode prods her to use her men to get on with God's business (as the poet conceives of it). Her Protestant lords are her rod that will bring Europe into line. Justice is not human but divine, and she is an executor of divine justice in her international policy. She must not behave like an Amazon or Petrarchist mistress and misdirect allegiance owed to her public body to the satisfaction of her private vanity. In her relations with Artegall and in the government of her realm, Radigund is a negative exemplar of female authority; she is a 'tyrannesse,' as the poet says repeatedly. Elizabeth must follow another model – Mercilla – but first Radigund must be overpowered.

Before Britomart becomes the agent of Amazonian Radigund's defeat, the last traces of the Amazon in her are excised. She finishes the process of becoming Radigund's opposite: a good woman who does not hate men and who does not desire to retain political authority but who is fully capable and willing to wield it when necessary. She is neither an Amazon nor an Amoret. This characterisation of Britomart is only incontrovertibly established in the representation of her meeting the challenge that Artegall's submission to Radigund presents to her.[12] Spenser first shows where Britomart stands emotionally and politically before she sets out to dispute Radigund's right to Artegall. He then represents her political education at Isis Church; finally, he shows her political act in her defeat of Radigund and her reorganisation of the government.

[. . .]

When Britomart receives the news of Artegall's thralldom to Radigund, she has become as helplessly feminine as Artegall. She is at home and has retired back into a traditional dependent female role of the kind revealed in Scudamour's account of his adventure at the Temple of Venus.[13] She is not wearing armor; she considers sending someone else to look for Artegall and only daydreams of going herself (vi. 6). And she indulges in jealous daydreams. After Talus tells her that Artegall is captive of a Tyranesse, she laments not 'as women wont, but . . . / Like a wayward childe' (xiii. 9–xiv. 1). She has regressed to the girlhood she so resolutely left behind when she donned armor and set out on her quest.

[. . .]

Britomart is jealous without any external provocation, and yet her nightmare is true – Artegall, although technically faithful, has submitted himself to another woman's authority. [. . .] Britomart's [situation] is resolved when she seeks more information from Talus and is converted into a political as well as a personal virtue when she visits Isis Church; Artegall needs to wait for her to liberate him.

Spenser begins to establish the equation between Britomart's chaste faith and justice at Dolon's house. Dolon and his sons mistake her for Artegall not only because she is with Talus but because of 'many tokens plaine,' and she survives Dolon's guileful attacks because she is faithful to her mission.[14] She remains in her armor instead of relaxing and going to bed, and she resists the efforts of her own eyes to relax their vigilance, although nothing in particular has happened to put her on guard. Her conduct contrasts with her behavior at Malecasta's Castle Joyous, when her utter ignorance of guile and of her own responsibilities led her to disarm and go to bed. She is ready now as she was not then. The similarity of the situation suggests that the faith illustrated here is an aspect of the chastity illustrated there.

The role of faith in her behavior is emphasised by the poet's contrast of her with Saint Peter. She reproaches her eyes three times, stays awake, and 'by God's grace, and her good heedinesse, she was preserued' (V. vi. 34). Her personal faith to her beloved takes on the aura of religious faith. Because of it, she conquers guile quite easily and arrives at Isis Church, where she encounters equity. The only transition between the end of the bridge where she fights Dolon's sons and the entry to Isis Church is the Narrator's paean to justice. It seems that her faithful victory over guile propels her into the church, whereas Artegall's unfaithful defeat by guile propels him into Radigund's dungeon.

At the church, the identification of Britomart's chastity with faith takes on its full political significance. The statement that the female goddess Isis figures equity (V. vii. 3) sets into motion the Platonic principle that forms the basis for Sir Thomas Elyot's proof of women's capacity for government: faith is the private face of equity; equity is the essence of justice and good government; therefore, women's capacity for faith makes them capable of justice and good government. Because chastity is a form of faith and faith a form of equity, Britomart's demonstration of chastity in Book III, friendship in Book IV, and justice in Book V, are all manifestations of the same virtue. This Platonic notion is an important part of Spenser's paradoxical defense of women and of gynecocracy because it values the feminine over the masculine. Woman does not ape masculinity in order to play a political role; she draws on a virtue that is inherent in her own sex and that she frequently demonstrates in private life.

Britomart's dream and the priest's interpretation of it reveal the Platonic lesson. In it, her personal sexual mission and her political function merge. Just as her initiations into sexuality and social relations were completed at the House of Busyrane and in hearing of the Temple of Venus, her initiation into politics is completed here; her prior knowledge of sexuality is applied to politics.[15] In the Garden of Adonis, the feminine tames male aggression into productive sexual activity; here Isis's rod directs the aggression of war to peaceful ends.[16] The statue of the goddess represents abstract virtue and exists in a realm outside time; her crocodile can always sleep. Britomart and her descendent Elizabeth represent virtue in this fallen world where force is necessary; they need to have relations with the savage crocodile, but, under feminine control, male aggression and sexual energy are productive of peace. The encounter between Britomart and the crocodile figures the union between feminine equity and masculine rough justice that has produced the (Protestant) lion of England that brings peace when it fights: '[he] shortly did all other beasts subdew' (viii. 16). The pacific predictions of this dream come true at the end of the book when Artegall fights wars to liberate a number of monarchies, all headed by female monarchs.[17] Just war liberated by chastity-equity brings peace.

Britomart's liberation of Artegall from Radigund puts the Amazonian alternative to rest. The Amazon is conquered by the woman who fights for the good of her family and nation. Britomart's victory is marked by her lack of mercy toward the woman who humiliated Artegall and her great mercy to everyone else – the citizens of Radigund's state and Artegall himself. She cuts off Radigund's head, prevents Talus from killing any more people than he already has, and supplies Artegall with masculine attire and a lecture on the transience of fleshly force when it is not supported by virtue.[18] His virtue restored, Artegall goes on his way, no longer tempted out of his path by pity for female evildoers.

Britomart's restoration of male sovereignty undoes Artegall's misplaced equity.

> . . . she there as Princess rained,
> And changing all that forme of common weale,
> The liberty of women did repeale,
> Which they had long vsurpt; and them restoring
> To mens subiection, did true Iustice deale:
> That they as a Goddesse her adoring,
> Her wisedome did admire, and hearkned to her loring.
>
> (V. vii. 42)

The people's joy at their return to patriarchal order asserts the rightness of Britomart's action.

The Narrator's denomination of the restoration of hierarchy as true justice recalls his statement in the proem to the canto

> For th'heuens themselues . . .
> . . . are rul'd by righteous lore
> Of highest loue, who doth true iustice deale
> To his inferiour Gods, and euermore
> Therewith containes his heauenly Common-weale:
> The skill whereof to Princes hearts he doth reueale.
>
> (V. vii. I)

Britomart is a reigning princess, and God has revealed the secret of government to her. She is an appropriate vehicle for this revelation because of her virtue. Like Elyot's Zenobia, she takes power when a man is lacking, but in this case the appropriate man is ready to hand and so, illuminated by the wisdom of God, she relinquishes power and withdraws into private life.

Britomart's restoration of patriarchy is not a betrayal of her self-reliant conduct in the earlier books, because she had never behaved in a way that ought to lead one to believe that she would sponsor a matriarchy. [. . .] Britomart's chastity leads directly to the belief in male-headed hierarchies because it is a form of justice.[. . .]

The stern language that Spenser attributes to Britomart here and to his Narrator in the earlier passage asserting the justice of male rule with only divinely sanctioned exceptions (V. v. 25) once again recalls Aylmer. The relationship of the entire episode and this stanza in particular to the contemporary English controversy about rule by women was expertly explicated by James Phillips in his pair of articles on Spenser's attitude toward female rulers. Phillips concludes:

> Because she demonstrates her ability to administer justice by forcing women into the 'base humilitie' to which they were born under 'mans well ruling hand,' Britomart clearly identifies herself as one of those exceptional women, instruments of divine justice, whom the heavens 'lift to lawfull soueraintie.' The episode of Radigund and Britomart, therefore, not only exemplifies Spenser's own expressed theory of gynecocracy, but also reaffirms our conviction that his position is precisely that of the moderate Calvinists. For it is with reference to the latter that we can most consistently explain his selection of a woman to overthrow the unnatural institution of female government.
>
> ('Woman' 233–4)

On the one hand, Britomart uses her sovereignty to divest herself of power, and her action shows that proven excellence in women – even her own – does not justify reversing the natural hierarchy of the sexes; on the other hand Britomart's very capacity to overthrow Radigund and reorganise the government demonstrates the natural capacity of womankind for office, should they be called. Spenser's stress on this latter quality continues to differentiate his approach from that of the 'moderate Calvinists,' even while he espouses the same political doctrine. His belief that chastity has a real connection to equity explains his choice of Britomart to depose Radigund better than the more cynical motives of a 'moderate Protestant' desirous of office. There is a philosophical spine to his work that is missing from the more openly opportunistic official works.

Mercilla

Mercilla's court is a fitting place to end this discussion of Spenser's defense of womankind, the feminine, and his queen because the trial of Duessa is an allegory of the legal defeat of Mary Stuart, the Catholic rival whose claim on the English throne kept alive the need to defend Elizabeth against criticism of gynecocracy for so many years after her accession. Once Mary was dead (1587), the pressing need to use biblical, legal, and historical grounds to distinguish Elizabeth from the other female claimant to the throne was greatly diminished.[19] As a result, Spenser could celebrate the capacities of womankind without appearing to support the enemy in the story of Britomart; he could celebrate the Queen's extraordinary status without becoming embroiled in the detailed evidence that proved her superiority in the encomiastic proems; and in the story of Radigund he could use Mary as a model of a kind of queenship that the Queen must always take care to renounce. The story of Mercilla is the exemplary life that completes the defense of womankind in *The Faerie Queene*. Her conduct of the trial of Duessa represents the positive alternative to the rule of Radigund; it shows how a good female ruler chosen by God disciplines her passions and wisely acts in the interests of her people.

The trial of Duessa presents the ceremonial judgment of the Amazonian model of female independence by a queen who displays none of its properties. Although she is not dressed as an Amazon, Duessa exemplifies the excesses of the Amazonian mode. She seduces Blandamour and Paridell, her male supporters, and corrupts them by offering them shadowy rewards (V. ix. 41); she does not have a legitimate claim to the throne that she attempts to acquire; she is not favored by God; and she claims her sex puts her outside the law. By contrast, Mercilla is 'a loiall Prince'; she has God on her side and is faithful to his law (V. ix. 42). She is 'the heyre of ancient kings' (V. ix. 29) and exercises her legitimate power wisely; she is not a tyrannical Amazon.

Mercilla's court benefits from her feminine sex; it is not perverted by it as Malecasta's and Radigund's (and Mary Stuart's) are. It is a commonplace of criticism of this episode that, in bringing Duessa to public trial and passing judgment on her, Mercilla enforces the principle of equity, as Elizabeth did in the case of Mary.[20] She thus brings into the open and exemplifies the special political benefits of feminine virtue that the poem has been suggesting from the moment it defined chastity as an active virtue, as the capacity for justice is the supreme public expression of private virtue.

Yet, as her name suggests, Mercilla goes beyond the cardinal virtues.[21] Until this point, we have seen political Elizabeth through the prism of Britomart, and Britomart, as the poet told us in the Proem to Book III, is not one of the mirrors of the Queen. She must struggle to abolish Amazonian tendencies from herself, and she feels no mercy for her mirroring opponent; she does not think or feel beyond her assertion that Radigund is not a special case. Mercilla, the ideal representative of the alternate feminine order in power, simultaneously enforces justice and feels 'the wretched plight' of her whom she must judge, unlike Artegall, who is consumed by his 'zeale of Iustice' (V. ix. 49). Although this capacity for mercy cannot actively intervene in the case of Duessa, it is nonetheless an all-important characteristic because it raises Mercilla's feminine Christian justice above masculine zeal and vengeance. Her mercy expresses itself in her tears, in her sheltering of Duessa from 'just vengeance' (V. ix. 50), in the honor she allows to Duessa's corpse, and in her conduct of cases that her subjects bring to her.

The aggressive force that Spenser associates with masculine women and with men is absent from Mercilla. The rusty sword that lies at her feet in the initial description of her (V. ix. 30) is an emblem of the benefits of feminine control of government. A support of order, but not its source nor its governing principle, it now lies at rest, but it dismays the world when she draws it. Like Britomart's lance and sword. Elizabeth's white rod, the boar's tusk, and Isis's crocodile, the masculine sword, pressed into service by the feminine ruler, brings about peace.[22] In this scene, the woman ruler is the ideal ruler because her feminine qualities are what the world needs.

Because the account of Mercilla does not explicitly distinguish the rightful queen from the wrongful one on the Calvinist grounds that the former was raised by God from her natural inferior status and the latter was not (as the other moments of celebration of Elizabeth discussed in this chapter do), the defensive tone, omnipresent elsewhere, is absent here. Yet, this encomiastic representation of the Queen is an ideal, of course, and like all encomia, it serves an advisory purpose.[23] By aligning the conflict between the Amazonian and the feminine models of queenship with the conflict between Catholic and Protestant theology and politics, the narrative of Mercilla's judgment of Duessa associates the triumph of Protestantism with the defeat of autocratic female rule. Because Mercilla's treatment of Duessa is exemplary of her behavior at all times, if Elizabeth is to be Mercilla, she must imitate herself and continue her past course of action; she must not lapse into Amazonian queenship now that the need to defend herself against her Amazon rival is past.

Critics of *The Faerie Queene* frequently argue about where the allegorical core of Book V lies. Certainly, if Spenser's development of the notion of the nature of woman is taken seriously, there can be no doubt. Important as Isis Church is to Britomart's and the reader's understanding of the relationship between chastity and equity, it is Mercilla who brings the long and complex sequence to a close. In her, the positive personal, social, and political value of the feminine – which has been so carefully constructed throughout Books III, IV, and V, in such diverse episodes as the Garden of Adonis, the encounter with Malecasta, and the meeting with Dolon, to name but a few – receives its final and most showy exposition. Mercilla is the fullest fulfillment of the capacities of womankind.

Notes

1. For extensive treatments of equity, see APTEKAR 54–7; PHILLIPS, 'Renaissance'; KNIGHT; KERMODE 49–59.
2. Spenser was not alone in his association of equity with the feminine. See JORDAN, *Renaissance Feminism*, for a discussion of equity in English law and thought and of 'Sidney's concern for equity as the feminine complement to justice.' She notes that in Book V equity is 'gendered as feminine and attributed especially to female magistrates' (236). O'CONNELL also stresses the 'essentially feminine quality of equity' (145).
3. From Radigund's point of view her suggestion that one-to-one combat be substituted for general battle is a wise strategy; on her own she is more likely to avenge Artegall's partial victory and save her people. Nothing in the presentation of the scene encourages us to accept her point of view, however. Her mind is troubled, she seeks revenge, and her terms are unchivalric.
4. SUSANNE WOODS discovers that 'Artegall becomes Britomart's vassal of his own free will. He becomes Radigund's slave because of her improper use of female beauty to effect political tyranny. She does not inspire with her beauty as do Britomart, the Faerie Queene, and Queen Elizabeth; she uses it to enervate her opponent' (152).
5. See BENDER for a comparison of the two scenes.
6. See APTEKAR, chapter 11, on the eroticism of Artegall's relationship with Radigund.
7. NORTHROP suggests that God's raising of Elizabeth is an example of equity. 'Spenser's contribution to the gynaecocratic controversy was to see the exceptions created by God as an instance of equity, in which the law of men's rule is put aside so that the principle of the rule of the superior will be followed by conferring sovereignty on the divinely endowed woman' (277–8).
8. I do not intend this interpretation to replace the readings of the episode as an allegory of Elizabeth's conflict with Mary Stuart begun by NEILL, but rather to show that a more general allegory of the dangers of gynecocracy is also present. See O'CONNELL for an excellent recent interpretation of the episode as an allegorisation of Elizabeth's relationship with Mary (140ff.). Also see NORBROOK (138).
9. O'CONNELL notes the similarity of Radigund, Belphoebe, and Britomart, and suggests that they are connected with 'the propaganda battle waged by supporters of Elizabeth and of Mary,' but distinguishes Radigund from the others because only 'she psychologically emasculates the men she encounters,' as did Mary (141–2).
10. See WOODS for a reading of this episode as representing Petrarchism favorably.
11. BOWMAN comes to a similar conclusion from a very different starting point. She argues that *Britomart* employs the same strategies to 'ease Artegall's fears of her power' that the Queen used 'to pacify her possibly anxious male courtiers'; yet she concludes that 'when Britomart kills her [Radigund],' she rejects 'the model of Elizabeth's court' (523–4).
12. For a recent reading of this episode in psychological terms, see BOWMAN, who argues that Britomart wants to 'avoid instilling fear in the man she loves . . . Inverting the Amazonian society enables her to respond to this dilemma' (512). Bowman finds evidence for this reading in the *Furioso*.

13. Although Spenser never says that she is at home and never gives the castle in which she waits any of the warm domestic coloring of her home in Book III, he does refer to 'her bed.'
14. PHILLIPS sees the Dolon episode as essential to 'the concept of equity exemplified in the central cantos' but he lays stress on Britomart's actions themselves and not the inner disposition they reveal. It exemplifies 'the capacity to administer justice, even Justice Absolute, in a woman who will be the exception to the law against the woman ruler' ('Renaissance Concepts' 113).
15. ROCHE has shown that this episode is connected with the Busyrane episode by Busiris, who is associated with Osiris (*Kindly* 81). APTEKAR demonstrates the episode's closeness to emblems of marriage (99–107). FLETCHER suggests that Britomart is initiated into her womanhood (268).
16. KATHLEEN WILLIAMS explored the relationship of Venus's Temple and Isis's (175).
17. '[T]he dream image of sexual *discordia concors* makes equity and the common law a fused whole of British justice' (O'CONNELL 145).
18. In Book III, Spenser introduces the notion that Britomart is indifferent to feminine beauty when she does not follow Florimell.
19. NORTHROP distinguishes 'two controversies that involved the defence of Elizabeth': 'the right of women to rule' and 'the justice of Elizabeth's actions as ruler' (277–8). Because it is couched in terms of defense, his discussion of the latter provides a useful supplement to my argument.
20. See O'CONNELL for details of the invocation of 'equitable procedure . . . in the unusual (and not notably merciful) trial of the Queen of Scots' (146); KNIGHT (286) and GRAZIANI (379) also note the historical invocation of the principle of equity.
21. See STUMP for the case for the importance of distinguishing mercy from equity in this scene (95–6). PHILLIPS ('Renaissance Concepts') sees this episode as belonging to the exposition of mercy, not equity. For a negative evaluation of Spenser's success in representing mercy, see O'CONNELL (153–4).
22. CHENEY offers a sensitive analysis of the precarious balance of action and inaction in Mercilla (166–7).
23. GOLDBERG offers an important corrective to the general tendency to find bland approval of the Queen's policies in this part of the poem. He stresses the contradiction and strain present in the Bonfont/Malfont episode and the trial of Duessa. Both raise questions about Spenser's relation to 'the discourse of power,' and the trial of Duessa lays bare the premises upon which sovereign power operates ('Poet's' 88).

Notes

APTEKAR, JANE. *Icons of Justice: Iconography and Thematic Imagery in Book V of* The Faerie Queene. New York: Columbia University Press, 1969.
BENDER, JOHN B. *Spenser and Literary Pictorialism*. Princeton: Princeton University Press, 1972.

BENSON, PAMELA JOSEPH. 'Rule Virginia: Protestant Theories of Female Regiment in *The Faerie Queene.' English Literary Renaissance* 15 (1985): 277–92.

BOWMAN, MARY R. ' "she there as Princess rained": Spenser's Figure of Elizabeth.' *Renaissance Quarterly* 43 (1990): 509–28.

CHENEY, DONALD. *Spenser's Image of Nature: Wild Man and Shepherd in* The Faerie Queene. New Haven: Yale University Press, 1966.

FLETCHER, ANGUS. *The Prophetic Moment: An Essay on Spenser.* Chicago: University of Chicago Press, 1971.

GOLDBERG, JONATHAN. 'The Poet's Authority: Spenser, Jonson, and James VI and I.' *Genre* 15 (1982): 81–99.

GRAZIANI, RENÉ. 'Elizabeth at Isis Church.' *PMLA* 79 (1964): 376–89.

JORDAN, CONSTANCE. *Renaissance Feminism: Literary Texts and Political Models.* Ithaca, NY: Cornell University Press, 1990.

KERMODE, FRANK. *Shakespeare, Spenser, Donne.* New York: Viking, 1971.

KNIGHT, W. NICHOLAS. 'The Narrative Unity of Book V of *The Faerie Queene*: "That Part of Justice Which Is Equity." ' *Review of English Studies* 21 (1970): 267–94.

NEILL, KERBY. 'Spenser on the Regiment of Women: A Note on *The Faerie Queene*, V, v, 25.' *Studies in Philology* 34 (1937): 134–7.

NORBROOK, DAVID. *Poetry and Politics in the English Renaissance.* London: Routledge & Kegan Paul, 1984.

NORTHROP, DOUGLAS A. 'Spenser's Defense of Elizabeth.' *University of Toronto Quarterly* 38 (1969): 277–94.

O'CONNELL, MICHAEL. *Mirror and Veil: The Historical Dimension of Spenser's Faerie Queene.* Chapel Hill: University of North Carolina Press, 1977.

PHILLIPS, JAMES E. 'Renaissance Concepts of Justice and the Structure of *The Faerie Queene*, Book V.' *Huntington Library Quarterly* 33 (1970): 103–20.

——. 'The Woman Ruler in Spenser's *Faerie Queene.' Huntington Library Quarterly* 5 (1941): 211–34.

ROCHE, THOMAS P., Jr. *The Kindly Flame: A Study of the Third and Fourth Books of Spenser's* The Faerie Queene. Princeton: Princeton University Press, 1964.

SHEPHERD, SIMON. *Amazons and Warrior Women: Varieties of Feminism in Seventeenth-Century Drama.* New York: St. Martin's Press, 1981.

SPENSER, EDMUND. *The Faerie Queene.* Ed. A. C. HAMILTON. Annotated English Poets Series. 1977. Rpt. London and New York: Longman, 1980.

STUMP, DONALD V. 'Isis versus Mercilla: The Allegorical Shrines in Spenser's Legend of Justice.' *Spenser Studies* 3 (1982): 87–98.

WILLIAMS, KATHLEEN. *Spenser's* The Faerie Queene: *The World of Glass.* Berkeley and Los Angeles: University of California Press, 1966.

WOODS, SUSANNE. 'Spenser and the Problem of Women's Rule.' *Huntington Library Quarterly* 48 (1985): 140–58.

10 The 'sacred hunger of ambitious minds': Spenser's savage religion*

ANDREW HADFIELD

This essay was first published as part of a collection designed to stress the importance of religion in early modern British culture, an area neglected by scholars – particularly New Historicists, despite the lead given by Stephen Greenblatt in *Renaissance Self-Fashioning* (see above, pp. 126–8). I wanted to show that despite the worth of many analyses of Spenser's religious beliefs, too many scholars had neglected to consider the relevance of his Irish experience to his conception of religion and the need to read the ongoing discussion of religion and politics in *The Faerie Queene* against the comments in the prose dialogue, *A View of the Present State of Ireland*. Ireland is traditionally only thought to be relevant to the later sections of the poem; I wanted to show that in the last three books which made up the second edition, many incidents specifically refer back to earlier events and invite the reader to go back and reformulate his or her judgements, broadening out an English context into an Irish one. Ireland, for Spenser, does not simply problematise certain relationships and make them more complex (although it does have that effect); 'it also exists as the site of potential chaos where Englishness and its attendant certainties (truth) are turned against themselves in an orgy of violence, never to be redeemed'.

The essay clearly owes a great deal to many contemporary theories of literature – deconstructionist, Marxist, New Historicist, cultural materialist – but in its stress upon the crucial role of the reader and Spenser himself as a rereader of his own poetic project, perhaps owes its greatest intellectual debt to American reader-response theory, especially the work of Stanley Fish.

Discussions of Spenser's religious affiliation usually try to determine the

*First published in Donna B. Hamilton and Richard Strier, eds, *Religion, Literature, and Politics in Post-Reformation England, 1540–1688* (Cambridge: Cambridge University Press, 1996), pp. 27–45.

177

precise nature of his faith from a scrupulous reading of his poetry. Critics have generally sifted through the evidence for doctrinal clues and lined these up against other contemporary writings to decide which label fitted Spenser best: Calvinist, Puritan, Anglican or Protestant.[1] But Spenser's religious views cannot be studied in isolation from other beliefs he might have held, or discourses he might have used, because for Spenser, an English exile in Ireland from (at least) 1580 until his death, there could be no easy separation of religious views and political position.[2] In Ireland in the last decades of the sixteenth century considerations of personal religious persuasion had to be perceived in the light of other forces determining cultural and national identity; Spenser was forced to define himself as an English protestant in order to distinguish himself from the Irish papists.[3]

Generally critics of the *Faerie Queene* have tried to circumscribe the influence of Spenser's Irish experience to the last three books, choosing to overlook the stubborn fact that the first edition of the poem did not appear in print until 1590, by which time Spenser had been resident in Ireland for ten years. Book I, for example, has usually been straightforwardly decoded by commentators from the early seventeenth century to the present day without reference to Ireland.[4] Una, the representation of religious truth, becomes separated from the Red-Cross Knight, who is later discovered to be Saint George, by the wiles of the catholic, Archimago; the primitive protestant church of England has become corrupted by catholic duplicity. The book narrates a series of adventures which culminate in the Red-Cross Knight and Una being re-united and betrothed after the Knight has killed the Satanic dragon.[5] It ends with the Knight promising to return after having served the Faerie Queene for six years, a number which corresponds to the days of the creation, and also to the length of the reign of Mary and Philip.[6] The book is said to look forwards to the religious triumphs of Elizabeth's reign, as England throws off its shackles.

But within Book I there is a troubling episode where Una is rescued from the Saracen knight, Sansloy, by a troop of fauns and satyrs who have been dancing in the wood. This 'rude, misshappen, monstrous rablement' (8) take her to the wood-god, Sylvanus, and proceed to worship her as a deity who exceeds their current religious knowledge and forms of representation. Therefore, she throws their notion of the sacred into crisis and inaugurates a whole new series of religious practices. Whilst 'the woodborne people fall before her flat, / And worship her as Goddesse of the wood', Sylvanus tries to figure her in terms of his previous conception of beauty. Sometimes he sees her as Venus ('But Venus never had so sober mood'), sometimes as Diana ('But misseth her bow, and shaftes, and buskins to her knee') (16); but eventually he comes to see in her a reminder of his dead love, Cyparisse, who pined away after Sylvanus accidentally shot his beloved hind (17).[7] The female wood-nymphs 'Flocke all about to see her lovely face: / But when they vewed have her heavenly grace, / They envie her in their malitious mind, / And fly away for feare of fowle disgrace'; the male satyrs, in contrast, reject their womenfolk and gaze, seeing everything that is beautiful as a part of her (18); eventually they transform her into an idol, and when she refuses that dubious honour they worship her ass, possibly recalling the exiled Israelites' idolatry in Exodus 32. Una becomes rather distressed at this unwelcome attention and tries to teach them more wholesome doctrine, but they remain transfixed with visual images:

> During which time her gentle wit she plyes,
> To teach them truth, which, worshipt her in vaine,
> And made her th'Image of Idolatryes;
> But when their bootlesse zeale she did restraine
> From her own worship, they her Asse would worship fayn.
>
> (I.vi.19)

Eventually, when the satyrs leave her alone, Una is rescued by Sir Satyrane (see below, pp. 189–90).

Usually the satyrs have been interpreted as representatives of a form of 'natural', animistic religion, ignorant primitive Christians, or even the Jews, Egyptians, Greeks and Romans.[8] But the satyrs are referred to as 'The salvage nation' (11), a description which links them to the series of representations of savages in Books V and VI.[9] This would suggest that the question of the identity of the satyrs ought to be read not simply in terms of the religious allegory of Book I, but also as part of the wider themes and debates running throughout the whole narrative of the unfinished poem. The representation of the satyrs early on within the epic, in a book which allegorises the legend of holiness, provocatively forces the reader to recognise that theological distinctions cannot be made without reference to questions of social being.

One of the most striking aspects of the verses detailing the reactions of 'the salvage nation' to Una is the diversity of their responses and attempt to understand Una in terms of their own experience of sacred images, a division noted in Una's fear of 'commit[ing] / Her single person to their barbarous truth' (12). She represents the fundamental indivisibility of a monolithic conception of religious 'truth', which their reactions split up into a variety of representations.

The story raises an important question about the nature of 'truth' and its representation: as many protestants who wished to refute what they saw as perverse and diabolic Christian thinking by an appeal to the literal 'truth' of the scriptures often had to recognise, 'truth' had to be represented in order to be expressed which meant that it had to be manifested as something which it was not, that is, in terms of figurative language. Una herself is a metaphorical representation of 'truth' within the overall pattern of the allegory. She has to be defined against a representation of falsehood, Duessa, her imitation. Furthermore, in being betrothed to the Red-Cross Knight, who is Saint George, she is a specifically English representation of 'truth' within a particular national language, English. In other words, she already exists as a representation herself within a series of differential signs and cannot possibly stand outside a system that is already in use. Readers of *The Faerie Queene* cannot securely assume that their understanding of their own religious representations and images avoids the misreadings, confusions and contradictions of 'the salvage nation's' inability to read something beyond their own system of representation. Admittedly, the separation of the Red-Cross Knight and Una can be read as a glaring example of dramatic irony, where the reader knows far more than the characters acting out the story; however, incidents like Una's encounter with 'the salvage nation' problematise this relationship of reader and text, putting the over-confident reader back to the same level of awareness as the hapless knight.

In this essay I want to demonstrate that the developing project of *The Faerie Queene* demands that not only can Book I not be read in isolation from the rest of the poem, but that its apparent assumption of a self-sufficient *Englishness* is significantly qualified in later books. Spenser's Irish experience envelops all aspects of his work, from his relationship with the Queen, his political pronouncements, to the very language of his epic poem. 'Savage' and sacred' are perhaps the foundational puns which link Spenser's poetry and prose, simultaneously expressing the hope of salvation and religious purity, and the fear of disintegration and damnation. Whilst Spenser's work deals with the question of transformation – salvaging what has been lost – such puns point in two directions at once, articulating the horror that what has to be transformed might well be precisely that which resists transformation. For Spenser, Ireland does more than problematise the relationship between religion and politics, and poetry and prose: it also exists as the site of potential chaos where Englishness and its attendant certainties (truth) are turned against themselves in an orgy of violence, never to be redeemed. In a sense, Ireland inhabited the English Spenser used, turning ('troping') the literal into the pun, threatening to collapse clear and distinct ideas and make the language of politics become the rhetoric of apocalyptic destruction.

In the second edition of *The Faerie Queene*, Spenser carefully linked representations and figures via deliberate verbal echoes, opening out the contexts of the poem and signalling different modes of discourse within which such images should now be read. Artegall, the Knight of Justice, is told at the start of Book V that his ultimate goal is to rescue

Irena, who is being held captive by the tyrant, Grantorto. In canto xi
Sir Sergis reminds Artegall of his promise 'To meete her at the salvage
Ilands side' (39), and in canto xii he duly crosses the sea and defeats
the giant. As has been frequently noted, Irena is clearly supposed to rule
Ireland and the fact that Artegall's quest should end there demonstrates
that a direct link is made between the articulation of an abstract concept
of justice and the establishment of Elizabethan rule in Ireland.[10]

The use of the term, 'the salvage Island', forces the reader to reread
incidents in the narrative so that their significance in the light of later
developments be considered; in other words, we are asked to go back,
reconsider and qualify our earlier judgements.[11] The reader is therefore
invited to regard the representation of Ireland in terms of images of the
savage and savagery which have preceded Book V (these include
'the wilde and salvage man' who tries to rape Amoret in IV.iv, Sir Satyrane
and Artegall himself), as well as in terms of the images which make up
a substantial part of Book VI (the Salvage man, the salvage nation and
the brigands who destroy the pastoral idyll).

This also means that the behaviour of 'the salvage nation' should be
read in conjunction with the behaviour of the inhabitants of 'the salvage
island'. These inhabitants only really appear in one verse, submitting
themselves to Irena with great gusto when Artegall finally cuts off
Grantorto's head:

> Which when the people round about him saw,
> They shouted al for joy of his successe,
> Glad to be quit from that proud Tyrants awe,
> Which with strong powre did them long time oppresse;
> And running all with greedie joyfulnesse
> To faire *Irena*, at her feet did fall,
> And her adored with due humblenesse,
> As their true Liege and Princesse naturall;
> And eke her champions glorie sounded over all.
>
> (V.xii.24)

Their submission to Irena – the legitimate English ruler of Ireland, who
stands as a representative of Gloriana (Elizabeth) – mirrors the worship
of Una by 'the salvage nation'.[12] Both incidents show savages recognising
a superior power which they depend on, but, whereas 'the salvage
nation' do not fully comprehend what it is they worship, the inhabitants
of 'the salvage island' are clearly making the right choice for the right
reasons in rejecting tyranny for legitimate authority. These savages are
clearly salvaged.

However, this moment of sovereign/colonial success is made
problematic in at least two ways. Firstly, Irena's position is undermined

by the recall of Artegall to the Faerie Court before he has been able to
use his sidekick, the iron-man, Talus, to root out elements hostile
to English rule and thoroughly reform 'the ragged common-weale' (26).[13]
Secondly, the 'savage' Irish are represented as if they had been loyal all
along and had only been led astray by the usurping force of the wicked
tyrant, Grantorto. In effect, Book V splits the Irish into two: there are
these obedient, savage Irish who worship Irena as a goddess; and there
are those like Malengin, the figure of guile, who is represented wearing
the Irish mantle in the same way that Irenius described the native Irish
in Spenser's prose tract, *A View of the Present State of Ireland*.[14] He is
slaughtered by Talus and dismembered so ferociously that his corpse
disappears (V.ix.19).[15] The premature recall of Artegall means that Talus
cannot extirpate such dangerous rebels who live on to threaten the safety
of English rule in Ireland and it remains a kingdom of divided loyalties.[16]

By the end of Book V the reader can be in no doubt that, as the narrative
of *The Faerie Queene* progresses, things which probably appeared clear
and distinct at the start of the poem, become inextricably interlinked.
Canto xii begins with a crucially important pun which forms an explicit
link between the desire for illicit territorial gain and the perversion of
religion:

> O sacred hunger of ambitious mindes,
> And impotent desire of men to raine,
> Whom neither dread of God, that devils bindes,
> Nor lawes of men, that common weales containe,
> Nor bands of nature, that wilde beastes restraine,
> Can keepe from outrage, and from doing wrong,
> Where they may hope a kingdome to obtaine.
> No faith so firme, no trust can be so strong,
> No love so lasting then, that may enduren long.
>
> (V.xii.1)

'Sacred' can mean both 'proceeding from God' – and, hence, a taboo not
to be violated – but also 'accursed'. The enterprise of Grantorto (literally,
'great wrong' from the Italian) is thus a supposedly religious one in its
aim of restoring catholicism to Ireland; for a protestant audience it is
therefore an accursed threat to true religion in its desire to replace the
Christian faith with that of the AntiChrist and is symptomatic of the Fall
itself.[17] Grantorto can be seen to represent the attempt of the Spanish
monarchy and papal authorities to help the Irish overthrow English rule
in Ireland: specifically, as Artegall is associated with Spenser's erstwhile
patron, Arthur, Lord Grey de Wilton, who was Lord Deputy from 1580
to 1582, the second Desmond Rebellion (1579–83), during which Spenser
may have witnessed the notorious massacre at Smerwick (1580) and, on

another occasion, the Irish forces marched into battle behind the papal banner.[18] His claim to Ireland is allegorised as totally spurious and without foundation and the opening verse places him beyond the laws of God, men and nature.[19]

The conflict between truth and falsehood moves out onto a wider stage. Book I can be seen as wholly concerned with a national issue: the marriage of Una (true religion) to the Red-Cross Knight (Saint George, a changeling in Faerieland, who is the offspring of 'ancient race / Of *Saxon* kings' (I.xi.65)) achieved in the face of an international catholic threat which claims to go beyond the bounds of sovereign integrity.[20] In Book V, Artegall (like the Red-Cross Knight, a changeling, a Briton, Arthur's half-brother (III.iii.26–7)) also has to face an international catholic threat in the form of Grantorto. But the nature of the conflict has altered, not least because Artegall has to cross the sea to Ireland.[21]

We have moved from an explicitly religious allegory concerned to establish the legitimacy of English Christianity to a consideration of religion as it applies to practical conceptions of justice in a world of contemporary political struggles.[22] The Proem to Book V acknowledges that the world has decayed from the Golden Age when 'simple Truth did rayne, and was of all admyred' (V, Proem, 3) to a Stony Age where such notions of truth have been turned upside down, 'vertue . . . Is now cald vice . . . Right now is wrong, and wrong that was is right, / As all things else in time are chaunged quight' (V, Proem, 4). The reader is informed that the distinction between truth and falsehood in the book of justice involves a difficult and delicate balancing act: the ancient principles of justice have to be isolated and applied to a world in which it is virtually impossible to separate truth and falsehood. In order to apply such principles and make them relevant they will have to be translated from their original pristine meanings into the language of duplicity with the attendant risk that in the process they will actually become the opposite of what they were meant to be, hence the frequent difficulty in the book of separating the means of implementing justice from what it is supposed to overcome.[23] The very nature of Artegall's quest involves the possibility that he will be unable to succeed because it will be too difficult to distinguish between what he is supposed to uphold and what he has to reject and, indeed, it is the Faerie Queene herself who aborts the project, the centre of power actually serving to undermine itself. The problem of difficulty has become more grave: it is no longer a question of the reader *misreading* and being corrected, but a suggestion that perhaps there is no path through the mass of details to the truth.

The book ends with Artegall and Talus crossing back over the sea to what is obviously England, having had to abandon the object of the quest, Irena, to an incompletely reformed commonwealth. There, they are attacked by two monstrous hags, Envy and Detraction, who proceed to

slander their policies, claiming that they had been unmercifully cruel and
that Grantorto had been treacherously put to death (V.xii.40).[24]
Eventually they set the Blatant Beast, a monster with a multitude of
tongues, on to them, and all three repeat a mass of vicious falsehoods.

Envy and retraction clearly represent the slander of English policy in
Ireland. But that is not all, as the allegory moves outwards onto its
wider stage, linking the religious representations of Book I with the
political message of Book V. In Book VI, the Blatant Beast expands in
significance, becoming the object of Sir Calidore's quest and, ultimately,
the antithesis of the Knight of Courtesy's failed attempt to establish a
correspondence between words and things: in other words, a
representation of untruth, like the villains of Book I, Duessa and
Archimago.[25] A narrative link between Books V and VI occurs in the first
canto when Calidore comes across Artegall returning to the Faerie Court
and enquires if he has seen the Blatant Beast. Artegall replies that he has
seen the 'Monster bred of hellishe race' since he left the 'salvage Island'
(VI.i.7–8). The ending of Book V retrospectively affirms that, like Book I,
it is also centrally concerned with the question of truth as the sequence
of images of specifically catholic untruth become absorbed into one which
threatens language, the very means of representation itself.

When Una was rescued from the 'lawlesse lust' of Sansloy by 'the
salvage nation' in Book I, her fear was described by the narrator in
terms of two antithetical beasts competing for her:

> She more amaz'd, in double dread doth dwell;
> And every tender part for feare does shake:
> As when a greedy Wolfe through hunger fell
> A seely Lambe farre from the flocke does take,
> Of whom he meanes his bloudie feast to make,
> A Lyon spyes fast running towards him,
> The innocent pray in hast he does forsake,
> Which quit from death yet quakes in every lim
> With chaunge of feare, to see the Lyon looke so grim.
>
> (I.vi.10)

Una has escaped from the wolf only to be ensnared by what she believes
to be a lion. Wolves were a staple feature of protestant pastoral satire,
especially when preying on lambs, representing God's flock, and were
almost inevitably associated with catholicism.[26] Sansloy, in terms of the
romance motifs of the plot, is a false pagan knight who, in the guise of
protecting Una, will prey on her as his spoil.

The comparison of 'the salvage nation' to a lion is a little more complex.
On the one hand a lion denotes menace to Una as God's threat to the
Israelites in *Jeremiah*, 5:6: 'Wherefore a lyon out of the forest shall slaye

them, and a wolfe of the wildernesse shall destroy them.' On the other, Una herself reads the salvage nation in terms of what she already knows – just as 'the salvage nation' read her. Because Sansloy's capture of her was achieved through killing the lion which had hitherto helped to protect her, she sees them as allies against the wolf, replacing the original lion and therefore opposing good and evil beasts. The lion had been tamed by Una when she had first become separated from the Red-Cross Knight and had been out 'Hunting full greedie after salvage blood' (I.iii.5). It becomes her companion and champion, accompanying her into the house of Abessa where they receive reluctant hospitality and slaying Kirkrapine, before his fatal encounter with Sansloy. The lion has usually been interpreted to be Henry VIII, an ambivalent figure in later Reformation histories, who inaugurated, limited and suppressed the spread of protestantism. This is exactly how the lion is portrayed here: he defends Una, is able to break down doors and offset some threats, but does nothing to stop their entry into the catholic Abessa's house ('Nine hundred *Pater nosters* every day, / And thrise nine hundred *Aves* she was wont to say' (I.iii.13)) and fails to protect her from Sansloy.[27]

Una's initial perception of 'the salvage nation' as akin to the lion who has just failed her implies that the savages might constitute a serious threat, they might prove inadequate, they might, in fact, be more successful than the real lion/Henry VIII in protecting her from the wolves. An ironic reversal has taken place: the lion was hunting for 'salvage blood' which would have included Una; she now sees 'the salvage nation' in terms of the lion. The savages actually succeed in preserving the figure who represents religious truth as well as the official founder of the English Reformation.

At the end of Book V there is a similarly ironic reversal, again, employing specifically protestant iconography. Envy and Detraction cry out against Artegall, 'As it had bene two shepheardes curres, had scryde / A ravenous Wolfe amongst the scattered flockes' (V.xii.38). The real wolves are, of course, Envy and Detraction, who constitute the serious threat to the flock; but, true to the nature of wolves, they appear in sheep's clothing, claiming that Artegall's legitimate policy of trying to reform Irena's land by rooting out hostile elements, is evil. In doing so, they are defending another wolf, the catholic Grantorto, and are therefore trying to halt the progress of both the Reformation and the establishment of true political authority. It is further implied that they have influenced the Faerie Queene; although the reason for Artegall's premature recall is left unstated, its disastrous effects are made clear. Just as Henry VIII as the lion is shown to be a flawed hero who hinders as much as helps the protestant cause, so is Elizabeth in her myopic policy towards Ireland; just as radical protestant satire saw the most dangerous threat to their existence coming from within, so does *The Faerie Queene*. Book I ended with the hope of religious reform and national greatness, of Elizabeth going beyond her father and correcting his errors whilst preserving his virtues; the events of the later books imply that her reign was a false dawn for protestants and that identical errors will be repeated. The central controlling figure of the book, the elusive Faerie Queene, turns out to be an impostor, as dangerous for her flock as those she is supposed to protect them from, so that the narrative progress of the work is under threat. There is no stable centre of truth.

This process manifests itself in other ways. The poem confronts the reader with two diametrically opposed representations of catholicism which cannot be separated from the series of representations of savagery. There is the image of the ignorant but well-meaning idolater who can be transformed into something better with proper education and the benefits of nurture, set against the evil desires of those who pervert religion and threaten the foundations of the state's moral and legal basis. This latter category includes both the wolves within and without, like Duessa and Grantorto, and also the cannibalistic 'salvage nation' which appear in Book VI, Canto viii, who attempt to sacrifice Serena. This salvage nation exists as the antithesis of 'the salvage nation' of Book I and practises diabolic natural religion:

> Unto their God they would her sacrifize,
> Whose share, her guiltlesse bloud they would present,
> But of her dainty flesh they did devize
> To make a common feast, and feed with gurmandize.
>
> (VI.viii.38)

What strikes this 'salvage nation' first is the beauty of Serena's face:

> but when her face
> Like the faire yvory shining they did see
> Each gan his fellow solace and embrace,
> For joy of such good hap by heavenly grace.
>
> (VI.viii.37)

There is the same rhyme here as there was in I.vi.18 (face/grace), and an identical situation occurs as the visage of the beloved triggers a series of religious responses, so that this episode has to be read in terms of the earlier one. Whereas the wood-nymphs reacted with a mixture of envy and fear to their exposure to 'heavenly grace', the 'salvage nation' elevate the status of eating to a religious one.

Serena is described in terms of a pornographic blazon akin to the language of much Elizabethan love poetry so that 'the cannibals' confusion of the two appetites of hunger and lust with the language of

a love-religion' actually forces the contemporary reader into a
recognition that such writing is part of his or her own cultural matrix
rather than that of the cannibals:

> Her yvorie necke, her alablaster brest,
> Her paps, which like white silken pillowes were,
> For love in soft delight thereon to rest;
> Her tender sides, her bellie white and clere,
> Which like an Altar did it selfe uprere,
> To offer sacrifice divine thereon;
> Her goodly thighes, whose glorie did appeare
> Like a triumphal Arch, and thereupon
> The spoiles of Princes hang'd, which were in battel won.
>
> (VI.viii.42)[28]

Spenser makes us see Serena's body as a construction of conceits which
is dismembered and sacrificed as much by the civilised reader's gaze
as the cannibals' knives. What should separate the reader from these
cannibals, the ability to represent using language, in fact draws the two
closer together.[29]

Spenser's prose dialogue, *A View of the Present State of Ireland*, contains
a similar discussion of the problem of religion and savagery. It opens
with one of the disputants, Eudoxus, asking what courses can be taken
for 'reducing that salvage nation to better government and Civilitye'.[30]
Irenius states that before he can suggest solutions, the evils of the country
must be enumerated and these can be divided up into three main
groups: laws, customs, and religion. He explains at great length that Irish
society is so barbarous and the people so degenerate that they cannot
be persuaded to obey civilised, English laws, but must be forced,
emphasising that it is no good applying laws without the threat of
punishment. Laws, and methods of imposing them, differ from state to
state and the Irish need stern laws which will be harshly applied. The
imposition of these laws will sweep away the savage Irish customs which
resist the advance of civilisation: intermarriage and fostering of children,
transhumance, wearing mantles and growing glibs (long moustaches), using
kerns and gallowglasses to fight tribal wars, chaotic and murderous
assemblies, keeping seditious bards who incite rebellion and improper
land tenure. These are all derived from the savage customs of the ancient
Scythians, one of the many ancestors of the contemporary Irish.[31]

Irenius's discussion of religion is much briefer because it is far easier
to explain as a social phenomenon: 'the faulte that I finde in religion is
but one and the same universall throroughe all that Countrye, that is that
they are all Papistes by theire profession but in the same so blindelye
and brutishly enformed for the moste parte as that ye woulde rather

thinke them *Atheists* or infidles' (p. 136). Just as in *The Faerie Queene* there is an explicit relationship between types of error which form a cluster of related forms – catholicism, devil worship, savagery, paganism – so is there in Irenius's description of Irish religion in the *View* (Eudoxus comments that it 'is trewlie a moste pitifull hearinge that so many soules should fall into the divells Iawes'). Irenius continues further to stress the innocence of the ignorant Irish whose religion developed in the way it did because they were converted via the direct command of the Pope rather than the true Christianity of the protestant church:

> The generall faulte Comethe not of anie late abuse either in the people or theire priestes who Cane teache no better than they knowe nor shew more lighte then they have sene but in the first Institution and plantinge of religion ... it is certaine that religion was generalie Corrupted with theire Popishe trumperie Therefore what other could they learne then such trashe as was taughte them And drinke of that Cupp of fornicacion with which the purple Harlott had then made all nacions drunken.
>
> (p. 137)[32]

The religion of the Irish represented in the *View* resembles that of 'the salvage nation' of Book I rather than Book VI as Irenius does not doubt the good faith of their mistaken belief. Later, he argues that the Irish understand their professed religion as little as they do protestantism and simply hate the latter 'thoughe unknowen even for the verye hatred which they have of the Englishe and theire government'. Thus, if St Patrick could convert them from idolatry and paganism to catholicism, 'how muche more easely shall godlie teachers bringe them to the trewe understandinge of that which they allreadye professe' (p. 221).

The logic of Irenius's argument would seem to imply that the innocence of the savage Irish can be cured by evangelical persuasion rather than military coercion and Eudoxus ventures an initial conclusion that what Irenius is saying is that he 'finde[s] no faulte with the people them selves ... but with the firste ordinance and institution thereof' (p. 138). Irenius refuses to draw such a moral because 'the sinne or ignorance of the Priestes shall not excuse the people'; the religion of the Irish is simply one of a number of factors which have led the land into rebellion against English rule ('the verye hatred they have of the Englishe and theire government'). The blame lies not only in individual wills,

> but the in Convenience of the time and troublous occasions wherewith that wretched Realme hathe Continuallie bene tormoyled. ffor instruction in religion nedethe quiett times and ere we seke to settle a sounde discipline in the Clergie we muste purchase peace unto the

Layitye for it is ill time to preache amongst swordes and . . .
impossible . . . to settle a good opinion in the mindes of men for
matters of Religion doubtfull which have a doubtlesse evill opinion of
ourselves for er a newe be broughte in the olde muste be removed.

(p. 138)

Irenius's argument is that a religious problem cannot be solved in
purely religious terms. The faith of 'the salvage nation' may be the
result of an innocent and understandable mistake, but its effects are far
more wide-ranging and destructive. The consequences of the most
benign error can be lethal, as Irenius's grim warnings imply. The point is
that the particular brand of Irish catholicism helps to make them a
threat to English government. English rule has to be established before
English protestantism can be spread effectively and meaningfully, and
this, according to Irenius, necessitates a full-scale military conquest as a
prerequisite to both processes. The *View* argues the case that religious
persuasion and national identity are mutually cohesive parts of the same
whole.[33]

Irenius's manipulative rhetoric can be read in other ways. In *The Faerie
Queene*, the second type of 'salvage nation' qualified our understanding
of the first; the first seemed at worst harmless, possibly good, the second,
an evil menace. The Irish in the *View* combine both representations of
savagery, being innocent in religious intent but guilty of serious
transgression in effect and therefore demanding harsh and immediate
suppression. The seeming paradox is that the excessive violence will
appear to come from the forces of order, but, in fact, is caused by the
errors of the subjects, however innocent they may be in terms of
the personal conviction of their faith. Eradicating savagery will, of
necessity, require the use of savage violence.

This harsh reality is explicitly signalled in the epic poem too: on the
third day of Satyrane's tournament an unknown warrior appears in
'salvage weed, / With woody mosse bedight, and all his steed / With
oaken leaves attrapt, that seemed fit / For salvage wight' (IV.iv.39).
Satyrane was the knight who had rescued Una from 'the salvage nation'
in I.vi, and had himself been brought up in the forest, 'noursled up in
life and manners wilde, / Emongst wild beast and woods, from lawes of
men exiled' (I.vi.23). The son of a human mother, Thyamis ('passion'), and
a satyr father, Therion ('wild beast'), Satyrane forms a link between the
virtues and vices of nature and nurture and is represented as a 'wild
man of the woods'.[34] The knight who appears at his tournament and
triumphs in violently bloody fashion – 'Hewing, and slashing shields,
and helmets bright, / And beating downe, what ever nigh him came'
(IV.iv.41) – is later revealed to be Artegall, who Merlin has prophesied
will marry Britomart in the previous book (III.ii.24–5), and who takes on

the role of the Knight of Justice in the subsequent book. He is dressed like Satyrane; the motto on his shield is *'salvagesse sans finesse'*, which the narrator explains shows 'secret wit' (IV.iv.39). Thus, a wild, or savage knight, takes the honours at the tournament of another savage knight.[35]

The brutal severity of the (as yet) unnamed savage knight's style of combat is mirrored later in his methods of applying justice in Book V; but, just as Irenius's perception of the Irish as religiously naive rather than wicked is carefully distinguished from his recommendation that the nation be reconquered in order to remove all recalcitrant elements and enable political order to be established, so is Artegall's role as justicer separated from the most horrifying aspects of his policy. The worst violence is performed by the dehumanised iron man, Talus, the sower of death, who 'brusht, and battred them without remorse, / That on the ground he left full many a corse . . . That they lay scattered over all the land, / As thicke as doth the seede after the sowers hand (V.xii.7). Artegall's growth to maturity, as the husband-to-be of the British maiden and typological precursor of Elizabeth, Britomart, does not involve a rejection of savage violence so much as an intensification and, simultaneously, a separation of the means from the implementation of brutality (Artegall is actually shown restraining Talus in V.xii.8, an absurdity given his close identification with the Irish policy of Spenser's erstwhile patron, Arthur, Lord Grey de Wilton).[36]

One possible way of reading Spenser's poetry and prose in a religious context is provided by a treatise deposited in the state papers (1572?), endorsed by Lord Burghley with the comment, 'Sent from Thos. Cecil to me, wrytten by Mr. Carleton, concerning a power of 1000 horsemen and 2000 cullivers. To suffer the precise sort to inhabit Ireland'.[37] The paper argues that there are three sorts of disaffected subjects within the realm of England, papists, atheists and protestants, and that all suffer equal favour and persecution: the first two groups are treated well because they are feared and persecuted because they are traitors and godless, the third favoured 'because wee, having some religion, feare to displease God in them' and persecuted because they are separatists. The author asserts that the good government of a state demands that papists and atheists ought to be 'removed' as 'they knowe no obedyence but under tyranny'. However, the protestants are a different matter as the reason for their disaffection is a noble one: 'as they hate all heresyes and poperye, so they cannot be perswaded to beare lykynge of the Queen's proceedings in relygion, by reason that oure churche here is not reformed'. Although they hold their own separate services and assemblies which will offend many supporters of the church settlement, they ought

> not to be punished for the same, because they are the Quene's owne
> bowells, her dearest subjects, the servants of God, and suche as doe

tread the straighte pathe of the Lorde to salvacion. So that eyther the church of Englonde must be framed to theire appetyte, or els they must be suffred, with out blame, to proseede as they beginne.

The author's solution to this problem is threefold: first, allow some to depart; second, allow some to remain in England and have their own churches; third, bestow upon those who want to go 'a porcion of the countrye of Irelond' and so help to 'beare a people to God's glorie and Englond's surety'. This last notion is the most satisfactory because it will 'not only worke the quyet of the Quene and State at home', but help to subdue a recalcitrant people who threaten the defence of the realm. There will, of course, be problems, the author concludes rather cryptically: 'I will say no more but that so Godly & noble a journey shall fynde more enemyes then friends; such is the sleighte of Sathan when God's kingdome shynthe'.

Mr Carleton's tract is another argument that religious persuasion cannot be considered in isolation as a phenomenon in an Irish context; as historians have frequently pointed out, after the Reformation was imposed upon Ireland, religious differences reinforced and transposed English notions of their cultural separation from the Irish.[38] Both Carleton's tract and Spenser's *View* argue that current English efforts to convert the Irish are grossly inadequate and need to be improved;[39] both express explicit fears that the proper way to reform Ireland will be scorned and rejected because the central authorities simply do not understand the problems involved (something also emphasised in *The Faerie Queene*).

Most importantly, Carleton's tract argues that the place of the truly godly in Elizabethan England is exile: their task is to shore up the realm from *outside*. A related but more pessimistic argument shadows the narrative of the extant fragment of *The Faerie Queene* where Spenser criticises Elizabeth's indifference towards her Irish subjects and refusal to intervene and crush the elements of rebellion. In the 'Two Cantos of Mutabilitie' there is a direct allegory of the Fall. Ireland is described as 'the holy-Island' (VII.vi.37), because in the past Diana (Cynthia) and her nymphs and satyrs used to come to relax:

> Whylome, when IRELAND flourished in fame
> Of wealths and goodnesse, far above the rest
> Of all that beare the *British* Islands name,
> The Gods then us'd (for pleasure and for rest)
> Oft to resort there-to, when seem'd them best:
> But none of all there-in more pleasure found,
> Then *Cynthia*; that is sovereigne Queene profest

Of woods and forrests, which therein abound,
Sprinkled with wholsom waters, more then most on ground.

(VII.vi.38)

After Faunus dares to see Diana naked whilst bathing she abandons and curses the island, so that it ceases to be a pastoral retreat and is instead populated by wolves and thieves who still menace current inhabitants (VII.vi.55).

In the *View*, Irenius remarks that Ireland's ancient name was '*sacra Insula*, taking *sacra* for *acursed*' (p. 145). What this short narrative – usually read as if it were only peripheral to the plot of the Cantos – informs us is that Ireland is the place where both the political stability of the British Isles is threatened and the religious certainties outlined in the earlier books of the poem are rendered problematic. Cynthia, as the letter to Raleigh attached to the first and subsequent editions of the poem stated, stood for Elizabeth, so that Ireland is said to have been the fairest of the British Isles she rules.[40] The fact that she curses Ireland and vows never to return must surely be read as a fierce criticism of her lack of concern for one of her kingdoms and her lack of intervention to prevent it from remaining as a dangerous and neglected land. Just as Ireland ceases to be an Edenic paradise and becomes instead a wilderness, so does an etymological change take place as its name ceases to mean 'holy' and becomes instead 'acursed'. The fact that the debate between Mutability and Jove to decide who rules the universe takes place in a land that is shown to be mutable also serves to undercut Nature's judgement that Mutability's arguments are self-defeating and hence fail to unseat Jove from his position.[41] Spenser has been forced to recognise where the most significant threat to his sense of a stable identity as a protestant Englishman came from and what it had been defined against.[42]

Lord Burghley is long thought to have been one of Spenser's chief political opponents and was possibly instrumental in having him permanently exiled to Ireland in 1580.[43] If so, it would seem likely that Spenser was regarded as akin to the protestants of Carleton's treatise, useful (or harmless) abroad but dangerous at home. Spenser, in turn, founded much of his discussion of religion and politics in both the *View* and *The Faerie Queene* on two related puns, sacra (holy/accursed) and salvage (savage/rescued) which meant that two seemingly separate concepts are always juxtaposed and a subversive reading can be set beside a more orthodox one. Hence lines such as 'O sacred hunger of ambitious mindes, / And impotent desire of men to raine' (V.xii.1), are offered as a general statement which is then specifically applied to Burbon (Henry IV of France), and the two tyrants Gerionio and Grantorto.[44] But in the context of the never-completed Book XII, it can clearly be used to refer directly to Gloriana and Elizabeth herself for her foolish policy of abandoning a half-reformed Ireland, so that the separation between holy/cursed protestant and catholic crusader is blurred and Artegall, the salvage knight, is not sure exactly what he is rescuing. Regarded another way still, the lines could be read in the more usual English sense – 'sacred' as 'holy' – in order to signify the problems Artegall has in completing his assigned task. Artegall has to be cruel to be kind and risk becoming what he is supposed to overcome: a gauntlet is continually laid down to the reader to condemn his enterprise. The point of this verse might be that Artegall has to go beyond all acceptable standards to complete his quest: 'the impotent desire of men to raign' could refer to either Artegall's ultimate failure or the futile desires of those who want to rule but are not prepared to break eggs to make an omelette. Analogously, on this reading, English protestants, like Spenser himself, could be said to have a holy desire to see the salvage island where they lived ruled properly, tragically frustrated by the vacillations and ignorance of the central authorities.

Notes

1. GRACE WARREN LANDRUM, 'Spenser's Use of the Bible and his Alleged Puritanism', *PMLA* 51 (1926), 517–44; VIRGIL K. WHITAKER, *The Religious Basis of Spenser's Thought* (Stanford University Press, 1950); ANTHEA HUME, *Edmund Spenser: Protestant Poet* (Cambridge University Press, 1984); JOHN N. KING, *Spenser's Poetry and the Reformation Tradition* (Princeton University Press, 1990), 'Appendix: Was Spenser a Puritan', pp. 233–8. My thanks to Lucy E. Hadfield for help with the typing of this essay.
2. For detail of Spenser's life see WILLY MALEY, *A Spenser Chronology* (Basingstoke: Macmillan, 1994).
3. See also ANDREW HADFIELD, 'Translating the Reformation: John Bale's Irish *Vocacyon*', in BRENDAN BRADSHAW, ANDREW HADFIELD and WILLY MALEY, eds, *Representing Ireland: Literature and the Origins of Conflict, 1534–1660* (Cambridge University Press, 1993), pp. 43–59.
4. See, for example, the comments of George de Malynes and John Hughes, cited in R. M. CUMMINGS, ed., *Spenser: The Critical Heritage* (London: Routledge & Kegan Paul, 1971), pp. 115, 263–4; GRAHAM HOUGH, ed., *The First Commentary on 'The Faerie Queene'* (privately published, 1964); VIRGIL K. WHITAKER, 'The Theological Structure of *The Faerie Queene I*', *English Literary History*, 19 (1952), 151–64; MICHAEL O'CONNELL, *Mirror and Veil: The Historical Dimension of Spenser's Faerie Queene* (Chapel Hill: North Carolina University Press, 1977), ch. 2; ELIZABETH HEALE, *The Faerie Queene: A Reader's Guide* (Cambridge University Press, 1984), ch. 1.
5. See HUME, *Edmund Spenser: Protestant Poet*, ch. 5.
6. HOUGH, ed., *First Commentary*, p. 10; O'CONNELL, *Mirror and Veil*, p. 61.
7. On Cyparissus see OVID, *Metamorphoses*, trans. MARY M. INNES

(Harmondsworth: Penguin, 1955), p. 228. All references to *The Faerie Queene*, ed. A. C. HAMILTON (London: Longman, 1977).

8. See the entry on 'satyrs' in A. C. HAMILTON, ed., *The Spenser Encyclopedia* (London: Routledge, 1990), p. 628; FRANK KERMODE, *Shakespeare, Spenser, Donne: Renaissance Essays* (London: Routledge & Kegan Paul, 1971), pp. 48–9.

9. For a general discussion see A. D. HADFIELD, 'The English Conception of Ireland, c.1540–1600, with special reference to the works of Edmund Spenser', unpublished D. Phil. thesis, University of Ulster at Coleraine, 1988, pp. 446–69. See also ROY HARVEY PIERCE, 'Primitivistic Ideas in *The Faerie Queene*', *Journal of English and Germanic Philology* 44 (1945), 139–51.

10. For a more sustained analysis see ANDREW HADFIELD, 'The Course of Justice: Spenser, Ireland and Political Discourse', *Studia Neophilologica* 65 (1993), 187–96, at pp. 192–3.

11. MARTHA CRAIG, 'The Secret Wit of Spenser's Language', in PAUL ALPERS, ed., *Elizabethan Poetry: Modern Essays in Criticism* (Oxford University Press, 1967), pp. 447–72.

12. On Irena and Ireland see SHEILA CAVANAGH, ' "Such was Irena's Countenance": Ireland in Spenser's Prose and Poetry', *Texas Studies in Literature and Language* 28 (1986), 25–50.

13 On the relationship between Artegall and Talus see RICHARD A. MCCABE, 'The Fate of Irena: Spenser and Political Violence', in PATRICIA COUGHLAN, ed., *Spenser and Ireland: An Interdisciplinary Perspective* (Cork University Press, 1989), pp. 109–25.

14. EDMUND SPENSER, *A Viewe of the presente state of Irelande discoursed by waye of a dialogue betwene Eudoxus and Irenius*, *Works: A Variorum Edition*, X, *The Prose Works*, ed. RUDOLF GOTTFRIED (Baltimore: Johns Hopkins University Press, 1949), pp. 39–231, pp. 99–102; GRAHAM HOUGH, *Preface to The Faerie Queene*, p. 194; HAMILTON, ed., *The Faerie Queene*, p. 590.

15. For comment see HADFIELD, 'The English Conception of Ireland', pp. 129–30.

16. See also the representation of the Irish rivers during the marriage of the Thames and the Medway (IV.xi.40–4) and the comments in HADFIELD, 'The English Conception of Ireland', pp. 499–500.

17. EDWIN A. GREENLAW, 'Spenser and British Imperialism', *Modern Philology*, 40 (1910/1), 347–70; BERNARD CAPP, 'The Political Dimension of Apocalyptic Thought', in C. A. PATRIDES and JOSEPH WITTREICH, eds, *The Apocalypse in English Renaissance Thought and Literature* (Manchester University Press, 1984), pp. 93–124 at pp. 95–9.

18. See the entry on 'Grantorto' in *The Spenser Encyclopedia*, p. 339.

19. ALASTAIR FOWLER, 'Spenser and War', in J. R. MULRYNE and M. SHEWING, eds, *War, Literature and the Arts in Sixteenth-Century Europe* (Basingstoke: Macmillan, 1989), pp. 147–64 at pp. 158–9.

20. On the protestant iconography of Book I see KING, *Spenser's Poetry and the Reformation Tradition*, ch. 5.

21. On the problem of ruling a British 'multiple kingdom' see CONRAD RUSSELL, 'The British Background to the Irish Rebellion of 1641', *Historical Research* 61 (1988), 166–82.

22. JUDITH ANDERSON, ' "Nor Man It Is": The Knight of Justice in Book V of Spenser's *Faerie Queene*', *PMLA* 85 (1970), 65–77.

23. JANE APTEKAR, *Icons of Justice: Iconography and Thematic Imagery in Book V of 'The Faerie Queene'* (New York: Columbia University Press, 1969), chs 6–7.
24. It is usually assumed that the slander refers to Grey's ruthless policy at Smerwick (1580), which Spenser defended in the *View*, pp. 63–4, 159–62.
25. ANNE FOGARTY, 'The Colonization of Language: Narrative Strategies in *View of the Present State of Ireland* and *The Faerie Queene*, Book VI', in COUGHLAN, ed., *Spenser and Ireland*, pp. 75–108, at pp. 93–104.
26. For an example see KING, *Spenser's Poetry and the Reformation Tradition*, p. 37.
27. See for example JAMES NOHRNBERG, *The Analogy of the Faerie Queene* (Princeton University Press, 1976), p. 218; HOUGH, *A Preface to the Faerie Queene*, p. 145. On the ambivalent image of Henry VIII for later protestants, see JOHN N. KING, *Tudor Royal Iconography: Literature and Art in an Age of Religious Crisis* (Princeton University Press, 1989), pp. 137–8.
28. DONALD CHENEY, *Spenser's Image of Nature: Wild Man and Shepherd in 'The Faerie Queene'* (New Haven and London: Yale University Press, 1966), p. 106.
29. JOHN PITCHER, 'Tudor Literature', in PAT ROGERS, ed., *The Oxford Illustrated History of English Literature* (Oxford University Press, 1987), pp. 59–111, at pp. 88–90.
30. *View*, p. 43. Subsequent references in the text in parentheses.
31. See A. D. HADFIELD, 'Briton and Scythian: Tudor Representations of Irish Origins', *Irish Historical Studies* 28, No. 112 (Nov. 1993), 390–408.
32. Compare the representation of Duessa in *Faerie Queene*, I.viii.13–14.
33. See above, n. 3.
34. CHENEY, *Spenser's Image of Nature*, pp. 62–5. More generally see RICHARD BERNHEIMER, *Wild Men in the Middle Ages* (Cambridge, Mass.: Harvard University Press, 1952).
35. The upbringings of Satyrane and Artegall are linked through a series of verbal echoes: compare I.vi.21–7 and V.i.5–8.
36. McCABE, 'The Fate of Irena'.
37. Extracts reprinted in *Calendar of State Papers, Domestic Series, Addenda, 1566–79*, pp. li–iv.
38. JOHN GILLINGHAM, 'The English Invasion of Ireland', in BRADSHAW et al., eds, *Representing Ireland*, pp. 24–42, at p. 26.
39. *View*, pp. 221–2; CARLETON, p. liii.
40. HAMILTON, ed., *The Faerie Queene*, p. 737.
41. For a more sustained argument see ANDREW HADFIELD, 'Spenser, Ireland and Sixteenth Century Political Discourse', *Modern Languages Review* 89 (1994), 1–18, at pp. 13–18.
42. See ANDREW HADFIELD and WILLY MALEY, 'Introduction: Irish Representations and English Alternatives', in BRADSHAW et al., eds, *Representing Ireland*, pp. 1–23.
43. RICHARD RAMBUSS, *Spenser's Secret Career* (Cambridge University Press, 1993), pp. 83–4, 90–1.
44. See the entries on 'Burbon' and 'Gerionio' in *The Spenser Encyclopedia*, pp. 121, 331.

11 The colonisation of language: narrative strategy in *The Faerie Queene*, Book VI*

ANNE FOGARTY

Critical readings of *The Faerie Queene* frequently depoliticise the poem, or treat its historical context – the author's involvement in the Munster Plantation – as irrelevant or an embarrassment. Anne Fogarty's interpretation of Book VI assumes that the text has been materially influenced by Spenser's support of the concerted New English attempt to colonise Ireland. Hence the essay treats the central images and themes of the book not simply as idealised abstractions but as metaphorical reflections of the complex, contradictory, and insidious motives of colonisation. The aim is not to posit simple parallelisms between the text and the author's world but to explore the multifarious ways in which the poem mediates, refracts, and even apparently subverts Spenser's political beliefs. Thus, although Fogarty argues that Book VI is a continuation of the poem's overall attempt to construct a colonialist aesthetics by drawing up lines of demarcation between forms of wildness and civility or 'courtesie', it also draws attention to contradictions and moments of breakdown in the narrative which threaten its coherence. While Spenser's political writings on Ireland may have allowed little room for doubt or for counter-currents of sympathy with the 'wild' Irish, his epic poem explores the political unconscious and the jarring ambiguities of the colonial ideals which he propounds and supports. The *sprezzatura* of Spenser's poetic creation leads to uncomfortable revelations of savagery, such as, for example, the voyeuristic description of Serena's depredation by the cannibals, which undermines the assured vision of the civilising influence of the followers of 'courtesie' which Book VI also unfolds. This essay was awarded the Isabel MacCaffrey Award from The Spenser Society of America.

Foucault's concept of the heterotopia is of use in describing the narrative

*Reprinted from PATRICIA COUGHLAN, ed., *Spenser and Ireland: An Interdisciplinary Perspective* (Cork University Press, 1989), pp. 92–108.

world of *The Faerie Queene*, Book VI, and of the colonial ideology which subtends it. In a posthumously published article, he propounds the theory that societies maintain themselves by incorporating within their structures 'other spaces', or oppositional sites, in which the many facets of their ideologies or belief systems may be simultaneously represented, contested and inverted.[1] While these counter-sites may involve an idealising moment, Foucault ultimately distinguishes them from the non-place of utopia and prefers instead to refer to them as heterotopias, that is places of Otherness or difference. Moreover, despite being 'absolutely different from all the sites that they reflect and speak about', heterotopias remain inseparably linked with reality.[2] As a result, Foucault positions them both inside and outside of social reality. He cites as examples such varied socio-cultural structures as ships, brothels, boarding schools, military academies, gardens, cemeteries, honeymoon trips, and cinemas. In addition, he suggests that two distinct kinds of heterotopia may be discerned: those which create real spaces imbued with order in the attempt to offset the jumbled and disordered nature of social reality, and those which create an illusory or fictional space so as to criticise and expose certain aspects of social and political regimes. There is, however, a glaring omission from this account of the role of other spaces within culture, namely literature and writing. It will be argued here that Book VI of *The Faerie Queene* conforms to Foucault's description of the heterotopia. Within the other space afforded by writing, it constructs a revised version of the social and political order while still acknowledging its connections with the material and historical circumstances in which it is embedded. Through the depiction of a feudal world of villainous knights and noble savages and of the attractions and vulnerabilities of the pastoral life, it acts out the difficulties encountered by the New English colonists in Ireland who likewise found themselves trapped between competing cultures and political systems and beliefs. In thus drawing attention to conflict and almost wilfully exposing the flaws within the colonial ideology which it apparently upholds, Book VI of *The Faerie Queene* corresponds to Foucault's notion of the illusory heterotopia which constructs an other space as much to test the contradictions within certain political values as to idealise them. Unlike *A Viewe of the Present State of Ireland* which aims at reducing everything to a levelling sameness, it openly invites the play of difference as a means of countermanding chaotic relations in the world beyond it. In the final event, however, the narrative of the poem is almost destroyed by the images of difference which it unleashes and the only recourse left to the poet is to undermine and censor his own creations in an attempt to stem the dangerous energies to which they expose him. It is as if the poem cannot finally sustain its own unflinching vision of the bloody conflicts of colonial warfare.

It is important, of course, to recognise the extent to which metaphors of colonialism are imbricated with Spenser's description of the imaginative process in *The Faerie Queene* as a whole. These images come particularly to the forefront in the proems to the successive books of the poem. In Book II, for example, it is claimed that 'the happy land of Faery' is not just a 'painted forgery', but is as real as the new worlds which have been placed on the map through the Elizabethan voyages of discovery:

> But let that man with better sence advize,
> That of the world least part to us is red:
> And dayly how through hardy enterprize
> Many great Regions are discovered,
> Which to late age were never mentioned.
> Who ever heard of th'Indian Peru?
> Or who in venturous vessel measured
> The Amazons huge river now found trew?
> Of fruitfullest Virginia who did ever vew?
>
> (II. Proem. 2)

The narrator, here, validates the truth of his creation by destabilising the relationship between reality and fiction. In fact, he goes so far as to assert that the method by which new countries are annexed in reality parallels the process by which the meaning of the poem unfolds. Thus, political rhetoric and the language of fiction are seen in terms of each other. Both ultimately depend on the colonisation of language and on the knowledge and mastery of words. It is implied too that if the book may be seen as world, then the world may also be seen as book. This is particularly stressed by the pun on the word 'to read' at the beginning of the stanza:

> But let that man with better sence advize,
> That of the world least part to us is red.

'Red', in this context, means both to reveal or disclose, and to read or interpret. Hence, for Spenser, we construe or read the world in the same way that we make sense of poetry. As a result, the interpretative skills of the reader are taxed in *The Faerie Queene* with particular intent. By problematising our ability to decipher and understand, the text aims at educating and controlling our political responses. Also, it will be seen that, in tandem with this process, the poem constantly subverts and questions its own rhetoric as a means both of revealing and of protecting the ideology it enshrines.

The primary problem with which we are confronted at the opening of Book VI is that of the seductiveness and endlessness of fiction itself.

Text and reality can no longer be held apart and the narrator depicts himself as aimlessly wandering in a world of language. Words have become inexhaustible and beyond any form of control:

> The waies, through which my weary steps I guyde,
> In this delightful land of Faery,
> Are so exceeding spacious and wyde,
> And sprinckled with such sweet variety,
> Of all that pleasant is to eare or eye,
> That I nigh ravisht with rare thoughts delight,
> My tedious travell doe forget thereby;
> And when I gin to feele decay of might,
> It strength to me supplies, and chears my dulled spright.
>
> (VI. Proem. 1)

This sense of impediment extends also to the subject matter of the book which is about to commence. The virtue of courtesie is missing in the real world of the court and subsumed entirely as fictive ideality in the figure of the queen herself. Elizabeth, as transcendent signifier, nullifies the narrator's efforts in advance. His words falter in their attempt to capture her presence, as the clumsy periphrases illustrate:

> ... where may be seene
> The goodly praise of Princely curtesie,
> As in your selfe, O soveraine Lady Queene,
> In whose pure mind, as in a mirrour sheene,
> It showes, and with her brightnesse doth inflame
> The eyes of all, which thereon fixed beene;
> But meriteth indeede an higher name:
> Yet so from low to high uplifted is your name.
>
> (VI. Proem. 6)

The echoing phrases of the final two lines bear witness to the difficulty of the poet's position. His aim is to exalt the transcendent authority of the queen – to lift her name from low to high – but yet, at the same time, he must recognise that his undertaking is doomed to failure before he even begins. The 'higher name' which he seeks will never be located and the words which he uses will always, as a consequence, be haunted by an absence or lack. In the end, the poem resigns itself to being an elaborate circumscription of the fictions of authority. Its circulation of meanings will reproduce in another guise the mechanisms by which power sustains its mystique in society:

> Then pardon me, most dreaded Soveraine,
> That from your selfe I doe this vertue bring,
> And to your selfe doe it returne againe:
> So from the Ocean all rivers spring,
> And tribute backe repay as to their King.
>
> (VI. Proem. 7)

It is noteworthy that Spenser derived this cameo narrative of fealty from the colonised topography of Ireland, as the tidal currents of the Shannon are given particular mention elsewhere in the poem.[3] Thus, the formalised obeisance of *The Faerie Queene* and of his defence of colonial rule in the *View* stems from a similar belief in the unassailable prerogatives of royal control.

Moreover, by including his work within the never-ending cycle of an ocean which feeds rivers which feed an ocean, the poet succeeds in enmeshing his private desire with the designs of power. It will be a signal feature of this desire that it sustains itself by trying to satisfy the lack which it wishes to fill, while at the same time always leaving it gaping. In this connection, two key images of the proem must be borne in mind, the motifs of a vision which is adumbrated but never fully revealed in stanza 6, and of the spiralling circularity of royal power in stanza 7:

> Right so from you all goodly vertues well
> Into the rest, which round about you ring,
>
> (VI. Proem. 7)

will be reflected and repeated in varying forms during the course of Book VI. Through such self-replicating structures, the narrative propels itself onwards while always acknowledging its ultimate status as the echo chamber of a power which remains obdurately remote and intangible. Thus, the irony of the central plot of the *Legend of Courtesie* is that it must constantly stress Elizabeth's presence as an absent cause and celebrate her as an outside authority which both upholds and permanently undermines its fictions.

From the outset, the quest of Calidore, the exemplary hero of Book VI, is linked with the problems of language and of narration. Indeed, it is underlined that this figure's plight is but a transposition of the narrator's dilemma. Both are afflicted by the endless nature of their undertaking. Thus, Calidore's first account of the enterprise which faces him immediately recalls the words of the proem:

> . . . now I begin
> To tread an endlesse trace, withouten guyde,
> Or good direction, how to enter in,

Or how to issue forth in waies untryde,
In perils strange, in labours long and wide.

(VI.i.6)

The task which he has been set is, of course, to hunt down and kill the Blatant Beast. This hybrid monster is never described directly, but seems to be a curious anthropomorphic mixture of dog, hydra, and wild boar. From the end of Book V onwards, it runs amok through the poem inflicting poisonous, festering wounds on several of the characters. Critics have generally seen in the Beast a figure of slander or detraction, one derivation of its name being from the Latin 'blatire', to babble or to bark.[4] The text, however, also intimates that the Blatant Beast represents all the abuses of rhetoric, in short, the disruptive and falsifying powers of language itself. Thus, the 'thousand tongs' of the Beast are described in Canto xii:

And therein were a thousand tongs empight,
Of sundry kindes, and sundry quality,
Some were of dogs, that barked day and night,
And some of cats, that wrawling still did cry,
And some of Beares, that groynd continually,
And some of Tygres, that did seeme to gren,
And snar at all, that ever passed by;
But most of them were tongues of mortall men,
Which spake reproachfully, not caring where nor when.

(VI.xii.27)

Hence, Calidore seeks to subdue and tame the anarchic forces of language, a mission which will inevitably remain unaccomplished. It is no surprise, then, that his attempts to close quarters with the proliferating babble of languages symbolised by the Beast seem so ineffectual and irrelevant.[5] Indeed, there are many indications that this monster represents a repressed libidinal aspect of the mannered world of courtesie, and that it is a splinter function of the seductive, chivalric heroes who abound in Book VI. Calidore's courtesie, for example, displays itself primarily through his ability to converse and to use words in order to manipulate situations.[6] Far more given to discourse than to action, he persuades Briana and Crudor to renew friendly relations, seals the peace between Priscilla and her father by treating him to a carefully edited version of her exploits, engages in dialogue with Meliboee concerning the relative merits of urban and rural lifestyles, and seeks to dispel Colin Clout's anger by luring him into a discussion of the blissful scene on Mount Acidale, which he had so fatefully interrupted. As a final flourish of irony, Pastorella in the gloom of the Brigants' cave recognises this most talkative of heroes by his voice.

A complex network of connections, in fact, links the Beast with the suppressed instinctual world which is the dark underside of courtesie. Its first appearance in the book coincides with Calidore's interruption of the love-play of Calepine and Serena. Far from being discomfited by this blunder, he displaces their previous activity with the 'delightfull pleasure' of conversation, thereby setting the scene for the eventual wounding of Serena by the Blatant Beast. Thus, Calidore substitutes the sublimations of language for the instinctual pleasures of physical satisfaction. He uses words as a means of rerouting and containing the motions of desire. However, the wound inflicted by the Beast marks the repressions or lack in such discourse. A similar juxtaposition occurs during Calidore's conversation with Colin Clout. While listening to the latter's explanations, he exhibits that greed for words which is one of his principal characteristics:

> In such discourses they together spent
> Long time, as fit occasion forth them led;
> With which the Knight him selfe did much content,
> And with delight his greedy fancy fed,
> Both of his words, which he with reason red;
> And also of the place, whose pleasures rare
> With such regard his sences ravished,
> That thence, he had no will away to fare,
> But wisht, that with that shepheard he mote dwelling share.
>
> (VI.x.30)

However, the next stanza cancels this moment of transport and reminds us of the wound of desire which impels Calidore's actions:

> But that envenimd sting, the which of yore,
> His poysnous point deepe fixed in his hart
> Had left, now gan afresh to rancle sore,
> And to renue the rigour of his smart.
>
> (VI.x.31)

Once again, the deflectionary pleasures of rhetoric are interrupted by the libidinal forces which they are designed to hold in check. The power of words to seduce is shown to be complementary to the Beast's power to erode and dissipate meaning. Calidore, who is associated with the voicing and expressiveness of words, is inevitably accompanied by the Blatant monster who allegorises that desire which both motivates and impedes the use of language. Thus, these two figures represent interlinked rather than opposing forces and, as a result, neither can ever succeed in definitely routing the other.

On another level again, the disruptive sorties of the Beast are emblematic of the meanderings and fracture of Spenser's narrative as a whole. The randomness of the monster's attacks and the devious trails which it lays for its pursuers mirror the constant ruptures in the plot of Book VI. All of the main protagonists, in contrast, show a deep-seated predilection for the symmetrical, harmonious endings of romance. Calidore unites Briana and Crudor, pairs off Tristram and the lady of the nameless, discourteous knight, salvages Priscilla's reputation, restores Pastorella to her parents, and is even granted a momentary Pyrrhic victory over the Blatant Beast itself. Calepine, who acts as a surrogate for Calidore, is no less industrious in the production of happy endings. He passes on the baby whom he has rescued to the childless Matilde, and saves Serena in the nick of time from the depredations of the cannibal race. Arthur, likewise, metes out punishment to the discourteous Sir Turpine, thus putting an end to his crimes, and rescues Timias, his squire, from the grips of Disdaine and Scorne. However, running counter to all these attempts to achieve conclusive and idyllic endings, is a far more powerful momentum which destroys any equilibrium which has been attained. As Harry Berger indicates, almost every episode after the first canto is left unresolved.[7] Stories are interrupted and then discontinued, despite the narrator's protestations that he will supply us with further information at a later point. Thus, the futures of Tristram, the noble Savage, Matilde's child, and of Priscilla and Aladine remain a blank. Calepine and Serena are abandoned at the moment of reunion and even the fate of Calidore and Pastorella is hedged with uncertainty. Mirabella, too, notwithstanding Arthur's exertions on her behalf, is left caught in the freeze frame of allegory, condemned continually to perform a penance which can never be completed:

> Here in this bottle (says the sory Mayd)
> I put the teares of my contrition,
> Till to the brim I have it full defrayed:
> And in this bag which I behinde me don,
> I put repentaunce for things past and gon.
> Yet is the bottle leake and the bag so torne,
> That all which I put in, fals out anon;
> And is behinde me trodden downe of Scorne,
> Who mocketh all my paine, and laughs the more I mourne.
>
> (VI.viii.24)

The suspensions created by the Ariostan endings, which occur seven times in various guises during the course of the book, also disturb the smooth progression of events. Each transition represents a lacuna, rather

than a moment of completion; the narrator either cuts across his own
recital and defers an ending until another occasion:

> Such chaunces oft exceed all humaine thought:
> That in another Canto shall to end be brought,
>
> (VI.iii.51)

or reminds us that events which we have just witnessed were, in fact, a
deviation from the central concerns of the plot and hence of minor
importance:

> But Calidore himselfe would not retaine
> Nor land nor for hyre of his good deede . . .
> There he remaind with them right well agreed,
> Till of his wounds he wexd hole and strong,
> And then to his first quest he passed forth along.
>
> (VI.i.47)

The Beast may, therefore, be seen as a symbol of that element of imbalance
in Spenser's text which constantly defies and prevents closure. Its very
name lends support to this argument. The *OED* states that one of the
possible roots of 'blatant' is an earlier form of the word 'to bleat'. In
this light, the Blatant Beast is a monstrous anti-type of the pastoral,
arcadian world which constitutes the core of Book VI. It signals in advance
that even the rounded harmony of this idyllic scene will also be
overthrown and dispelled by the turbulence of Spenserian narrative.[8]

Indeed, this pastoral episode is one of the major cruxes in the *Legend
of Courtesie*. It has been declared a glaring desertion of duty on Calidore's
part and seen as conclusive evidence that he willfully plays truant from
the quest which he has beeen assigned.[9] However, one of the prime
objectives of this departure into rural idyll is that it allows the poet to
establish a heterotopic sphere from which the problems of the court
may be reviewed. Just as Ireland in the *View* functions as the place of
difference in which the lineaments of order may be traced, so too Calidore's
sojourn amongst the shepherds serves to consolidate and redefine the
virtue of courtesie. Frank Kermode makes the point that 'the first
condition of Pastoral is that it is an urban product'.[10] Thus the pastoral
interlude permits a meeting of contraries and aims at counterposing
and ultimately reconciling the conflicting values of court and country.
The further purpose which this episode serves is to continue a sequence
of images set in motion in the proem. A recurring *leitmotif* in Book VI is
a scene of scopic desire which centres on the iconic figure of a woman
whose presence can only be partially captured and represented.[11] In the
wake of the impeded vision of the queen in the proem, the text attempts

by various subterfuges to produce a successon of metonymies for this vital, but perpetually blurred, originary point. This method of duplicating similar images by infinitely embedding them in each other may be likened to the heraldic device of the *mise en abîme* where a miniature version of the overall design is inset at the centre of a shield.[12] Through this process of interior duplication, Spenser's text repeats and reworks a central scene in an effort to combat the tensions with which it is laden.

The first and most disturbing of these scenes is that of Serena amongst the cannibals. It acts as a nightmare inversion of the visionary idealism which marks the opening of this book. Serena is described in terms of the voyeuristic lust of the cannibals, who feast their eyes as a prelude to the ultimate consumption which they eagerly await:

> So round about her they them selves did place
> Upon the grasse, and diversely dispose,
> As each thought best to spend the lingering space.
> Some with their eyes the daintest morsels chose;
> Some praise her paps, some praise her lips and nose;
> Some whet their knives, and strip their elbows bare:
> The Priest him selfe a garland doth compose
> Of finest flowres, and with full busie care
> His bloudy vessels wash, and holy fire prepare.
>
> (VI.viii.39)

She is dissected and violated by the invasive seeing of this 'salvage nation' and of the narrator who shares their point of view. The scene culminates with a triumphant blazon which tries to provide an exhaustive inventory of her beauty:

> Her yvorie necke, her alablaster brest,
> Her paps, which like white silken pillowes were,
> For love in soft delight thereon to rest;
> Her tender sides, her bellie white and clere,
> Which like an Altar did it selfe uprere,
> To offer sacrifice divine thereon;
> Her goodly thighes, whose glorie did appeare
> Like a triumphall Arch, and thereupon
> The spoils of Princes hang'd, which were in battel won.
>
> (VI.viii.42)

However, as Barthes has argued, such enumerative descriptions always fall short of their objects.[13] The more Serena is exposed to the rapacious eyes of those surrounding her, the more she is anatomised, and the more she disappears from sight. In the course of this fragmentation, she is reduced, in Barthes's phrase, to a kind of 'dictionary of fetish objects'.[14] Ultimately, Spenser lets loose the ravening gaze of desire in order to curb it and place it under restraint. Thus, even barbarism in the poem is discovered to have its limits. In the final reckoning, it is answerable to the dictates of a rudimentary 'civilitie'. As a result, two moments of censorship cut short this episode. First, the cannibals check their own impulses and are prevented by their priest from defiling Serena because, as the text informs us, 'religion held even theeves in measure' (VI.viii.43). Then, the entire scene is curtailed by the providential arrival of Calepine. In the closing moments of the canto, the two principal figures are left sitting in the dark. Serena's nakedness becomes its own disguise; she is denuded, but shrouded in darkness. She both can and cannot be seen. The poet, like the cannibals, refuses any further intrusions. The scene is truncated and Serena is thereby effectively removed from our field of vision, never to be seen again, despite the narrator's promise to the contrary:

> So all that night to him unknowen she past.
> But day, that doth discover bad and good,
> Ensewing, made her knowen to him at last:
> The end whereof He keepe untill another cast.

(VI.viii.51)

In the final two visionary scenes of Book VI, both of which occur during Calidore's stay in the world of arcadian innocence, the symbolic female figures assume a more idealised shape, and appear increasingly nebulous and elusive. Pastorella, for example, is depicted simply as a stock pastoral character, namely, the youthful maiden, who is the epitome of uncorrupted beauty:

> And soothly sure she was full fayre of face,
> And perfectly well shapt in every lim,
> Which she did more augment with modest grace,
> And comely carriage of her count'nance trim,
> That all the rest like lesser lamps did dim:
> Who her admiring as some heavenly wight,
> Did for their soveraine goddesse her esteeme,
> And carolling her name both day and night,
> The fayrest Pastorella her by name did hight.

(VI.ix.9)

Her very name obscures; it depends on an omission and on those elliptical strategies which Richard Cody identifies as a fundamental aspect of pastoral fiction.[15] We learn only that she is a beautiful shepherdess and the perfect accoutrement of the fictional world in which she resides. Later, she loses even this identity when Calidore returns her to her parents, Claribell and Bellamour. She becomes ultimately an incarnate but cryptic sign. The purple rose birthmark on her breast allows her genuine origin to be ascertained. But, in the final event, she remains anonymous, as her real name is never revealed in the poem. Pastorella metamorphoses before our eyes, and in the end, like Serena, she foils the attempts of language to fix or establish her presence in any definitive way.

In the final, climactic vision on Mount Acidale, a tension is set up between Calidore's wish to understand and interpret, and his longing for passive voyeuristic pleasure:

> He durst not enter into th'open greene,
> For dread of them unwares to be descryde,
> For breaking of their daunce, if he were seene;
> But in the covert of the wood did byde,
> Beholding all, yet of them unespyde.
> There he did see, that pleased much his sight,
> An hundred naked maidens lilly white,
> All raunged in a ring, and daucing in delight.

(VI.x.11)

However, in this case, the perspectives provided by the text are even more blurred and confused than in the previous scenes of scopic desire. Only with difficulty does the eye focus on the fourth Grace who is the central aspect of this phantasmic scene. It does not zoom in on her as in the description of Serena. Instead, this new icon of beauty remains indistinct and framed by her Otherness:

> And in the middest of those same three, was placed
> Another Damzell, as a precious gemme,
> Amidst a ring most richly well enchaced,
> That with her goodly presence all the rest much graced.

(VI.x.12)

The qualifying comparison which is unfolded in the following stanza deliberately deflects our attention from this 'damzell' whose presence has been so fleetingly evoked. We are forced to look in another direction:

> Looke how the Crowne, which Ariadne wore . . .
> Being now placed in the firmament,
> Through the bright heaven doth her beams display,
> And is unto the starres an ornament,
> Which round about her move in order excellent.

(VI.x.13)

A final attempt at description also runs aground. The poet, recognising the futility of his task, foreshortens his account of events, and simply repeats his earlier comments in slightly altered form:

> Such was the beauty of this goodly band,
> Whose sundry parts were here too long to tell:
> But she that in the midst of them did stand,
> Seem'd all the rest in beauty to excell,
> Crownd with a rosie girlond, that right well
> Did her beseeme . . .
>
> (VI.x.14)

Ultimately, the entire spectacle is dislodged and fragmented into further 'sundry parts' by the explanatory interjections of the narrator, and the long disquisition held by Calidore and Colin Clout concerning the meaning of the episode. The anatomising scrutiny of allegorical interpretation has replaced the fetishising gaze of the cannibals' greed. The language of exegesis succeeds in dismantling the arcane scene on Mount Acidale. In this way, it protects it from further profanation, while still subjecting it to the scopic regime of reading. It is as if the poem can continue only through the secession of its own rhetorical constructs. Thus, the discontinuities, rather than the unity, of the vision are foregrounded. In particular, we are reminded that the ethereal 'fourth Mayd' is but a further figure in the chain of metonymies which represents the queen with ever-increasing obliquity:

> Sunne of the world, great glory of the sky,
> That all the earth doest lighten with thy rayes,
> Great Gloriana, greatest Maiesty,
> Pardon thy shepheard, mongst so many layes,
> As he hath sung of thee in all his dayes,
> To make one mimime of thy poore handmayd,
> And underneath thy feete to place her prayse,
> That when thy glory shall be farre displayd
> To future age of her this mention may be made.
>
> (VI.x.28)

Elizabeth is, once again, appealed to as the absence upon which the text is predicted. While she is responsible for the fissures in the poem's surface, it is through probing such insufficiencies and through highlighting the struggle of language both to express and to contain desire that *The Faerie Queene* performs its complex act of homage to the incontrovertible right of authority.

Spenser has been called the poet of 'second thoughts' and indeed, the recursive patterns of his writings and their self-conscious efforts to mould and manipulate language are the primary strategies which he uses to articulate his political convictions.[16] As analysis has shown, the final book of Spenser's epic poem presents an equivocal and divided account of the political ideologies which it wishes to sustain. The 'other spaces' which it projects of a primordial pastoral innocence and of the incontestable moral imperatives of feudal knighthood are realised with great difficulty. The tensions which shape and inform the poem impede any possibility of resolution; we are confronted instead with a narrative which flirts with and is threatened by its own ultimate breakdown. In addition, the meandering and dilatory character of *The Legend of Courtesie* results from a deep-rooted conflict between the stimulus of language and the necessity to keep this incitement in check. It polices, interrogates, and probes its own rhetoric in an attempt to protect and control the fictions of authority which it manages to construct. Anxieties about the political order are contained by being deflected onto the realm of language, but rise persistently to the surface in the form of irresolvable ambiguities and lines of narrative which are stifled, cut off, and abandoned. Due to this continual struggle between the attractions and the prohibitions of narrative and language and the tensions caused by a political ideal of civility which yet depends on a policy of limitless violence, Spenser's text is, in the final reckoning, founded on its own impossibility. The Blatant Beast, that haunting spectre of unaccommodated Otherness, will always remain at large in the world and the ultimate goal, that of the colonisation of language, will never be attained.

Notes

1. MICHEL FOUCAULT, 'Of Other Spaces', *Diacritics* 16 (1987), 22–7.
2. FOUCAULT, p. 24.
3. *The Faerie Queene*, IV.iii.27.
4. ARNOLD WILLIAMS, *Flower on a Lowly Stalk* (Michigan, 1967), declares that 'the Blatant Beast is merely the essential evil of slander, indeed of all discourtesy: it hurts someone' (p. 68).
5. J. C. MAXWELL, 'The Truancy of Calidore' in WILLIAM MUELLER and DON CAMERON ALLEN (ed.), *That Soveraine Light: Essays in Honor of Edmund Spenser, 1552–1952* (Baltimore, 1952), pp. 63–9, notes that Calidore's fight with the Beast represents something of an anti-climax, while HUMPHREY TONKIN, *Spenser's Courteous Pastoral* (Oxford, 1972), contends that Calidore renders the Blatant Beast 'almost irrelevant to the central concerns of the book' (p. 33).
6. See SHORMISHTHA PANJA, 'A Self-Reflexive Parable of Narration: *The Faerie Queene* VI', *Journal of Narrative Technique* 15, 3 (1985), 277–88, who observes

that Calidore is the most loquacious of Spenser's heroes and points out that discourse forms the main activity of Book VI.

7. HARRY BERGER JNR., 'A Secret Discipline: *The Faerie Queene*, Book VI' in WILLIAM NELSON (ed.), *Form and Convention in the Poetry of Edmund Spenser* (New York, 1961), pp. 35–75.

8. KENNETH GROSE, *Spenserian Poetics: Idolatry, Iconoclasm and Magic* (New York, 1985), p. 230, treats this role of the Beast as a type of anti-pastoral in greater detail.

9. MAXWELL, pp. 65–6.

10. FRANK KERMODE, *English Pastoral Poetry* (London, 1952), p. 14.

11. See CHRISTIAN METZ, *The Imaginary Signifier: Psychoanalysis and the Cinema* (Bloomington, Indiana, 1982), pp. 58–78, for an account of the scopic drive. Metz explains that the desire to see 'represents the absence of its object in the distance at which it maintains it and which is part of its very definition' (p. 59). In all of Spenser's scenes of voyeuristic viewing the object of desire is either destroyed and thus banished, or else it disappears and fades away from sight.

12. For a recent discussion of this concept of the *mise en abîme* see STEPHEN W. MELVILLE, *Philosophy Beside Itself: On Deconstruction and Modernism* (Minneapolis, 1986), pp. 96–7.

13. ROLAND BARTHES, *S/Z* (tr.) RICHARD MILLER (New York, 1974): 'As a genre, the blazon expresses the belief that a complete inventory can reproduce a total body, as if the extremity of enumeration could devise a new category, that of totality: description is then subject to a kind of enumerative erethism: it accumulates in order to totalise, multiplies fetishes, in order to obtain a total defetishised body' (p. 114). See also JONATHAN GOLDBERG, *Endlesse Worke: Spenser and the Structures of Discourse* (Baltimore, 1981), p. 16, for a further discussion of this passage in Barthes.

14. BARTHES, p. 114.

15. RICHARD CODY, *The Landscape of the Mind: Pastoralism and Platonic Theory in Tasso's Aminta and Shakespeare's Early Comedies* (Oxford, 1969). Cody argues that pastorals are concerned with hidden comparisons and allusive signs which insist on remaining indecipherable. He claims that the fascination of pastoral literature derives from 'the difficulty of coming to a just appreciation of what the poet does not say' (p. 161). Pastorella, in Spenser's text, seems just such an example of the elliptical 'non-articulation of experience' inherent in pastoral fiction which Cody describes.

16. WILLIAM BLISSETT, 'Florimell and Marinell', *Studies in English Literature, 1500–1900* V (1965), 87–104 (p. 89).

12 Mapping mutability: or, Spenser's Irish plot*

Julia Reinhard Lupton

'Mapping Mutability' first appeared in an interdisciplinary collection of essays dealing with early modern Anglo-Irish relations, which sought to juxtapose and combine the insights of historians and literary critics. Julia Lupton's essay considers a variety of interrelated significant problems; she traces the different meanings of the word 'plot' – a map or survey and a plan or project – in the Irish State Papers in order to reconstruct an interpretative framework for Spenser's *A View of the Present State of Ireland*; she attempts to connect Spenser's disagreement with the Irish magnate Lord Roche concerning the title to the Kilcolman estate with Mutability's 'trial to ... Titles and best Rights' in *The Faerie Queene*, Book VII; she suggests that Ovid's poetry – both his metamorphic verse and his writings from exile – might provide a way of conceptualising Spenser's Irish career in literary as well as political terms. Acteon, the figure whom Ovid cites in the *Tristia* as the model of his own error, implicates the extreme localisation of the exiled autobiographical voice in the scattered world of mythopoesis, and thus offers a model for Spenser's Irish reflections in the *Cantos of Mutability*.

Lupton's essay is valuable both for its sophisticated discussion of Spenser's Irish contexts and for its focus on the generic intertextuality of individual works – a major concern of New Historicist and deconstructionist critics alike, as other essays in this collection illustrate. Any direct transcription of Spenser's Irish activities into his poetry is problematic, as poetic conventions and motifs more often refer to each other than to a world outside, and poets in particular are given to refigure personal experience through complex meditations on the literary tradition.

---

*Reprinted from Brendan Bradshaw, Andrew Hadfield and Willy Maley, eds, *Representing Ireland: Literature and the Origins of Conflict, 1534–1660* (Cambridge: Cambridge University Press, 1993), pp. 93–115.

In Spenser's *View of the Present State of Ireland*, Eudoxus listens attentively to Irenius' proposed deployment of English forces in key positions across Ireland:

> in what places would yow sett their garrison that they might ryse out most Convenientlie to service and though perhapps I am ignorante of the places yett I will take the mapp of Ireland before mee and make my eyes in the meane while my scholemasters to guide my understanding to judge of your plott.[1]

Spenser's casually concrete reference to a 'mapp of Ireland', presented here as a means of illuminating Irenius' 'plott' or policy for the country, emblematises what I will call the Elizabethan genre of the *Irish plot*, a phrase encompassing English strategies for Irish reform, the cartographic projects of surveying and mapping which furthered them, and, more generally, a geographical, antiquarian approach to Irish history which marks Spenser's poetics as well as his politics. As we shall see, the key word in Spenser's Irish plot is *waste*: Spenser's tract defines Ireland as wasteland (desolate, depeopled, and unpossessed) in order to defend an active policy of further wasting followed by restorative 'plantation'. It is in consonance with this geographical delineation of Ireland that Spenser writes an etiology of the Irish landscape in the *Mutabilitie Cantos*: the mock-Ovidian narrative of Faunus which mythologises the wasting of Arlo Hill, a landmark of Spenser's Irish home. In these *Cantos*, Spenser's reliance on Ovid entails not only the borrowing of the Acteon tale, but also a dependence on and thematisation of 'the Ovidian' as such, understood as both a narrative mode – the genealogy of landscape in the *Metamorphoses* – and an authorial posture – the autobiography of exile in the *Tristia* and *Ex Ponto*. This double Ovidian legacy underwrites Spenser's Irish plot as it passes between his policy and his poetry, a plot in which the etiology of Ireland as wasteland supports a poetics of exile which in turn justifies and masks the Tudor project of imperial dispossession. Read together, Spenser's *View of Ireland* and the *Cantos of Mutabilitie* map Ireland as a desert in order to defend its further wasting through systematic depopulation, geographic re-inscription, and georgic recolonisation. At the same time, the internal contradictions of the *View's* spatialising fantasies threaten to interrupt the dream of cartographic order from within, cracking, piercing and mutating the plane surfaces of English space with enclaves of Irish alterity. In the *Mutabilitie Cantos*, these residual strata of Irish waste are figured through the digressive etiologies of Ovid, whose poetics of exile and metamorphosis come to describe not only the stance of the English poet in Ireland, but also the acts of dispossession which found his Irish home.

In tracing Spenser's Irish plot across these two texts, I am
simultaneously mapping my own place in criticism: namely, the *topos* and
utopos (no-place) of intertextuality as the network of discourses which
enables and conditions every poetic and critical act. For the Spenser of
this essay, these discourses include the literary genres of pastoral and
epylion, the authorial example of Ovid, and their intersection with the
available political and legal vocabularies that defined Ireland for the
English. Although these discourses together inform Spenser's attempt
to map Ireland as a certain kind of place, they could do so only insofar
as they themselves constitute a mutable landscape of rhetorical *topoi*
whose very historical over-determination dislocates them from the
discrete moments in space and time which they none the less continue
to index. The landscape of intertextuality, with its multiple sources,
crossing currents, and shifting boundaries, is reticulated and punctuated
above all by the classical landmarks of literary history whose shifting
contours subtend the motifs and motives of a particular political agenda.
It is here that my own approach may finally differ from that of the 'new
historicism', whose salutary expansion of the textual field threatens at
times to overlook, forget, or misrecognise the specific efficacies and logics
of the literary canon and its discontents.

Waste of Shame: Spenser's Ireland

Spenser's reference in the *View* to a 'mappe of Ireland' flags a series of
connections between cartography and conquest which illuminates not
only the political *content* or argument of Spenser's tract but also its *mode
of discourse*, its enabling fantasies of political representation. The
continuum between the political sciences of cartography and policy-
making is already announced in the title of Spenser's dialogue, a *view*
of Ireland. 'View' is initially defined in the *OED* as 'A formal inspection
or survey of lands, tenements or ground, for some special purpose', a
definition abstracted into 'a survey, a general or summary account' (*OED*,
12), and projected forwards as 'an aim or intention; a design or plan;
an object or purpose' (*OED*, 12).[2] Reflecting these multiple valences,
Spenser's 'view' of Ireland is at once a programme and a survey, a
military and cultural agenda supported by geographic and ethnographic
arguments. The book falls into three sections: a critical summary of current
policy (pp. 3–48), a cultural and historical account of Gaelic barbarism
(pp. 48–120), and Spenser's own modest proposal for the reformation
of Ireland (pp. 121–220). The text offers, that is, a view, re-view, and pre-
view of Ireland's present, past and future; in each case, Spenser's work

remains a survey *of the land*, a fundamentally geographical perspective
in which the topographic, synchronically systematising, and visually
ordering connotations of 'view' comprehend and organise the text's
chronological moments.

Thus, in the central section on Gaelic customs, Spenser couches Irish
history as *natural history* by representing events not so much in military
or dynastic as in racial terms: Ireland emerges as the registration of the
undulating displacements of barbarian peoples (Scythians, native
Spaniards, Africans, Gauls, Brittons), migrations legible in the
'comparison of tymes, lykenes of manners and customes, affinitie of
wordes, & names, properties of Natures and uses resemblances of rights
and ceremonies monumentes of Churches and Tombes, and manye other
lyke Circumstances' (p. 52). The *View*'s antiquarian concern with
language, law and custom is a function of Spenser's fundamentally
geographical approach to Ireland's history and culture, in which the
remaining monuments of culture rather than the suspect chronicles of
its barbaric bards best tell the story not of a family, *polis*, or empire, but
of a 'land', understood as the fortuitous collision and collusion of
geography and race. The *View*'s geographical and anthropological
impulses find ample precedent in the long tradition of English writings
on Ireland; for example, the most influential account of Ireland in
medieval and Renaissance England was Giraldus Cambrensis'
Topographia Hiberniae (1187), a description of the land, wild-life, barbarous
customs and 'immigrations' of Ireland with a view to justifying and
celebrating the recent Anglo-Norman conquest of the island.[3] Far from
anticipating a liberal humanism of cultural difference – as Sheila
Cavanagh has implied – Spenser's antiquarian approach, like Giraldus'
before him, is racial in focus and racist in intent.[4]

In the *View*, Eudoxus refers to 'the map of Irelande' in a military context.
English maps of Ireland were almost always designed for military and
legal purposes, in order to establish strategies of attack and defence,
and, in consolidating military success, to (re)determine the boundaries of
property – bluntly pragmatic concerns which distinguish these documents
from the humanist, antiquarian, patriotic, scientific or aesthetic ambitions
of printed atlases by cartographers such as Saxton, Camden or Ortelius.[5]
Eudoxus signals the strategic function of Irish maps through the word
'plot', a term whose valences indicate mapping as a structural principle
of Spenser's text. Here, the word 'plot' most directly indicates 'strategy'
or 'plan', a use recurrent in official correspondence concerning Ireland
during the period, as in Lord Pelham's 1580 'Plot for Munster' or
Nicholas White's 1584 'Ireland – A Plate [plot] conceived how that realm
may be governed with contentation of the inhabitants and surety of the
estate'.[6] Spenser's *View* follows in part what I call the genre of the Irish

'plot', the numerous manuscript proposals for reforming Ireland which are scattered throughout the calendars of Tudor state papers.

These Irish plots, as Nicholas Canny has argued, document the rise of a professional class of English colonist-bureaucrats. Protestant in religion, humanist in education, and drawn from ' "the younger houses of gentlemen" ',[7] these 'New English' officials were opposed not so much to the barbaric 'mere Irish' – the Celtic peoples with little or no legal claim to land under British rule – as to the 'Old English' or 'Anglo-Irish': the heirs of the original Norman conquerors of Ireland whose titles were English but whose style of rule tended towards the Gaelic and whose religion remained resolutely Catholic. Like the *View*, these 'New English' documents tend to prefer military solutions to reformist ones, since war followed by colonisation could most effectively displace and disperse the prerogatives of the Anglo-Irish. Thus John Davies, a later New English apologist, wrote,

For the husbandman must first break the land before it be made capable of good seed; and when it is thoroughly broken and manured, if he do not forthwith cast good seed into it, it will grow wild again, and bear nothing but weeds. So a barbarous country must be first broken by a war before it will be capable of good government; and when it is fully subdued and conquered, if it be not well planted and governed after the conquest, it will eftsoons return to the former barbarism.[8]

Like the *View*, such tracts employ agricultural language to defend a violent solution; if Virgil's *Georgics* counseled the transformation of swords into ploughshares, the counter-georgics of the Irish 'plantation' used extended metaphor to turn ploughshares back into swords.

'Plot' (like 'View') can also mean 'map' (*OED* 3a). One of the chief cartographers of Ireland in the period, Francis Jobson, titling one of his maps a *'plotte* of the greatt countey of Lymbrick', describes its contents: 'Also you shall finde the *plotte formes*, with the just proportion & simitrie of all the perticuler percells of grounds, as I have surveyed & measured, of her Ma[jes]ties lands escheated within the said country' (emphasis added). A map is called a 'plot' because it establishes 'plots' (or here, 'plotte formes') of land: parcels of property demarcated by their borders, in colours, we are told, of red, yellow and green depending on the type of land tenure.[9] Read within the context of its creation – the context moreover of Spenser's Irish career – Jobson's description of geographical description reveals the functional relation between mapping and the definition of property. Jobson's maps were made under a commission appointed in 1584 to survey Munster in the wake of the Desmond rebellion which had ravaged the region. The survey was needed to determine the boundaries of escheated lands and to 'compound' –

that is, convert to English tenure – the lands not held by the Crown.[10] All of this was necessary groundwork for establishing the proper borders and individual plots of the Munster plantation, the colony of English settlers in which Spenser would participate from its inception in 1586 till the burning of his property during the Tyrone rebellion in 1598.[11] The results of such a survey included most obviously the redistribution of property from the rebels to the English 'undertakers' via the Crown. In addition, the act of 'composition' entailed conversion to a fundamentally different relation to the land, based not on the brief leases and nomadic displacement of Brehon law, but on the fixed, transmittable 'plots' of what we now call private property; thus the establishment of English tenure was seen not only as a legal convenience facilitating settlement and taxation, but also as a crucial means of 'civilising' the Irish by tying them down to the domestic responsibilities and values of the English home.[12] Finally, the act of mapping and surveying had the inevitable effect of transforming the names of places, whether through the substitution of Gaelic words by English transliterations and outright replacements, or through the redefinition of traditional county lines and regional divisions.[13]

While the *View* refers to maps like Jobson's and borrows topoi from the geographical tradition of Giraldus Cambrensis' *Topographia Hiberniae*, Spenser's approach to the land of Ireland is not 'topographical' in the sense of detailed chorographic description, so much as 'topological', supported by and articulating a generalised theory and ideology of place. In the pioneering Spenserian topology of Great Britain, the georgic enterprise of 'planting' is underwritten by the definition of Ireland as a wasteland: uninhabited, uncultivated, devastated, deserted, outside the law. Again and again, the *View* presents an image of the Irish landscape as wasteland: 'desertes, and Mountaines' (p. 18), 'the mountaine and waste wilde places' (p. 64), 'great mountaines and waist deserts' (p. 64), 'waste places farr from danger of lawe' (p. 67). It is a landscape of occluded corners where the Irish, 'shutt upp within those narrow corners and glens' (p. 21), 'lurketh in the thycke woodes and streight passages' (p. 67). This 'view of the present state of Ireland' as desert – this 'plot' in the sense of map or survey – motivates and reinforces the retrospective and projective 'plots' of Spenser's text. Spenser's Irish 'plot' is repeatedly one of *waste*, as he tells the story of Ireland's repeated devastations, surveys its present geography, and puts forward a programme of depopulation, displacement, and geographic transformation – a programme whose unspoken fantasy is of a land as flat, empty and inscribable as the 'mappe of Irelande' which Eudoxus holdes before him.

In the historical episodes recounted in the *View*, the agents of 'wasting' shift between the Irish and their conquerors, while the site of desolation appears alternately as the natural terrain of a barbaric people and as a civilised land subject to wilful devastation. Spenser describes the adventures of

> Murrogh en ranagh, That is Morris of the ferne or waste wylde places, who gatheringe unto him all the relickes of the discontented Irishe eftsones surprized the said Castle of Clare, burnte and spoyled all the Englishe there dwellinge . . . whence shortelye breakinge forth lyke a suddaine tempest he overran all Mounster, and Connaught, breakinge downe all the holdes and fortresses of the Englishe, defacing and utterlie suvertinge all corporate townes that were not stronglie walled . . . So in shorte space he cleane wiped out manie greate townes . . . some of which there is nowe noe memorie nor signe remayninge . . . For yt was his pollicie to leave noe houldes behinde him, but to make all plaine and waste.
>
> (pp. 21–2)

Here Morrough 'en Ranagh' O'Brien, who led a rebellion in 1382, is represented as both arising from 'the ferne of waste wylde places' and as 'burning and spoyling all the English', re-absorbing the fragile outposts of British civilisation into the Irish desert surrounding it. In the crucial description of Morrough making 'all plaine and waste', Ireland emerges as a kind of mapped surface subject to continual reinscription: the 'defaced' towns of Mounster and Connaught have been 'cleane wyped out' so that, like erased markers on a map, 'there is now noe memorie nor signe remayninge' of them.

It is no accident that Spenser lingers on this episode from Irish history, since Morrough's wasting of Munster prefigures the infamous *English* wasting of the same region during the Desmond rebellion under Spenser's employer, Arthur Lord Grey de Wilton, the 'Artegall' of the *Faerie Queene*. In the *View*'s most quoted passage, Spenser puts forth the military benefits of famine:

> Although there should none of them fall by the sworde, nor be slaine by the soldyer, yet thus beinge kept from manurance, and there cattle from runninge abroad by this hard restrainte they would quicklie consume them selves and devoure one another. Thee proof whereof I sawe suffycientlie ensampled in those late warrs in Mounster, for notwithstanding that the same was a most rich and plentifull Countrye . . . yet err one yeare and a half, they were brought to such wretchednes, as that any stonie harte would have rewed the same, out of everie Corner of the woodes & glennes they came creeping forth upon their hands, fr theire legges could not beare them, they looked Anatomies of death, they spake like ghostes cryinge out of their graves,

they did eate of the dead Carrions . . . and yf they founde a plotte of
water cresses or shamrockes, there they flocked as to a feast for the
tyme, yet not able longe to contynewe therewithall, that in shorte
space there were none almost left and a most populous and plentyfull
Countrye suddenlie left voyde of man or beast.

(p. 135)

In this passage, Spenser deploys the motif of Irish cannibalism, a
commonplace of the antiquarian topographic tradition, in support of
a policy of starvation; the English are thus portrayed as simply bringing
out the self-wasting propensities of the Irish. These flesh-eating natives
appear, and then disappear, in a man-made desert, 'a most populous and
plentyful Countrye suddenlie lefte voyde of man or beast'.
Topographically, the passage counterpoints two kinds of wasteland, the
Irish desert of wooded 'Corners', and the English desert of land literally
cleared by famine and war. One goal of Spenser's policy is to get the
Irish out of their 'waste places farr from danger of lawe' (p. 67) and
into the *English* desert of pure visibility.[14] As in Morrough en Ranagh
O'Brien's making of Munster 'all plaine and waste', the topography of
the desert reinforces representational features of mapping: Spenser's ideal
Ireland would be a plane surface, open and visible, conveniently
unpeopled for the purposes of more orderly re-population, a surface
capable of infinite articulation, erasure, and reordering. In Spenser's
'Anatomy of death', *surveillance* and *surveying* merge in the ideal of an
emptied, flattened landscape without 'corners' – except perhaps paper
ones.

'Ensampling' how Ireland can best be reformed, the devastation of
Munster functions for Spenser as the interface of (past) history and
(proposed) policy, the narratival and strategic senses of 'plot'. The
'wasting' of Munster conveniently fed into a specific legal sense of the
word: 'a piece of such land not in any man's occupation, but lying
common' (*OED* 2). If Spenser and his New English contemporaries
could successfully define Ireland as waste, they could in turn better justify
the appropriation and cultivation of its lands. Robert Dunlop, an
historian of both the Munster plantation and sixteenth-century maps of
Ireland, has isolated 'one particular fact' that distinguished Munster
from earlier projects and strongly influenced its planners: 'the utter
depopulation of the province'. The consequences were ideological as
well as practical, since, Dunlop continues, 'the "repeopling of Munster",
therefore, if not in truth the cause of the plantation, furnished at any
rate a plausible excuse for it'.[15] Following this logic, the Queen in one
directive declared without any apparent sense of paradox that, whereas
the province had been 'utterly wasted, unpeopled, and made desolate',
she, in her 'gracious disposition' and 'zealous care' of the realm, would

'encourage and enable our loving subjects ... to inhabit and repeople that province of Munster'.[16] The same logic governs Spenser's Irish plot and grants Munster its exemplary status: if Ireland is (made) a desert – desolate, uninhabited, and *unowned* – then its colonisation becomes a right and a duty.

In laying out his proposal for Ireland, Spenser extends the Munster experience into a general programme which continues to articulate the ideal of Ireland as a map, both surveyed and surveyable, a fantasy in which the cartography of the desert – flat and empty, 'plaine and waste' – becomes a figure of *the cartographic as such*.[17] In discussing the limits of humanist reform and the need for more radical military action, Eudoxus remarks that 'the whole ordynance and institucion of that Realmes government, was both at first when yt was placed evill plotted, and also since through other oversighte, Run more out of square ... lyke as twoe indyrect lynes the further they are drawen out, the further they goe asunder' (p. 121). Eudoxus presents Ireland as a badly drafted, 'evill plotted' drawing whose lines are not parallel, a metaphor which embodies the fantasy of mapping motivating the operations and goals of Spenser's military strategy.[18] Eudoxus had referred to 'the mapp of Ireland' in the context of the 'setting' of garrisons, a phrase which evokes the role of the map not only as a tool for military strategy, but more fundamentally as a structuring fantasy, *a fantasy of structure*, which informs the text's colonising desire for spatial mastery. Spenser's plan for the 'newe framinge' of Ireland (p. 121), explicitly and implicitly develops the ideal of colonised space as a map, an image most clearly visible for Spenser on the ground of the Munster plantation, which had been cleared by war and famine, intensively surveyed by the Queen's commission, and 'repeopled' (not, as we shall see, without contention) by English settlers.[19]

According to J. H. Andrews, however, for all this dream of a paper landscape, the surveying of the Munster plantation was a 'false start', a project faulted not only by political expedience, bad weather, and rough territory, but by the impasses of its own conceptual framework: 'With almost every farm a rectangle or triangle, the whole design was suffused with ... the land surveyor's mentality ... it carried the demand for professional expertise all the way down the socio-agricultural hierarchy'.[20] The geometric perfection of the initial survey of Munster led to its immediate replotting in a number of commissions, first to resurvey the land, and later to try the legality of its borders (p. 32). So, too, if cartographics inform the *View*, this sixteenth-century text cannot yet approximate the Cartesian plane of homogeneous, calculable space. To borrow William Boelhower's semiosis of the early modern map, the *system of the line* – 'an invisible network of abstract structural ties and infinite possibilities of calculation'[21] – does not yet dominate the two other fundamental signifying systems of cartography, *the word* and *the image*, which both dislocate the universality of space with the specificity of place. The flattened, rational space of Spenser's ideal Ireland is insistently punctured by those intransigent 'corners' and 'coverts' of locality, a pocketing or pock-marking of the paper plane with non-integrated hollows of cultural and terrestrial difference. It is here that the landscape of the Ovidian *oeuvre* operates as both a poetic analogue and a counterdiscourse linking the Ireland of the *View* to the *Cantos of Mutabilitie* by distending the hollows of alterity which twist and pit the *View's* spatial dream.

Metamorphosis Ex Ponto: Spenser's Ovid

During the discussion of Irish antiquities in the *View*, Eudoxus asks Irenius, 'Is yt possible, how comes yt then that they are soe barbarous still and so unlearned, beinge so old scollers: For learninge as the Poete sayth: *Emollit mores ne sinit esse feros* [softens the customs and permits it not to be cruel] whence then I praye yow could they have those lettres' (p. 53). Distinguishing his speech from that of the barbarians through the definitively humanist act of classical citation, Eudoxus quotes Ovid's *Ex Ponto* (II. ix. 48), the exile's complaint from a barbarous land at the edges of empire. The citation from 'the Poete' suggests the textual and structural affiliations between the Irelands of Spenser's *View* and the *Mutabilitie Cantos*. While the Ovidian tale of Faunus and Diana exercises a learned wit – the entire Canto is written, it seems, with a forced smile – the darker purpose of the episode is to give an account of Irish desolation, a mythopoetic analogue to the *View's* narrative of waste. This etiology of the Irish desert situates the legal plaint of Mutabilitie in a landscape whose Ovidian physics infuse the medieval metaphysics of the poem's formal debate with the political fictions of the westward enterprise.

The mock-epic flow of Canto VI, describing the virago Mutabilitie's bid for power, branches into the 'soft delights' of pastoral digression at 'Arlo-Hill', the Irish mountain where Nature will hear Mutabilitie's case in Canto VII:

> And, were it not ill fitting for this file
> To sing of hilles & woods, mongst warres & Knightes,
> I would abate the sternesse of my stile,
> Mongst these sterne stounds to mingle soft delights;
> And tell how *Arlo* through *Dianaes* spights

(Beeing of old the best and fairest Hill
That was in all this holy-Islands hights)
Was made the most unpleasant, and most ill.
Meane while, O *Clio*, lend *Caliope* thy quill.

(vi. 37)

Whylome, when IRELAND flourished in fame
Of wealths and goodnesse, far above the rest
Of all that beare the *British* Islands name,
The Gods then us'd (for pleasure and for rest)
Oft to resort there-to, when seem'd them best.

(vi. 38)

Ireland, Spenser proposes, was once a pastoral resort for the Olympian
gods; through the shameful voyeurism of Faunus, a latter-day Actaeon,
however, the island has fallen from a *locus amoenus* to a region 'most
unpleasant, and most ill'. The temporal contrast between resort and
desert doubly confirms Ireland's subjected conditions. Anticipating the
'vacationscape' of modern Ireland's tourist industry, Spenser's zoning
of the island 'for pleasure and for rest' projects an originary leisure world
which the georgics of the Elizabethan 'plantations' aim to restore.[22]
Spenser's 'IRELAND' spatially registers the temporal (non)difference
between two discourses of place: the arche-colonial pasture of the gods'
Irish 'resort' as it slips into and implies the language of a debased and
urgently contemporary realism of waste.

The episode ends with Diana's departure from Arlo-Hill:

Nath'lesse, *Diana*, full of indignation,
Thence-forth abandoned her delicious brooke;
In whose sweet streame, before that bad occasion,
So much delight to bathe her limbes she tooke:
Ne onely her, but also quite forsooke
All those faire forrests about *Arlo* hid,
And all that Mountaine, which doth over-looke
The richest champain that may else be rid,
And the faire *Shure*, in which are thousand Salmons bred.

Them all, and that she so deare did way,
Thence-forth she left; and parting from the place,
There-on an heavy haplesse curse did lay,
To weet, that Wolves, where she was wont to space,
Should harbour'd be, and all those woods deface,
And Thieves should rob and spoile that Coast around.
Since which, those Woods, and all that goodly Chase,

221

>Doth to this day with Wolves and Thieves abound:
>Which too-too true that lands in-dwellers since have found.
>
>(VI. 54–5)

Diana's desertion of Ireland clearly echoes in a humorous key the departure of Astrea which frames the iron world justice of Book V, a mythographic and intratextual link which intimates the bearing of Irish politics on the *Mutabilitie Cantos*. The final stanza of the canto is marked by the vocabulary of the *View*: like 'Morris of the ferne or waste wylde places', the aggressively anti-pastoral Irish wolves 'deface' the woods, natural counterparts to the nameless 'Thieves' whose vocation to 'rob and spoil' implicitly opposes the nomadic shepherds' economy of the Irish natives to the georgic virtues of English private property. In the final line, 'Which *too-too true* that lands in-dwellers since have found', Spenser flags the intrusion of this 'realistic' discourse into the pastoralism of the preceding narrative, a translation facilitated by Ovid as the poet of quick changes.[23]

As a digression on geography, the Faunus episode also effects a digression within the geographical mode itself, inhabiting and exaggerating the ravines of locality faulting the spatial ideal of the *View*. If, in Boelhower's semiosis of the map, 'every toponym . . . contains the story of its own origin, a trap door . . . opened in the written surface of the map'[24] the Ovidian landscape of mutability, with its rhetorical mythography of place, its digressive textuality, and its insistence on metamorphosis, confirms the de-cartesian tendency in Spenser's topology of Ireland. The 'too-too true' of contemporary Ireland signals the obdurate enclaves of alterity that transform the 'many woods, and shady corners' of Diana's sylvan pastoral (VI. 41) into 'those narrow corners and glens' of the lupine Irish (*View*, p. 21).

Spenser's self-conscious reworking of the Actaeon story locates his text in the Ovidian geography of metamorphosis while simultaneously enunciating the Ovidian poetics of exile. In the *Tristia*, Ovid compares his error to that of Actaeon:

>cur aliquid vidi? cur noxia lumina feci?
>cur imprudenti cognita culpa mihi?
>inscius Acteon vidit sine veste Dianam:
>praeda fuit canibus nun minus ille suis.

[Why did I see anything? Why did I make my eyes guilty? Why was I so thoughtless as to harbour the knowledge of a fault? Unwitting was Acteon when he beheld Diana unclothed; none the less he became the prey of his own hounds.][25]

Here Ovid inscribes his autobiographical letters of exile into his epic of metamorphosis by identifying the *persona* of the *Tristia* with the figure of Actaeon. Indeed, the allusion was prominent enough to deserve mention in George Sandys's 1621 annotated translation of the *Metamorphoses*, which uses the Actaeon of exile to gloss the Actaeon of mythopoeis: 'But this fable was invented to shew us how dangerous a curiosity it is to search into the secrets of Princes . . . Some such unhappy discovery procured the banishment of our *Ovid*: who complaining of his misfortunes, introduceth this example' (p. 151).[26] Spenser's citation of Actaeon in the Faunus episode, then, confirms and extends Michael Holahan's suggestive comments on the merging of the two Ovids – via the two Actaeons – in the *Mutabilitie Cantos*: 'Spenser gestures pointedly to his Ovidian source [the *Metamorphoses*] but in a manner that implies critical revision. His selection of an Irish locale represents Ovidian myth in exile, its rustication so to speak (as if in ironic accord with the poet's Black Sea fate)'.[27] The reference to Actaeon neatly overlays two versions of Ovidian displacement: the sea changes of endless metamorphosis, and the *tristes tropiques* of exile.

The textual *spargamos* of Actaeon across the *Metamorphoses*, the *Tristia*, and the *Mutabilitie Cantos* indicates the affinity between the metamorphic etiology of waste and the authorial stance of exile: the first mythologises the *locus* from which the *genius* expressed in the latter can emerge. If, as Harry Berger, Junior, has argued, the poet's voice is increasingly lyricised in the unfolding of the *Mutabilitie Cantos*, I would suggest that it is precisely the mythopoetic demarcation of the poet's home-away-from-home which permits the appearance of a more concretised narrative persona.[28] Combining etiology with etymology and blurring both through paronomasia, the play of the Latinate 'Faunus' against the Celtic 'Fanchin' dramatises the diaspora of classical culture, situating Ovidian metamorphosis at Pontus, and Spenserian epylion at Kilcolman. So, too, in the condensation of 'Mulla' and 'Moles' in Spenser's 'old father *Mole*', the mountain whose 'highest head' is Arlo-hill, the Irish landscape is doubly 'italicised': both given the typographic emphasis of the toponym and *rendered Italian*, charged with the cachet of the classical in exile.[29] Through these subtle operations, the desert of exile is reclaimed as the most fertile ground for both the rising poet and the new gentleman.

Like Colin's song of the Bregog and Mulla Rivers in *Colin Clouts Come Home Again*, the Faunus episode gives a fanciful etiology to physical features of Spenser's Irish estate and its environs – here, the 'marriage' of the 'Molanna' [Behanagh] River to the Fanchin or Funcheon.[30] While lacking the architectural focus and topographic specificity of the great country house poems of the seventeenth century, Spenser's Ovidian etiologies share with them an interest in the landmarks of property. The Irish setting helps determine the humorous pessimism which

distinguishes Spenser's mytho-topology from the epideixis of the later
country house poems: we have here not the neo-georgic praise of a
patron's benevolent manorialism, but rather a tragi-comic narrative
describing the poet's own estate of exile. The toponym *Arlo-Hill*, a signifier
of the 'too-too true' infolded in the interlocking Ovidian poetics of
displacement, locates Spenser's authorial voice as fundamentally dis-
located; at once poems of property and poems of expatriation, *Colin Clouts
Come Home Again* and the *Mutabilitie Cantos* channel the Ovidian pathos
of exile via narratives of metamorphosis into Spenser's sense of Irish
place.

'Triall of Their Titles and Best Rights': An Historical Allegory

That sense of Irish place doubly involves exile: not only Spenser's distance
from the centre of English life, but also the acts of dispossession which
made the English plantations possible – again, not the displacement of
the 'mere Irish' so much as their Anglo-Irish lords. It was members
of this class who led the great revolts of the sixteenth century, including
the Desmond rebellion which cleared the land for the Munster
plantation. While Munster, as we have seen, was basically depopulated
by flight and famine in the wake of the Desmond uprising, the New English
undertakers were constantly plagued by the return of previous
inhabitants, primarily Anglo-Irish landholders, who claimed rights to
the property. This situation led to the establishment in 1588 of 'a
commission for the trial of the pretended titles in Munster';[31] at stake
was precisely the reliability of the survey made of the lands, an initial
mapping whose sloppy execution, impeded by the inclemencies of the
physical and political climate, plagued the groundwork of the plantation
with ambiguous and inaccurate measurements.[32] As J. H. Andrews
concludes, 'The failure of the Munster surveys – for failure it was –
extended to almost every aspect of the work'.[33] While these
contradictions in the initial survey contributed to the ultimate failure of
the Munster plantation in the 1590s, the trial of the titles was decided
in favour of the settlers: of eighty-one cases heard by the commission,
only one was honoured.[34] One plaintiff was Maurice Lord Roche, whose
claims against a number of undertakers were dismissed by the
Commissioners, 'as they were informed that the witnesses for Her
Majesty have been sinisterly seduced by Lord Roche'.[35] The following
year, the same Lord Roche, complaining that he is 'like to be
dispossessed of his ancient inheritance', raised claims against Edmund
Spenser, whom he accused of having 'wasted 6 ploughlands of his

Lordship's lands'.[36] While Lord Roche disputed Spenser's title to the land, Spenser countered by impugning Roche's loyalties: 'He speaketh ill of the government and hath uttered words of contempt of her majesty's laws, calling them unjust'. Spenser eventually lost two ploughshares to another undertaker, Nicholas Synan, in 1592, but none to Lord Roche.[37]

In these trials of titles, then, the strategic and cartographic discourses – the 'plots for reform' and the 'plotting of land' – produced around the establishment of the Munster plantation were publicly displayed in their structuring limitations and internal contradictions: the fact that every boundary leads to displacement, the intransigence of both the land and the people to cartographic reinscription, and the palimpsestic character of the terrain as a history of contested titles whose erasure is always imperfect. I mention these trials because of their parallels with the legal hearing of Mutabilitie, parallels that concern not the 'characters' or personalities involved, but rather their 'titles', in both the legal and the typographic senses. If *Arlo-Hill*, a landmark of Spenser's Irish property, is the setting of Mutabilitie's plaint, to what extent is the local history of Kilcolman – Spenser's title to his property and his poetry – registered in the debate which unfolds there?

When Jove rejects Mutabilitie's claims, she appeals to Dame Nature:

> Eftsoones the time and place appointed were,
>   Where all, both heavenly Powers, & earthly wights
> Before great Natures presence should appeare,
>   For triall of their titles and best Rights:
>   That was, to weet, upon the highest hights
> Of *Arlo-Hill* (Who knows not *Arlo-Hill?*)
>   That is the highest head (in all men's sight)
> Of my old father *Mole*, whom Shepheards quill
> Renowmed hath with hymnes fit for a rural skill.
>
>   (VI. 36)

For triall of their Titles and best Rights: while the scene clearly enunciates the medieval genre of the debate, an allegorical form elaborated in the pageants of Canto VII, the location of the trial on Spenser's own property resituates the medieval form in the national geographics of contemporary Ireland. As Eiléan Ní Chuilleanáin writes of Canto VII's Munster setting, 'Mutabilitie's chief witnesses, the laboring Months with their aura of georgic festivity, figuratively recolonize the wilderness'.[38] Like Spenser's *View*, the *Mutabilitie Cantos* first waste Ireland in order to recolonise her, a procedure which Mutabilitie serves both to justify – as a figure of primordial chaos requiring the ordering of Nature – and to resist – as a sign of the contradictions mortgaging Spenser's Irish home. Mutabilitie states her case to Jove:

> I am a daughter, by the mother's side,
> Of her that is Grand-mother magnifide
> Of all the Gods, great *Earth*, great *Chaos* child:
> But by the father's bloud (whereon I build)
> Then all the Gods, though wrongfully from heaven exil'd.
>
> (VI. 26)

Like the Old English, Mutabilitie's claims are conservative, based as were Lord Roche's on 'ancient inheritance'. As the daughter of Earth, she is linked to the land in its most primitive, inchoate guise; as the daughter of 'Titan', she stems from a line of originary revolt, the battle of the Titans against Saturn and Jove, a myth which functions in Spenser to implicate political rebellion in primeval, unredeemed nature.[39] Mutabilitie's claims are thus both ancient and intrinsically chaotic, since they derive not from the classical antiquity of the Olympian gods but from the counter-classical disorder of the chthonic deities.

The claim to be 'wrongfully ... exil'd' shifts from Mutabilitie to Jove, finally victorious 'against that *Titanesse* / That him of heavens Empire sought to dispossesse' (VII. I). Jove counters Spenser's arguments from antiquity with the same reasoning used against the Irish and the Anglo-Irish:

> But wote thou this, thou hardy *Titanesse*,
>   That not the worth of any living wight
>   May challenge ought in Heavens interesse;
>   Much lesse the Title of old *Titans* Right;
>   For, we by Conquest of our soveraine might,
>   And by eternall doome of Fates decree,
>   Have wonne the Empire of the Heavens bright;
>   Which to our selves we hold, and to whom wee
> Shall worthy deeme partakers of our blisse to bee.
>
> (VI. 33)

Jove opposes the argument from inheritance – 'the Title of old *Titans* Right' – to the prerogative of conquest. '[T]he Empire of the Heavens bright' has been wrested from the powers of ancient darkness by the new generation of Apollinian deities, a drama of inheritance in which, like the story of Isaac and Esau, the younger brother inherits in the place of the elder. In a move which I would argue is characteristically Spenserian, the poet here legitimates the current hierarchy through the traditional conservative argument, 'what is, should be', yet frees it from the accompanying reliance on precedent, 'what is, has always been'. This vision of conservative innovation mirrors the project of the *View*, an Elizabethan defence of that Elizabethan anathema, political change, aimed at displacing the 'Old English' by the 'New'.[40] So, too, Canto VII's trial of titles does not end with a *rejection* of change, but rather with a celebration of natural order within change; the poem offers a theory and poetics of 'change for the better', enacted in its stylistic progression through classical, medieval, and Renaissance modes of representation.[11] In Chuilleanáin's reading, this historiographical progression also effects a *recolonisation*, a georgic reordering of pastoral waste narrated and localised as intransigently Irish in the Faunus episode.

While Spenser's concerns throughout the *Cantos* are largely philosophical, the setting of the debate on Spenser's much-debated property gives the abstract questions of the poem the local habitation of a name: *Arlo-Hill*. Arlo-Hill is doubly a site of survey. As a vantage point, 'that Mountaine, which doth over-looke / The richest champain that may else be rid / And the fair *Shure*, in which are thousand Salmons bred' (VI. 54), it offers a view of the present state of Ireland, a place from which to see and over-see the land below as a mapped surface, topographically etched by the SHURE river and iconically designated by its local associations ('thousand Salmons bred'). As a landmark of Spenser's plantation property, it is also a site of legal surveying whose procedures and results are contestable. Spenser's 'title' to *Arlo-Hill* in its italicised, toponymic specificity is bound up in Spenser's 'title' to his poetry. In his setting of the scene, 'For trial of their Titles and best Rights: / That was to weet, upon the highest hights of *Arlo-Hill* (Who knows not *Arlo-Hill*?)' (VI. 36), the advertised familiarity of Arlo-Hill, borrowed from *Colin Clouts Come Home Again*, functions as an authorial signature mapping the *locus* in the poetic landscape of Spenser's *oeuvre*. In this, the tag functions much like his pastoral persona, Colin Clout; the rhetorical question, 'Who knows not *Arlo-Hill*?' pointedly echoes Book VI's similarly pointed query, 'Who knows not *Colin Clout*?' Once again, the Spenserian voice emerges from and as a position of fundamental dislocation: the incessant, reflexive shifts of wasting and dispossession that measure out his home away from home, a landscape of Mutabilitie which describes at once the geographic, linguistic, and ethical bounds of his poetry.

Far from pressing the analogy between Mutabilitie's trial of titles and those held in Munster to the level of conscious intention, I would suggest instead the unconscious inscription or 'sub-titling' of Arlo-Hill by its legal determination and indeterminations. I offer this analogy as an 'historical allegory', understood not as a set of fictional masks for contemporary personages, but as the symptomatic metastasis of discursive tensions across a text which relates to other texts not as its outside or its before, but as the field of its articulation. The *Cantos of Mutabilitie* emerge as the set of intersections and cross-sections, positive and negative, between a series of discourses which knot the colonial and the classical, the proto-Cartesian and the insistently Ovidian, the singing contests of pastoral and the legal contests of titles. In this sense, 'historical allegory' can be read backwards and forwards: allegory is historical in the sense that it enacts the temporality of signification and the stratification of discourses, while history is allegorical insofar as it is only available through the textuality of competing views and contested titles. Finally, 'historical/allegory' suggests a fundamental oxymoron, a disjunction between the physical world and the representational systems which attempt to map it. In Spenser, this disjunction is manifested not in the distance between real and ideal but in the pocketing of the one within the other; the 'too-too true' of the Irish corners de-facing the cartographic fantasy maps the waste of shame inscribed in the Spenserian expanse of spirit, not beneath or before or beyond but within it, as its decisive condition of possibility.

In the inter- and intra-textuality of Spenser's Ireland, Arlo-Hill emerges as the confluence, the discursive river-marriage, of a series of rhetorical currents: the New English apologetics of the 'Irish plot', the antiquarian, topographic tradition of Anglo-Irish representation, Ovidian *metamorphosis ex Ponto*, and the legal contest of titles and best rights. Together, these discourses share a topology of Ireland which 'plots waste'. In the *View*, the Irish geography of 'waste wyld places' (p. 172) needs to be transformed by means of English military, legal and surveying techniques into a new kind of desert, a depopulated, wasted, 'open' terrain ready to be written anew by its English settlers. In the *Mutabilitie Cantos*, the Ovidian tale of Faunus and Diana, staged specifically to mythologise the desolate condition of Spenser's Irish estate, establishes the unstable foundation of Mutabilitie's plaint to Nature, a scene whose physics and metaphysics distantly register the legal history of Kilcolman. To cite the toponym of 'Arlo-Hill' is not an act which the authorial Spenser can fully control, since the *topos* brings with it a local history whose signifiers – 'titles', 'dispossesse', 'deface', 'too-too true', 'Empire', 'waste' – manifest the continuing contradiction of the author's double stance as exile from England and home-maker in Ireland.

Notes

Research for the essay began under the auspices of the NEH Summer Seminar, 'Rethinking an Intellectual History for Shakespeare's Age', directed by J. Leeds Barroll at the Folger Library in 1989. I thank Terence Murphy for advice on historical research, and Kenneth Reinhard and Richard Rambuss for commenting extensively on the draft.

1. EDMUND SPENSER, *A View of the Present State of Ireland*, ed. W. L. RENWICK (London: Eric Partridge, 1934), p. 128. All subsequent references are in parentheses in text.

2. Compare with SIR HENRY SIDNEY's 1576 report to the Privy Council, which presents various 'plots' for Ireland in the process of describing his trip through different parts of the country; J. S. BREWER (ed.), *Calendar of the Carew Manuscripts, 1515–1624*, 6 vols. (London: Longmans, Green, Reader and Dyer, 1867–73), II, pp. 38–44.

3. The conquest is narrated in the *Topographia*'s companion piece, the *Expugnatio Hibernica* (1189).

4. Cavanagh appears pretty much alone in her eloquent but forced defence of the comparative liberality of Spenser's policies. See SHEILA T. CAVANAGH, ' "Such was Irena's Countenance": Ireland in Spenser's Poetry and Prose', *Texas Studies in Literature and Language* 28 (1986): 24–50. On the collusion between topographic antiquarianism and political racism in a later moment of Irish history, see MARY HAMER, 'Putting Ireland on the Map', *Textual Practice* 3 (1989): 15–31.

5. On sixteenth-century maps of Ireland, see R. DUNLOP. 'Sixteenth-Century Maps of Ireland', *English Historical Review* 20 (1905): 309-37; J. H. ANDREWS, *Ireland in Maps: Catalogue of an Exhibition mounted in the Library of Trinity College Dublin* (Dublin: Dolman Press, 1961); *A Paper Landscape: The Ordnance Survey in Nineteenth-Century Ireland* (Oxford: Clarendon Press, 1975); *Plantation Acres: An Historical Study of the Irish Land Surveyor and his Maps* (Omagh, Co. Tyrone: Ulster Historical Foundation, 1985). For a military map pertinent to Spenser's experience, see the 'Sige of Smyrvick, in Irelande, 1580' cited in DUNLOP, 'Sixteenth-Century Maps', p. 322. For a recent analysis of Elizabethan poetics and cartography, see RICHARD HELGERSON, 'The Land Speaks: Cartography, Chorography, and Subversion in Renaissance England', *Representations* 16 (1986): 51–85. Unfortunately, Helgerson's discussion does not include Ireland.

6. Pelham's plot, paraphrased in H. C. HAMILTON (ed.). *Calendar of State Papers, Ireland (CSPI) 1509–1596*, 5 vols. (London: Longman, Green, Longman and Roberts, 1860–90), VI, pp. 284–7, presents ' "A probable Discourse, how, upon the extinguishing of this rebellion, the province of Mounster may be kept from any revolt hereafter, how it may bear the charge of 1,200 men, yield revenue to her Majesty, and in short time repay the charge of the war" '. For 'Ireland – A Plate', see BREWER (ed.), *Carew Calendar*, II, p. 397; cf. p. 412.

7. Cited in A. C. JUDSON, *The Life of Edmund Spenser*, vol. 8 of EDWIN GREENLAW *et al.* (eds.), *The Works of Edmund Spenser: A Variorum Edition*, 8 vols. (Baltimore: Johns Hopkins University Press, 1938), p. 125.

8. Cited in N. P. CANNY, *The Elizabethan Conquest of Ireland: A Pattern Established, 1565–76* (New York: Barnes and Noble, 1976), p. 15.

9. Jobson's description continues: 'All which perticulers is severally circumferenced with redde colours, & all such freeholds adjacent circumferenst with yellow, & the Queen's demaynes in lease circumferenst with greene; all the rest of the Queen's lands, escheated within the said country, in this plott is not as yet placed'. For convenience, I have conflated the descriptions attached to the two versions of the same map by Jobson. Cited in DUNLOP, 'Sixteenth-Century Maps', p. 321.

10. R. Dunlop, 'The Plantation of Munster, 1584–89', English Historical Review 3 (1888): 250–69 at p. 267.

11. For a brief account of the Desmond Rebellion and Munster Plantation, see T.W. Moody et al. (eds.), *A New History of Ireland*, 9 vols. (Oxford: Clarendon Press, 1976–), iii, pp. 105–14. On the Munster Plantation more specifically, see Dunlop, 'The Plantation of Munster'. On earlier plantations, see Canny, *Elizabethan Conquest*, passim.

12. Spenser discusses the distinction between English and Irish tenure and the domesticating influence of the former in the *View*, pp. 105–8. I have discussed Spenser's Irish homemaking at length in 'Home-Making in Ireland: Virgil's Eclogue I and Book VI of the *Faerie Queene*', in Patrick Cullen and Thomas P. Roche Jr. (eds.), *Spenser Studies* vii (New York: AMS Press, 1990): 119–45.

13. One such document associated with the commission redefines Munster in terms of 'South, North, West, East, and Middle Munster'; the divisions, clearly generated by the logic of map-making, cross and break up traditional county lines; e.g., 'North Munster . . . all of the whole county of Waterford, and most part of the county of Cork' (Hamilton, *CSPI*, iii, p. 284). For a discussion of the similar effects of the nineteenth-century Ordnance Survey of Ireland, see Hamer, 'Putting Ireland on the Map'; for a detailed history of the Ordnance Survey, see Andrews, *Paper Landscape*.

14. A few pages earlier Spenser had advised winter wars, since instead of having a hidden enemy in 'Corners nigh the woodes and mountains', one fights an 'open enemie havinge all his Countrie wasted, what by himself and what by the soldyr findeth then succor in noe place, Townes there are none of which he may get spoyle, they are all burnte, Countrye howses and farmers there are none, they be all fledd . . .' (pp. 131–2).

15. Dunlop, 'Sixteenth-Century Maps', pp. 250–1.

16. *CSPI*, iii, p. 549.

17. Compare Eudoxus' assertion that they deal with the rebel 'Feagh mac Hugh' by 'drawinge all the Inhabytantes of those next borders awaye and leaving them utterlie waste', which Irenius rejects as less convenient than 'the planting of garrisons' (pp. 153–4).

18. On 'writing Ireland', see David Cairns and Shaun Richards, *Writing Ireland: Colonialism, Nationalism and Culture* (New York: Manchester University Press, 1988); see also the critique by Willy Maley, 'Review of *Writing Ireland*', *Textual Practice* 3 (1989): 291–8. In his edition of the *View*, Renwick compliments Spenser for having 'the strategic geography of all Ireland in his head' (p. 241).

19. The *View*'s desire to reduce Ireland to the orderly, inscribable visibility of a mapped surface manifests itself in such literal mapping projects as the conversion of land tenure and administrative redivision. Irenius' plan for 'setting the land into signories' refers directly to the Munster survey discussed earlier, whose task was 'the meeting and bounding into seignories of Her Majesty's escheated and attainted lands' (pp. 166–7). In a linked proposal to 'shire' Ireland, the country would be subdivided into groups of ten ('tythings'), each member of which bears responsibility for the acts of the others. Shiring, that is, involved a re-mapping of the land for the purpose of policing, manifesting once more the link between 'survey' and 'surveillance'. So, too, Irenius suggests the strategic relocation of capital cities from the 'Corner' of each province to the center so that the governor 'should bee contenewallie

abydinge in the myddest of his charge, that he might . . . looke out alike into all places of his government' (*View*, p. 171).

20. ANDREWS, *Plantation Acres*, pp. 30, 31.

21. WILLIAM BOELHOWER, 'Inventing America: A Model of Cartographic Semiosis', *Word and Image* 4 (1988): 475–97: 494.

22. 'Vacationscape' is the term currently used in the tourist and development trade to describe countries or regions – usually impoverished – whose main industry is tourism. The vacationscape tends to become a kind of theme-park simulation of itself. See, for example, BOB SHACOCHIS, 'In Deepest Gringolandia', *Harper's Magazine* July 1989: 43–50.

23. See CAVANAGH's commentary on this line: 'Spenser and his contemporaries' "too-too" clear recognition of the prevalent danger in Ireland from wolves and thieves evinces the poet's method of using myth and reality for mutual verification' (' "Such was Irena's countenance" ', p. 37).

24. BOELHOWER, 'Inventing America', p. 494.

25. OVID, *Tristia* and *Ex Ponto*, trans. ARTHUR LESLIE WHEELER (Cambridge, Mass.: Harvard/Loeb, 1924), II, ll, 103–8.

26. The citation from the *Tristia* follows. I thank Elizabeth Dodge for pointing out the Sandys passage to me.

27. MICHAEL HOLOHAN, '*Iamque opus exegi*: Ovid's Changes and Spenser's Brief Epic of Mutability', *English Literary Renaissance* 6 (1976): 244–70 at p. 261. ROSEMOND TUVE has also commented on Spenser's identification with Ovid as a poet of exile; ' "Spenserus" ', in MILLAR MACLURE and F. W. WYATT (eds.), *Essays in English Literature from the Renaissance to the Victorian Age, presented to A. S. P. Woodhouse* (Toronto: Toronto University Press, 1964), pp. 3–25.

28. On the 'Mulla'/'Moles' pun, see *Spenser Variorum*, VI, p. 424.

29. HARRY BERGER, Jr., 'The *Mutabilitie Cantos*: Archaism and Evolution in Retrospect', in HARRY BERGER, Jr. (ed.), *Spenser: A Collection of Critical Essays* (Englewood Cliffs, NJ: Prentice Hall, 1968), pp. 146–76; p. 150.

30. *Spenser Variorum*, VI, p. 424.

31. *CSPI*, III, p. 496.

32. DUNLOP, 'The Plantation of Munster', p. 269.

33. ANDREWS, *Plantation Acres*, p. 39.

34. DUNLOP, 'The Plantation of Munster', pp. 261–5.

35. *CSPI*, III, p. 24.

36. *CSPI*, IV, p. 246.

37. JUDSON, *Life of Spenser*, p. 135.

38. EILÉAN NÍ CHUILLEANÁIN, 'Ireland, the Cultural Context', in A. C. HAMILTON (ed.), *The Spenser Encyclopedia* (Toronto: University of Toronto Press, 1990), pp. 403–4 at p. 404.

39. ANN PRESCOTT, 'Titans', in *Spenser Encyclopedia*, p. 691.

40. See DAVID BAKER, ' "Some Quirk, Some Subtle Evasion": Legal Subversion in Spenser's *View of the Present State of Ireland*', *Spenser Studies* VI (1987): 147–63. Baker argues that the *View* was censored not because it 'subversively' undermines the Elizabethan spectacle of horror, but because it counsels for laws more absolute and innovative than those already in place.

41. The best account of the stylistic dynamics of the poem and their historiographical implications remains HARRY BERGER, Jr., 'The *Mutabilitie Cantos*'.

Notes on contributors

Pamela Joseph Benson is Professor of English at Rhode Island College. She is the author of *The Invention of the Renaissance Woman* (1992) and editor of *Italian Tales from the Age of Shakespeare* (1995), as well as numerous articles on English and Italian Renaissance literature. She is currently working on a study of English translations of Italian texts and reception of Italian culture.

Anne Fogarty is a lecturer in the Department of English, University College, Dublin. She is the author of articles on Spenser, John Davies and Aphra Behn, and has also written essays on gender and representation in the work of modern Irish writers including Eavan Boland, Kate O'Brien, and Mary Dorcey. She is currently at work on a book entitled, *Colonial Plots: Edmund Spenser and Representations of Ireland, 1534–1634.*

Jonathan Goldberg is Sir William Osler Professor of English Literature at The Johns Hopkins University. His most recent book is *Sodometries: Renaissance Texts, Modern Sexualities* (1994). He is the editor of *Reclaiming Sodom* (1994) and of *Queering the Renaissance* (1993) and co-editor (with Stephen Orgel), of *Milton* (1995).

Stephen Greenblatt is The Class of 1932 Professor of English at the University of California, Berkeley, and the author of, among other books, *Shakespearian Negotiations* (1988) and *Marvellous Possessions* (1991).

Andrew Hadfield is Lecturer in English at the University of Wales, Aberystwyth. He is the author of *Literature, Politics and Identity: Reformation to Renaissance* (1994), co-editor with Brendan Bradshaw and Willy Maley of *Representing Ireland: Literature and the Origins of Conflict, 1534–1660* (1993) and co-editor with John McVeagh of *Strangers to that Land: British Perceptions of Ireland from the Reformation to the Famine* (1994). He is currently working on a book about Spenser and Ireland to be published in 1997.

Richard Helgerson is Professor of English at the University of California, Santa Barbara. He is the author of *The Elizabethan Prodigals* (1976), *Self-Crowned Laureates: Spenser, Jonson, Milton and the Literary System* (1983) and *Forms of Nationhood: The Elizabethan Writing of England* (1994).

Julia Reinhard Lupton is Associate Professor of English and Comparative Literature at the University of California, Irvine. She is the co-author with Kenneth Reinhard of *After Oedipus: Shakespeare in Psychoanalysis* (1993) and the author of *Afterlives of the Saints: Hagiography, Typology, and Secular Literature* (1995).

David Lee Miller is Professor of English at the University of Kentucky. He is the author of *The Poem's Two Bodies: The Poetics of the 1590 Faerie Queene* (1988) and co-editor of several volumes, including *The Production of English Renaissance Culture* (1994) and *Approaches to Teaching Spenser's Faerie Queene* (1994). He is currently at work on 'Filial Pieties', a study of masculine and filial sacrifices in Virgil, Shakespeare, Dickens and Freud.

Louis Montrose is Professor of English Literature and Chairman of the Department of Literature at The University of California, San Diego. He has published widely on Elizabethan culture and on theory and method in the historical analysis of literature, and has recently completed a book on Shakespeare and the cultural politics of the Elizabethan theatre.

Richard Rambuss teaches Renaissance literature and cultural studies in the English Department at Tulane University. He is the author of *Spenser's Secret Career* (1993) as well as a number of essays on Chaucer, Donne, Herbert, Crashaw and Traherne. He is completing a new book, *Closet Devotions*, on questions of devotional desire and embodiment, and materialism and subjectivity in seventeenth-century English religious culture.

Lauren Silberman is Professor of English at Baruch College of the City University of New York. She is the author of *Transforming Desire: Erotic Knowledge in Books III and IV of The Faerie Queene* (1994) and has published articles on Spenser, Jonson and mythography.

Further reading

Note: these categories are simply designed to help readers and are not to be taken as watertight distinctions. As will be obvious to any reader of this volume, very little Spenser criticism can be subsumed under any one title. I have tried not to include too many articles in specialist journals which may not be available to the general reader.

Introductory

HAMILTON, A. C., ed., *The Spenser Encyclopedia* (London: Routledge, 1990). The basic starting point for any Spenser scholar at whatever level.

HEALEY, TOM, 'Civilisation and its Discontents: The Case of Edmund Spenser', in *New Latitudes: Theory and English Renaissance Literature* (London: Arnold, 1992), pp. 84–109. A provocative reading of Spenser's cultural politics and poetics, suggesting interesting connections with contemporary issues.

ROBERTS, GARETH, *The Faerie Queene* (Buckingham: Open University Press, 1992). Useful on ways of reading the poem.

SHIRE, HELENA, *A Preface to Spenser* (London: Longman, 1978). The best short introduction to Spenser's work in its cultural context, especially the Irish issue.

History, Ideology, Politics

COUGHLAN, PATRICIA, ' "Some secret scourge which shall by her come unto England": Ireland and Incivility in Spenser', in PATRICIA COUGHLAN, ed., *Spenser and Ireland: An Interdisciplinary Perspective* (Cork: Cork University Press, 1989), pp. 46–74. Uses theories of dialogue to explore Spenser's articulation of Irish incivility. The whole volume is recommended.

GREENBLATT, STEPHEN, 'Murdering Peasants: Status, Genre and the Representation of Rebellion', in STEPHEN GREENBLATT, ed., *Representing the English Renaissance*

(Berkeley: University of California Press, 1988), pp. 1–29. Considers the politics of rebellion in Durer, Spenser, Sidney and Shakespeare.

HADFIELD, ANDREW, ' "Who Knowes not Colin Clout?"': The Permanent Exile of Edmund Spenser', in *Literature, Politics and National Identity: Reformation to Renaissance* (Cambridge: Cambridge University Press, 1994), pp. 170–201. Argues that Spenser's work has to be read in terms of Elizabethan anxieties about national identity.

HELGERSON, RICHARD, *Self-Crownde Laureates: Spenser, Jonson, Milton and the Literary System* (Berkeley: University of California Press, 1983). Studies the development of the professional author in Renaissance England.

—— 'Two Versions of the Gothic', in *Forms of Nationhood: The Elizabethan Writing of England* (Chicago: The University of Chicago Press, 1992), pp. 19–62. An analysis of the power of forms in early modern England, reading Spenser's and Milton's epics.

JONES, ANN ROSALIND and PETER STALLYBRASS, 'Dismantling Irena: The Sexualizing of Ireland in Early Modern England', in Andrew Parker et al., eds, *Nationalisms and Sexualities* (London: Routledge, 1992), pp. 157–71. On the gendering of the Irish context.

MONTROSE, LOUIS, 'The Elizabethan Subject and the Spenserian Text', in PATRICIA PARKER and DAVID QUINT, eds, *Literary Theory/Renaissance Texts* (Baltimore and London: The Johns Hopkins University Press, 1986), pp. 303–40. A fascinating exploration of the power of representation and the representation of power in terms of Spenser's portrayal of Elizabeth.

NORBROOK, DAVID, *Poetry and Politics in the English Renaissance* (London: Routledge, 1984). Essential reading on the political context.

PATTERSON, ANNABEL, 'Reopening the Green Cabinet: Clement Marot and Edmund Spenser', in *Pastoral and Ideology: Virgil to Valery* (Berkeley: University of California Press, 1987), pp. 106–32. Considers the ideological contexts of *The Shepheardes Calender*.

SCHOENFELDT, MICHAEL C., 'The Poetry of Conduct: Accommodation and Transgression in *The Faerie Queene*, Book 6', in RICHARD BURT and MICHAEL JOHN ARCHER, eds, *Enclosure Acts: Sexuality, Property, and Culture in Early Modern England* (Ithaca, NY: Cornell University Press, 1994), pp. 151–69. On the relationship between courtesy and violence.

SHEPHERD, SIMON, *Spenser* (Hemel Hempstead, 1989). The only introductory Marxist reading of Spenser. Often crude in both its readings of the text and theoretical underpinning.

SINFIELD, ALAN, *Literature in Protestant England, 1560–1660* (London: Croom Helm, 1983).

—— *Faultlines: Cultural Materialism and the Politics of Dissident Reading* (Oxford: Clarendon Press, 1992). Both refer to Spenser only in passing, but are essential for an understanding of British cultural materialist readings of the early modern period.

STALLYBRASS, PETER, 'Time, space and unity: the symbolic discourse of *The Faerie Queene*', in Raphael Samuel, ed., *Patriotism: The Making and Unmaking of British National Identity, Volume III: National Fictions* (London: Routledge, 1989), pp. 199–214. Considers the way in which Spenser's 'invented nation was forced to contemplate its own dissolution'.

Edmund Spenser

Narrative, Deconstruction, Genre

BERGER, HARRY, JR., *Revisionary Play: Studies in the Spenserian Dynamics* (Berkeley: University of California Press, 1988). New Criticism meets modern theory: some fascinating explorations into the narratives of *The Shepheardes Calender* and *The Faerie Queene*.

BERNARD, JOHN D., *Ceremonies of Innocence: Pastoralism in the Poetry of Edmund Spenser* (Cambridge: Cambridge University Press, 1989). Thorough, if somewhat distorted, discussion of the importance of a crucial Renaissance genre.

DENEEF, A. LEIGH, *Spenser and the Motives of Metaphor* (Durham, NC: Duke University Press, 1982). Suggests that there is more conscious control in the poetry than many post-structuralist critics do, but shares many affinities with such work.

GOLDBERG, JONATHAN, 'Consuming Texts: Spenser and the Poet's Economy', in *Voice, Terminal Echo: Postmodernism and English Renaissance Texts* (London: Methuen, 1986), pp. 38–67. Considers Spenser's role as an author in *The Shepheardes Calender* in the light of postmodern theory.

GLESS, DARRYL J., *Interpretation and Theology in Spenser* (Cambridge: Cambridge University Press, 1994). Some useful thoughts on reading narrative in the introduction.

GUILLORY, JOHN, *Poetic Authority: Spenser, Milton and Literary History* (New York: Columbia University Press, 1983). Discusses how *The Faerie Queene* deals with questions of origin and authority.

KINNEY, CLARE REGAN, 'The end of questing, the quest for an ending: circumscribed vision in *The Faerie Queene* Book VI', *Strategies of Poetic Narrative: Chaucer, Spenser, Milton, Eliot* (Cambridge: Cambridge University Press, 1992), pp. 70–121. Applies narrative theory to the text.

Gender studies

BERRY, PHILIPPA, *Of Chastity and Power: Literature and the Unmarried Queen* (London: Routledge, 1989), ch. 6. Explores Spenser's resentment of his female ruler in *The Faerie Queene* in the context of the cultural politics of the 1590s.

CAVANAGH, SHEILA T., *Wanton Eyes and Chaste Desires: Female Sexuality in The Faerie Queene* (Bloomington: Indiana University Press, 1994). Argues that women are excluded from a male-gendered conception of virtue in the poem.

DAVIES, STEVIE, *The Feminine Reclaimed: The Idea of Woman in Spenser, Shakespeare and Milton* (Lexington: University of Kentucky Press, 1986). Useful, but somewhat decontextualized and over-sympathetic to Spenser.

HARVEY, ELIZABETH D., *Ventriloquized Voices: Feminist Theory and English Renaissance Texts* (London: Routledge, 1992). Some useful comments on Britomart and Radigund.

PAGLIA, CAMILLE, 'Spenser and Apollo: *The Faerie Queene*', in *Sexual Personae: Art and Decadence from Nefertiti to Emily Dickinson* (New Haven: Yale University Press, 1990), ch. 6. Enthusiastic endorsement of Spenser's pagan pictorialism.

PARKER, PATRICIA, 'Suspended Instruments: Lyric and Power in the Bower of

Bliss', in *Literary Fat Ladies: Rhetoric, Gender, Property* (London: Methuen, 1987), pp. 54–66. Reads the incident in terms of a male desire to escape from and nullify female power.

QUILLIGAN, MAUREEN, *Milton's Spenser: The Politics of Reading* (Ithaca, NY: Cornell University Press, 1983). Considers the question of the female reader in the Renaissance.

SHEPHERD, SIMON, *Amazons and Warrior Women: Varieties of Feminism in Seventeenth-Century Drama* (Brighton: Harvester, 1981), chs 1–2. Considers Spenser's representation of women as the start of a tradition.

SILBERMAN, LAUREN, *Transforming Desire: Erotic Knowledge in Books III and IV of* The Faerie Queene (Berkeley: University of California Press, 1994). Argues that Spenser uses his fictional work to explore the problems of sexuality and the ideology of gender.

THICKSTUN, MARGARET OLOFSON, 'Spenser's Brides Errant', in *Fictions of the Feminine: Puritan Doctrine and the Representation of Women* (Ithaca, NY: Cornell University Press, 1988), ch. 2. Deals with the moral ambiguity of female sexuality in *The Faerie Queene*, Book III.

Index